Human–Computer Interaction Series

The *Human-Computer Interaction Series*, launched in 2004, publishes books that advance the science and technology of developing systems which are effective and satisfying for people in a wide variety of contexts. Titles focus on theoretical perspectives (such as formal approaches drawn from a variety of behavioural sciences), practical approaches (such as techniques for effectively integrating user needs in system development), and social issues (such as the determinants of utility, usability and acceptability).

HCI is a multidisciplinary field and focuses on the human aspects in the development of computer technology. As technology becomes increasingly more pervasive the need to take a human-centred approach in the design and development of computer-based systems becomes ever more important.

Titles published within the Human–Computer Interaction Series are included in Thomson Reuters' Book Citation Index, The DBLP Computer Science Bibliography and The HCI Bibliography.

More information about this series at http://www.springer.com/series/6033

Evangelos Kapros · Maria Koutsombogera
Editors

Designing for the User Experience in Learning Systems

Springer

Editors
Evangelos Kapros
Science Gallery Dublin, Trinity College
The University of Dublin
Dublin, Ireland

Maria Koutsombogera
School of Computer Science and Statistics, Trinity College
The University of Dublin
Dublin, Ireland

ISSN 1571-5035 ISSN 2524-4477 (electronic)
Human–Computer Interaction Series
ISBN 978-3-030-06915-5 ISBN 978-3-319-94794-5 (eBook)
https://doi.org/10.1007/978-3-319-94794-5

Softcover re-print of the Hardcover 1st edition 2018

This Springer imprint is published by the registered company Springer Nature Switzerland AG
The registered company address is: Gewerbestrasse 11, 6330 Cham, Switzerland

It is in the very nature of the human condition that each new generation grows into an old world, so that to prepare a new generation for a new world can only mean that one wishes to strike from the newcomers' hands their own chance at the new.

Hannah Arendt,
The Crisis in Education, 1954

Preface

Technology-enhanced learning has been a subject of discussion since the very early days of computer science and human–computer interaction. However, many of these early promises, such as intelligent tutors or personalised learning, were never realised. Several of these ideas were technology oriented, and the popularisation of user-centred information systems made apparent that user-centred design techniques were appropriate for technology-enhanced learning too.

In this spirit, we co-chaired a conference session with Aimilia Tzanavari of the University of Nicosia, Cyprus, initially titled 'Dissecting the User Experience when the User's Objective is to Learn', and then 'User Experience in and for Learning Technology'. The session found a good home at the International Conference on Learning and Collaboration Technologies (LCT) as part of the Human-Computer International conference (HCII) for several years.

The idea for the book was born as a result of these sessions. Over the years, a community of tens of experts in these sessions has contributed their ideas to the body of knowledge; however, we did not select the material for this book to be exclusively by these authors, and instead issued an open call so as to include more contributions. We believe we managed to give the opportunity for fresh ideas in designing learner experiences to come forward.

We would like to thank Aimilia Tzanavari, now at Proto.io, for the years we co-organised the session; Panayiotis Zaphiris and Andri Ioannou, of the Cyprus University of Technology, Cyprus, for organising LCT as part of HCII; Gavriel Salvendy, of Purdue University, USA, and Tsinghua University, Beijing, P.R. of China, and Constantine Stephanidis, of University of Crete/Foundation for Research and Technology—Hellas (FORTH), Greece, for organising HCII.

In addition, we would like to acknowledge Trinity College Dublin, the University of Dublin, for their flexibility which allowed us to prepare this book. Evangelos would like to thank his colleagues at the Science Gallery Dublin and Maria at the School of Computer Science and Statistics.

The research of Evangelos Kapros has received funding from (a) the Learnovate Centre at Trinity College, the University of Dublin, under the Technology Centre Programme through the Government of Ireland's state agencies Enterprise Ireland

and IDA Ireland and (b) SySTEM 2020, from the European Union's Horizon 2020 Research and Innovation Programme under Grant Agreement No. 788317.

The research of Maria Koutsombogera has received funding from the European Union's Horizon 2020 research and innovation programme under the Marie Skłodowska-Curie Grant Agreement No. 701621 (MULTISIMO).

This book could not have been completed without the help of many people. We sincerely thank all the authors for warmly supporting this endeavour through contributing to this book with their chapters and for engaging in peer-reviewing. We would also like to thank Beverley Ford and Nancy Wade-Jones at Springer (London, UK) for their invaluable support and assistance in publishing this book in a timely fashion.

Barcelona, Spain
Dublin, Ireland
June 2018

Evangelos Kapros
Maria Koutsombogera

Contents

Contributors

Erica Andreotti University College Leuven-Limburg, Limburg, Belgium

Manolis Chaniotakis Ellinogermaniki Agogi, Pallini, Greece

Salman Cheema Arizona State University, Tempe, AZ, USA

Thomas Fischer Ellinogermaniki Agogi, Pallini, Greece

Evita Fotinea Athena Research and Innovation Center, Athens, Greece

Renaat Frans University College Leuven-Limburg, Limburg, Belgium

Muriel Garreta-Domingo ICT Department, Universitat Pompeu Fabra, Barcelona, Spain

Davinia Hernández-Leo ICT Department, Universitat Pompeu Fabra, Barcelona, Spain

Elaine Hoter Talpiot College of Education, Holon, Israel

David Joyner College of Computing, Georgia Institute of Technology, Atlanta, GA, Georgia

Evangelos Kapros Science Gallery Dublin, Trinity College, The University of Dublin, Dublin, Ireland

Zoltan Karpati Leopoly, Budapest, Hungary

Vassilis Katsouros Athena Research and Innovation Center, Athens, Greece

Kathy Kipp Endurae, Aurora, IL, USA

Maria Koutsombogera School of Computer Science and Statistics, Trinity College, The University of Dublin, Dublin, Ireland

Pierre Laborde Cabrilog, Grenoble, France

Joseph J. LaViola Jr. University of Central Florida, Orlando, FL, USA

Marcus Liwicki University of Fribourg, Fribourg, Switzerland

Daniel Martín-Albo Wiris, Barcelona, Spain

Mirjam Neelen Accenture, Dublin, Ireland

Ian O'Keeffe Learnovate, Trinity College Dublin, Dublin, Ireland

Branden Ogata Department of Information and Computer Sciences, University of Hawaii at Manoa, Honolulu, HI, USA

Michael-Brian Ogawa Department of Information and Computer Sciences, University of Hawaii at Manoa, Honolulu, HI, USA

Pilar Orero Universitat Autònoma de Barcelona, Barcelona, Spain

Robert Piechaud Institut de Recherche et de Coordination Acoustique Musique-IRCAM, Paris, France

Fotini Simistira University of Fribourg, Fribourg, Switzerland

Peter B. Sloep Open University of the Netherlands, Heerlen, The Netherlands

Umida Stelovska parWinr Inc., Sunnyvale, CA, USA

Jan Stelovsky Department of Information and Computer Sciences, University of Hawaii at Manoa, Honolulu, HI, USA

Petros Stergiopoulos Ellinogermaniki Agogi, Pallini, Greece

Irene Tor-Carroggio Universitat Autònoma de Barcelona, Barcelona, Spain

Eddie Walsh Learnovate, Trinity Technology & Enterprise Campus, Dublin, Ireland

Manal Yazbak Abu Ahmad Sakhnin College for Teacher Education, Sakhnin, Israel

Chapter 1
Introduction: User Experience in and for Learning

Evangelos Kapros and Maria Koutsombogera

Abstract This chapter serves as the introduction to the edited volume 'Designing for the User Experience in Learning Systems'. It sets out to frame design for learning, including the description of some design principles for learning systems, and then proceeds to set the goals of the volume, indicate some prior work in this area, and summarise the contributions of the chapters in terms of addressing the goals.

1.1 Introduction

Learning technology has been widely used to support the learning and teaching processes, but has also served as a mechanism for knowledge creation and acquisition. The field of learning technology faces some specific challenges. Two of these challenges, described in more detail below, are the diversity of learning experiences, and the multiple stakeholders that are central in learning. Research in designing learning systems that seeks to address challenges in these aspects in a combined way is scarce; this volume attempts to fill this gap.

Learning experiences can be different from other ones, but also between them. The experience of an assessment can be very different to the experience of consuming educational content; however, contemporary user-centred (UCD) and user experience (UX) design methods treat them identically. It is possible to perform tasks that evaluate the functional usability of a piece of technology without investigating its educational usefulness; similarly, it is possible to investigate if a certain learning strategy, including a specific technology, produces learning benefits without investigating the usability of the experience. While the recent introduction of user-centred

E. Kapros
Science Gallery Dublin, Trinity College, The University of Dublin,
Dublin 2, Ireland
e-mail: ekapros@tcd.ie

M. Koutsombogera (✉)
School of Computer Science and Statistics, Trinity College, The University of Dublin,
Dublin 2, Ireland
e-mail: koutsomm@tcd.ie

E. Kapros and M. Koutsombogera (eds.), *Designing for the User Experience in Learning Systems*, Human–Computer Interaction Series,
https://doi.org/10.1007/978-3-319-94794-5_1

methods in learning technology is more than welcome, it has not always been clear in how the fruits of these methods have led to better learning outcomes.

In addition, learning technology has the attribute that the end users, the learners, are often not in control of which learning technology they will use or why, something for which the role of the instructor is often responsible—neither are the learners in control of what content, activity, or assessment they will consume or perform. Moreover, the purchaser or approver of a learning technology is more often than not someone other than the learner, and often other than the instructor. These attributes persist throughout the learning landscape, where the learner, instructor, and purchaser can be either a student, teacher, and parent, or an employee, trainer, and human resources/talent management department, respectively for K-12 and corporate learning. This role distinction is non-existent in consumer software applications, in which e.g. a music player software application is typically used by the purchasers, who also directly select the content of the musical content they will consume.

Therefore, the principles that govern the design of user experiences for learning need to satisfy the challenges that are unique to learning systems. The following section frames the context and introduces such high-level principles.

1.2 Framing Design for Learning

1.2.1 Design Principles

1.2.1.1 Design for the Educative Relationships Triangle

The Educative Relationships Triangle, often called "The Iron Triangle" of education (cf. Fig. 1.1), informs us that the Learner-Instructor-Knowledge relationships are of paramount importance in their entirety for learning to flourish. Learner-centric design should facilitate all three points of the triangle, rather than be learner-only design; as the latter would be to the expense of the Learner-Instructor, Learner-Knowledge, and Instructor-Knowledge[1] relationships.

Specifically, a design that would focus on the Learner-Teacher relationship but would neglect Content/Knowledge, would potentially create a pleasant social interaction at school or at corporate training. However, it would not necessarily be educational, if the content is not present strongly enough or is not appropriate. Similarly, a design that would focus on the Learner-Content relationship but would neglect the Teacher could result in the Learner engaging with potentially fun content, but without the mediation of the teacher this fun content might not be useful for learning. Finally, a design that would focus on the Teacher-Content relationship may end up

[1]Knowledge and Content are used interchangeably in most depictions of the Triangle, and also here. The aim is to point that, in this context, Content should not be understood as a static piece of text in a book as in previous times, but could be an interactive activity on a tablet, a project in a laboratory, or an assessment. It is in this way that the more generic term Knowledge can be used instead.

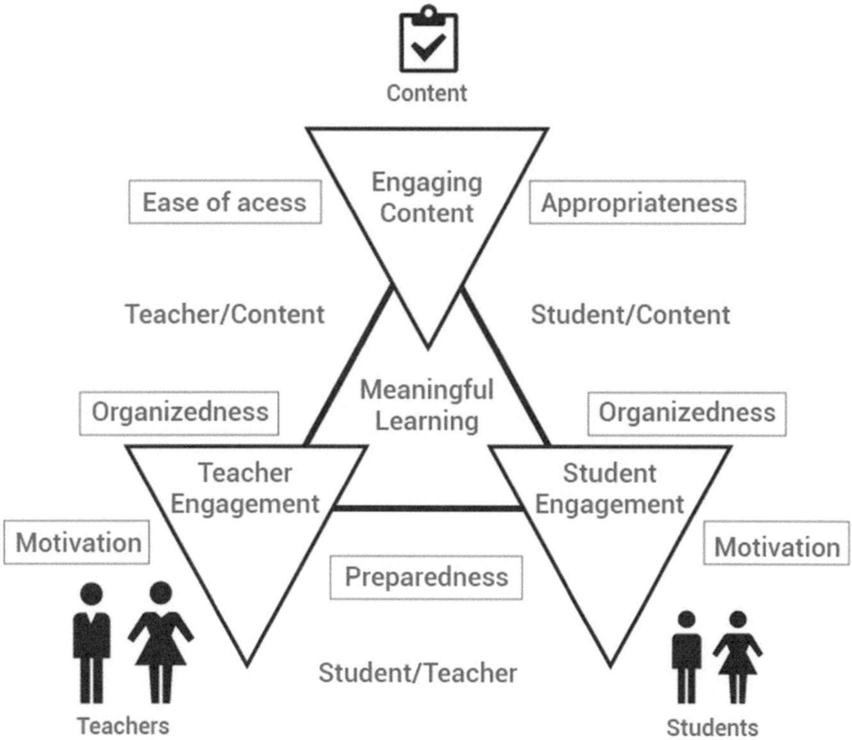

Fig. 1.1 The "Iron Triangle" of educative relationships triangle

with teachers teaching all the content they prefer, but with the learners not necessarily learning something from it.

Thus, a learner-centric design should have a scope that includes the teacher and content, so as to facilitate meaningful teaching and assessment (cf. Fig. 1.2). In this case the user would know that the teaching and assessment are done for content that is appropriate, by teachers who have organised the delivery of it, and by students that are prepared for it.

1.2.1.2 Focus on Learning

Education is, ultimately, a human enterprise: technology should facilitate it, but it should not be an end in itself. Thus, our focus must always be on education. We must design services to help people facilitate and enable learning. While technological advancements in the field are laudable, they will not lead to improved learning outcomes on their own.

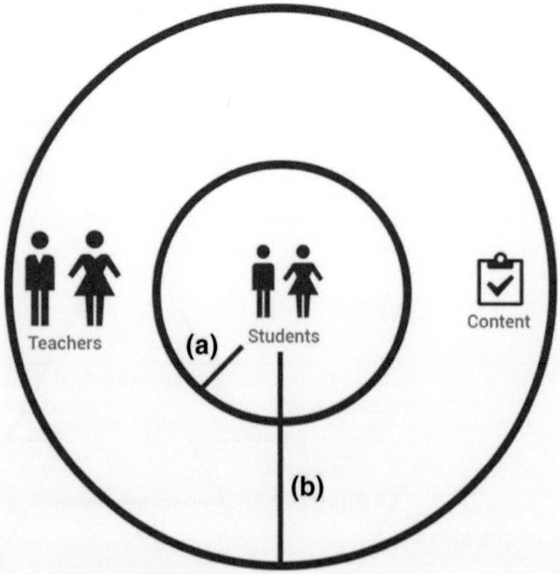

Fig. 1.2 **a** Inner circle: a student-centred system design whose scope excludes Teachers and content. **b** Outer circle: a student-centred design whose scope is intended for including the educative relationships triangle

1.2.1.3 Pedagogically Inclusive Design

Apart from the traditional definitions of disability and accessibility mentioned above, a pedagogically inclusive design should also cater for different **learning** needs. To this end, we embrace **broad definitions of accessibility** (Inclusive Design Research Center n.d.) which include user diversity in terms of their educational needs, and can have a big impact in designing for varying and diverse learning needs. Pedagogically inclusive design often requires **a high level of empathy** (Kapros 2016) for the learners.

1.2.1.4 Pedagogical Appropriateness

Understanding the pedagogical premises of a proposed solution in a learning environment project is key in designing said solution. The pedagogical frameworks used are one source of information about actual user needs and should be used in par with user input. Should a conflict between user input and pedagogy arise, understanding where the input and the pedagogy came from often helps resolve or mediate the conflict, and makes apparent the actual user needs instead of their preferences. This includes following age-appropriate guidelines, such as the ones in Hourcade (2015).

1.2.2 Goals

While the focus of the UX research and design discipline and the Learning Sciences and instructional design disciplines is often similar and almost always tangential, there seems to exist a gap, i.e. a lack of communication between the two fields. Not much has been said about how UX Design can work hand-in-hand with instructional design to advance learning. Thus, the goal of this book is to bridge this gap by presenting work that cuts through both fields.

To illustrate this gap in more detail, we provide a combined view of UX Research and Design and Educational Technology. While the traditional view has perceived the Learning Experience Design as a field of Instructional Design, we will highlight its connection with UX, an aspect that has become increasingly relevant.

The book also aims to present research on learning technology that is truly learner-centric, and treats the human experience as a solution to the problems faced by contemporary education.

Our focus on user experience research and design has a unique emphasis on the human learning experience: we strongly believe that in learning technology the technological part is only mediating the learning experience and we do not focus on technological advancements per se, as we believe they are not the solution, in themselves, to the problems that education is facing.

Moreover, UX and HCI research has typically focused on the experience of an individual learner, and specifically on aspects other than learning; examples include, but are not limited to, playfulness, engagement, fun, or "traditional" usability. These aspects re-enforce an individualistic understanding of learning, as opposed to a collective experience of learners functioning as parts of a larger system. This transfer of methods from UX/HCI without the additional domain expertise in learning can lead to misguided projects; to name an example scenario, engagement has been found to have no correlation with improvement in learning (Garon-Carrier et al. 2016; McConney et al. 2014; Ryan and Deci 2002), but is commonly used as a metric in learning technology projects, simply because of the familiarity of UX designers with it as a metric of commercial success in non-educational systems.

This book aims to lay out the challenges and opportunities in this field and highlight these, through research presented in the various chapters. The content of this contributed volume covers a relatively broad spectrum of detailed research topics encompassing both design aspects and use case studies. Contributions span human-centred and accessibility design approaches, assessment methodologies of transversal skills, innovative pedagogical frameworks and tutoring systems to multicultural learning experiences in the Middle East. Thus, this book presents a unique opportunity to represent areas of learning technology that go very far beyond the MOOC and the classroom technology. It provides an outstanding overview and insights in the area and it aims to serve as a significant and valuable source for learning researchers and practitioners.

Emphasis has been recently put on the user-centred design, an approach where the user feedback loop informs each step of the design (ISO 2010). The challenge lies in that the philosophy of human-centred design needs to be integrated into learning technologies and apps, in terms of processes (i.e. in the design of learning activities and educational technology), but also in terms of methods, i.e. learning design. Such design is heavily based on use cases that represent the distinct phases of a usage scenario, and that can be understandable by both developers and end users (Cockburn 2000). In this sense, the more accurate and inclusive a use case is, the more engaging it will be to the end users. The design of use cases faces some challenges that the relevant stakeholders and the related research need to address by introducing new methodologies. These challenges refer to insufficient definitions and documentation, as well as lack of collaboration in structuring use cases, resulting in poorer quality.

An important aspect in evaluating a user interface is the assessment of its usability. Usability evaluation takes into account the functionalities of an interface and assesses its ease of use and attractiveness (Bias and Mayhew 2005). Evaluation methods have been developed using robust, reliable and objective metrics to measure whether an interactive system is usable and to what extent. A common tool to evaluate learning environments is a usability survey. As regards collaborative aspects, such surveys should include questions assessing the facilitation of collaboration and results should be exploited in such a way that will improve future versions of the interactive interface.

Learning software or system development may be evaluated with traditional methodologies or via heuristic evaluation. A typical process involves the user interacting with the system following a scenario that indicates activities that the user has to carry out, and these activities are observed and measured. Mobile instruction and mobile learning (Quinn 2000) make the evaluation issue more complex, as it is hard to track the multiple users and the multiple devices they use, together with the flexibility and the multitude of ways they can use a learning platform or a game.

The above are only a few, but important, reasons why we think that Learning Experience Design can and should expand itself and cross-pollinate itself with UX/HCI research and practice, in order to infuse Instructional Design so as to result to meaningful learning experiences.

1.3 Challenges and Opportunities Addressed in this Book

The aim of this book is to provide a common ground for learning researchers, learning practitioners and UX experts to present their perspectives and their needs. In this respect, the chapters included in this book discuss the state of the art and aim to build a shared understanding of open challenges in our "Design for Learning" framework and the way the related UX research and design could accommodate the related pedagogical design principles. It includes application areas, components of pedagogical design to be implemented in software tools, as well as types of tools themselves from the learner-centric perspective.

1.3.1 Prior Work

A recent trend that has been adopted in learning delivery is that of Mobile Learning (Kearney et al. 2012; Traxler 2010). The use of mobile technologies in formal and informal educational settings is claimed to provide personalised educational experience following a user-centred approach. While the benefits of Mobile Learning regarding ease of access and cost effectiveness have been highlighted, there are still several challenges to be addressed, including further qualitative research on aspects of content delivery and UX design, as well as on defining the interconnections between formal and informal settings.

Improving student engagement has been a focus in the design of learning technologies and pedagogical environments (Zyngier 2008). In this respect, the design and deployment of serious and immersive games can significantly help towards this direction, by providing an approach that pursues engagement in a platform where an activity, a game, stimulates learning and social skills in an interactive and playful manner. Serious games are a non-traditional learning environment that can motivate, stimulate and engage students and learners in general, to overcome challenges and discover or acquire new knowledge (Peirce et al. 2008; Prensky 2003). They can be employed for independent learning as well as additionally to traditional pedagogical methods (Mach 2009) and give learners the opportunity to use them on their own time and pace as well as to acquire essential skills before they continue in more complex areas. The related interfaces in principle follow an integrated design approach (e.g. attractive storyline, highly interactive 3D environment) to achieve a stimulating learning experience.

Similarly to serious games, virtual worlds as a learning environment encourage collaboration, interaction and shared understanding among people from different locations, but also from different cultural backgrounds. Given the positive impact of virtual worlds on the learning outcomes of students (regarding e.g. knowledge transfer and social skills) (Freeman et al. 2017; Pellas et al. 2017), the challenge of the pedagogical model and the UX design of virtual worlds becomes increasingly important.

Multimedia learning environments often include embodied characters of pedagogical nature. Such animated agents can impact the learning process (Baylor and Kim 2004), therefore their design is a crucial issue. Aspects of their design take into account appearance and social cues in an attempt to make them more effective and appealing to learners. From this perspective, it has been claimed that learners are attracted by agents who present a set of similar features with them (Byrne 1971) (and that gender orientation is an important factor that may influence interactions Ridgeway and Smith-Lovin 1999).

Computer Supported Collaborative Learning tools are claimed to provide shared space for communication and co-construction of knowledge (Stahl et al. 2006). A two-fold objective for CSCL Computer Supported Collaborative Learning tools is (a) their design in a way that it promotes skills such as reflection, critical thinking etc. (Fischer et al. 1993), and (b) the investigation of the way they influence group learning in terms of effective practices that facilitate group learning.

Another paradigm that benefits from the intersection of UX and learning design is that of active or constructive learning, a learning-by-teaching concept where students are actively involved in their own education (Duran 2017; Bishop and Verleger 2013). With the use of supporting technologies, learners construct their own material, which is related to their course. This process enables them to acquire a deep understanding of the learning material through the resources that themselves or their peers create.

Furthermore, in the recent years innovative pedagogical frameworks have emerged, that exploit user-centred design and enabling technologies to connect concepts and skills of different fields, that have been previously considered unrelated (Honey et al. 2014). A relevant example are efforts towards extending STEM education to include Arts subjects in curricula (Kim and Park 2012; Quigley et al. 2017) with the aim of cultivating creative skills to maximize students' engagement and the learning impact.

Transversal or 21st century skills are nowadays considered highly linked to the productivity and competitiveness aspects occurring in the workplace (Voogt and Roblin 2012). The need to develop and assess those skills has lead to their integration not only in the higher educational sector but also into the K-12 context, through teaching and learning in schools. Consequently, this need has been driving research towards new pedagogical design elements and related design choices for the supportive technology and applications (Reeves 2010; Griffin and Care 2015). Therefore, developing and (self-) assessing transversal skills is yet another topic that demands the interaction between pedagogical design and UX design. In parallel to traditional areas such as formal learning and vocational training, an emerging application area for learning environments is that of professional development that addresses modern business needs, including corporate environments. In the same spirit, competency-based-education aims to tackle the challenge of capturing and objectively assessing employees' competencies in the workplace. The assessment of transversal competencies is a challenging issue because of including both professional and behavioral aspects (Hoekstra and Sluijs 2003).

In this respect, learning technologies are considered, in addition to traditional methods, to assist in assessing and supporting communication and collaboration competencies (e.g. peer feedback) that are critical for the work environment.

Traditional methodologies of evaluating the usability of pedagogic software involve actual end users in a lab or classroom setting (Nielsen 1994). Given the nature of modern technological learning solutions (such as mobile learning), where end users can be anywhere, more flexible evaluation solutions are required, such as heuristic evaluations (Nielsen 1995) in order to test solutions before they are out on the market.

A related issue is that of safety and security in collaborative learning environments. Web 2.0 tools provide a creative environment to interact and to share knowledge, thus making it appropriate for learning purposes as well (Parmaxi and Zaphiris 2017). However, major concerns have been expressed about potential risks that these technologies entail to the security aspects of such environments, and especially issues related to content, interaction with other users and privacy protection (OECD 2011). Further research is therefore required on tools and methods for monitoring the safety of students and instructors that make use of Web 2.0.

A horizontal aspect encompassing recently many endeavours in developing learning environments is that of the open learning education practice. Open Education and learning has been claimed to drive learning innovations and achieve higher learning quality by opening up education (Stracke 2017). Moreover, it offers another perspective on the learning process; that of the learners' access to learning opportunities and building their achievements themselves. In that respect, Open Education tools and Massive Open Online Courses (MOOCs) aim to improve learning experiences and facilitate high quality education in an attractive manner (Daniel 2012). This different perspective creates a need for a different way of assessing open education and MOOC results mainly because their design usually does not take into account the quality development (Stracke 2017). Therefore, there is a need to identify for new quality strategies and measures, as the traditional assessment (e.g. drop-out rates) is a no one-size-fits all measure. Instead, MOOC quality assessment should be measured individually and consider the individual learner's requirements and intentions. Similarly to the assessment, MOOC design should also reflect this personalised dimension regarding the diversity of different personal motivations and intentions of the learners.

A related challenge is that of accessibility aspects in MOOC design, because of the diverse requirements from different user groups (Seale 2014); the presence of such features has been often questioned (Sanchez-Gordon and Lujn-Mora 2017), thus making it necessary that accessibility design elements need to be integrated in all steps of the MOOC design process and that persons with disabilities, as foreseen users, need to be involved in this process. Though the MOOCs quality is often questionable (Margaryan et al. 2015; Global survey on the quality of MOOCs n.d.), their potential in providing innovative learning experiences is also highlighted and current research efforts address and investigate the evaluation of Open Education.

Because of the omnipresence of learning environments that complement or even replace the classroom experience, it is thus substantial, if not beneficial, to investigate the user experience from both the perspectives of interface design and learning design. Both perspectives present similarities and differences that serve two aspects of the user experience, that of dynamic interaction and that of learning gains. Deeper investigation of this intersection of interface design and learning design, mainly through theoretical support and evaluations of user interfaces will shed more light on the positive learning effects that this intersection yields.

1.3.2 Chapters of this Book

This book is organised in two parts. *Part I* is titled *Foundations, Frameworks, and Principles*, and deals with first principles and opportunities for the collaboration between education, technology, and design, and *Part II* is titled *Applications and Case Studies* and showcases practical applications of and results from applying ideas such as the ones outlined in Part I.

While this book does not set out to address each and every individual aspect of previous work described in the section above, the papers do break new ground in this general area, mainly by combining expertise in different fields ranging from Human-Computer Interaction to Learning and Development, K-12 Education, and inter-cultural communication.

A brief description of each chapter is presented below.

1.3.2.1 Part I: Foundations, Frameworks, Principles

Chapter 2 by Garreta et al. discusses the necessity for a novel conception of the role of design in education and they focus on human-centred design in the context of technology-enhanced learning. It addresses the design of both learning activities and educational technology and they stress the importance of engaging and empowering educators as designers and team members.

Chapter 3 by Kipp et al. describes a framework and learning mobile application that brings together innovative pedagogy and supportive technology to promote the practice, development and self-assessment of '21st Century Skills' in K-12, evaluating design elements and activities related to Universal Access to self-assessment for '21st Century Skills'.

Chapter 4 by Hoter et al. provides an empirical study about a new model for interactive learning in virtual worlds and they report on challenging issues encountered, as well as on the usefulness/impact of this teaching environment in enhancing online collaboration and intercultural competences.

Motivated by the increase in user interface design for educational contexts, Chap. 5 by Joyner illustrates the intersection of interface design and learning design through a case study on a human-computer interaction class and discusses shared principles/underlying similarities and blurred lines between interface design and online education (learning design).

This last chapter for Part I, with a subtitle of "Blurring the Lines between User Interfaces and Learner Interfaces", also blurs the line between frameworks and case studies, and is thus a good transition chapter moving forward to Part II, which is structured as follows below.

1.3.2.2 Part II: Applications and Case Studies

Chapter 6 by Orero et al. is inspired by the human right of access to education and discusses design approaches and options for MOOCs towards guaranteeing access to educational e-content and applications that will lead to the implementation of accessibility features in the production phase of learning materials.

Chapter 7 by Katsouros et al. introduces an innovative pedagogical framework actively involving both secondary school students and teachers. It approaches a user-centered development of integrating cutting-edge technological tools in novel activity environments, innovative pedagogy, educational scenarios and lesson plans to promote STEAM pedagogy research.

Chapter 8 by Neelen et al. presents a novel approach to assessing workplace transversal competencies through event-based, continuous peer-feedback based on workplace events, such as meetings and discussions, that was evaluated within multiple organisations and provides added value to traditional competency assessment methods.

Chapter 9 by Stelovsky et al. presents an instructional methodology that supports both students and instructors, within the concept of constructive Learning, where students actively create teaching materials, i.e. quizzes, that enable them to acquire a deep understanding of the learning material through the resources that themselves or their peers create.

Finally, Chap. 10 by Cheema et al. presents a prototype sketch-based physics tutoring system that provides animation support and visual feedback for a range of kinematics problems, with the aim to enrich the learning experience for the student by exploiting the solutions that the students themselves provide to construct the related animations.

1.4 Summary

This book gathered chapters that understand and apply “Design for Learning” in various contexts: formal education, corporate training, accessibility, inter-cultural communication, and others. Despite the variation in context, all authors share the view of applying certain design principles to advance their research or practice. However, these principles are not always explicit, and a lack of a unifying framework is evident. We hope that the four principles stated earlier in this chapter (design for the educative relationships triangle, focus on learning, design for pedagogical inclusion, and for pedagogical appropriateness) are a helpful, albeit minimal, guide for moving forward.

In addition, we do hope that this book and this chapter are a starting point in amplifying the very necessary discussion between the Human-Computer Interaction and the Learning Science communities about aligning our fields more closely, to the benefit of both better technology-enhanced learning, and improved human-computer interaction research and practice in learning environments.

References

Baylor AL, Kim Y (2004) Pedagogical agent design: the impact of agent realism, gender, ethnicity, and instructional role. In: Lester JC, Vicari RM, Paraguacu F (eds) Intelligent tutoring systems. Springer, Berlin, Heidelberg, pp 592–603

Bias RG, Mayhew DJ (2005) Cost-justifying usability: an update for the internet age. Morgan Kaufmann, Amsterdam
Bishop J, Verleger MA (2013) The flipped classroom: a survey of the research. In: ASEE national conference proceedings. American Society for Engineering Education
Byrne DE (1971) The attraction paradigm. Academic Press, New York
Cockburn A (2000) Writing effective use cases, 1st edn. Addison-Wesley Longman Publishing Co. Inc., Boston, MA, USA
Daniel J (2012) Making sense of MOOCs: Musings in a Maze of Myth, Paradox and possibility. Ubiquity Press. https://jime.open.ac.uk/articles/10.5334/2012-18/. Accessed on 31 May 2018
Duran D (2017) Learning-by-teaching. Evidence and implications as a pedagogical mechanism. Innov Educ Teach Int 54(5):476–484. https://doi.org/10.1080/14703297.2016.1156011
Fischer G, Nakakoji K, Ostwald J, Stahl G, Sumner T (1993) Embedding critics in design environments. Knowl Eng Rev 8(4):285–307. https://doi.org/10.1017/S026988890000031X
Freeman A, Adams Becker S, Cummins M, Davis A, Hall Giesinger C (2017) NMC/CoSN Horizon report: 2017 K-12 Edition. The New Media Consortium. https://www.nmc.org/publication/nmccosn-horizon-report-2017-k-12-edition/. Accessed on 31 May 2018
Garon-Carrier G, Boivin M, Guay F, Kovas Y, Dionne G, Lemelin J-P, Tremblay RE (2016) Intrinsic motivation and achievement in mathematics in elementary school: a longitudinal investigation of their association. Child Dev 87(1):165–175. https://onlinelibrary.wiley.com/doi/abs/10.1111/cdev.12458. https://doi.org/10.1111/cdev.12458
Global survey on the quality of MOOCs (n.d.). http://www.survey.MOOC-Quality.eu/. Accessed on 31 May 2018
Griffin P, Care E (2015) Assessment and teaching of 21st century skills: methods and approach. Springer, Dordrecht
Hoekstra H, Sluijs Ev (2003) Managing competencies: implementing human resource management. GITP
Honey M, Pearson G, Schweingruber H (2014) STEM integration in K-12 education: status, prospects, and an agenda for research. National Academies Press, Washington, District of Columbia
Hourcade J (2015) Child-computer interaction. University of Iowa, Iowa City
Inclusive Design Research Center. (n.d.). What is inclusive design. https://idrc.ocadu.ca/about-the-idrc/49-resources/online-resources/articlesand-papers/443-whatisinclusivedesign. Accessed on 31 May 2018
ISO (2010) ISO 9241–210:2010: Ergonomics of human system interaction–Part 210: Human-centred design for interactive systems (Standard). International Organization for Standardization, Geneva, CH
Kapros E (2016) The role of empathy in designing for education. Learnovate, Trinity College Dublin. http://www.learnovatecentre.org/empathy-in-designing-for-education/. Accessed on 31 May 2018
Kearney M, Schuck S, Burden K, Aubusson P (2012) Viewing mobile learning from a pedagogical perspective. Res Learn Technol 20(0). https://journal.alt.ac.uk/index.php/rlt/article/view/1225. https://doi.org/10.3402/rlt.v20i0.14406
Kim Y, Park N (2012) The effect of steam education on elementary school student's creativity improvement. In: T-h Kim et al (eds) Computer applications for security, control and system engineering. Springer, Berlin, Heidelberg, pp 115–121
Mach N (2009) Gaming, learning 2.0, and the digital divide. In: Siemens G, Fulford C (eds) Proceedings of edmedia: world conference on educational media and technology 2009. Honolulu, HI, USA: Association for the Advancement of Computing in Education (AACE), pp 2972–2977. https://www.learntechlib.org/p/31901
Margaryan A, Bianco M, Littlejohn A (2015) Instructional quality of massive open online courses (MOOCs). Comput Educ 80(C):77–83. https://doi.org/10.1016/j.compedu.2014.08.005
McConney A, Oliver MC, Woods-McConney A, Schibeci R, Maor D (2014) Inquiry, engagement, and literacy in science: a retrospective, crossnational analysis using PISA 2006. Sci Educ

98(6):963–980. https://onlinelibrary.wiley.com/doi/abs/10.1002/sce.21135. https://doi.org/10.1002/sce.21135
Nielsen J (1994) Usability inspection methods. In: Conference companion on human factors in computing systems. ACM, New York, NY, USA, pp 413–414. https://doi.org/10.1145/259963.260531
Nielsen J (1995) Heuristic evaluation: how-to. https://www.nngroup.com/articles/how-to-conduct-a-heuristic-evaluation/. Accessed on 31 May 2018
OECD (2011) The protection of children online (No. 179). https://www.oecd-ilibrary.org/content/paper/5kgcjf71pl28-en. https://doi.org/10.1787/5kgcjf71pl28-en
Parmaxi A, Zaphiris P (2017) Web 2.0 in computer-assisted language learning: a research synthesis and implications for instructional design and educational practice. Interact Learn Environ 25(6):704–716. https://doi.org/10.1080/10494820.2016.1172243
Peirce N, Conlan O, Wade V (2008) Adaptive educational games: providing non-invasive personalised learning experiences. In: 2008 second IEEE international conference on digital game and intelligent toy enhanced learning, pp 28–35. https://doi.org/10.1109/DIGITEL.2008.30
Pellas N, Kazanidis I, Konstantinou N, Georgiou G (2017) Exploring the educational potential of three-dimensional multi-user virtual worlds for stem education: a mixed-method systematic literature review. Educ Inf Technol 22(5):2235–2279. https://doi.org/10.1007/s10639-016-9537-2
Prensky M (2003) Digital game-based learning. Comput Entertain 1(1):21–21. https://doi.org/10.1145/950566.950596
Quigley CF, Herro D, Jamil FM (2017) Developing a conceptual model of STEAM teaching practices. School Sci Math 117(1–2):1–12. https://onlinelibrary.wiley.com/doi/abs/10.1111/ssm.12201. https://doi.org/10.1111/ssm.12201
Quinn C (2000) mLearning: mobile, wireless, in-your-pocket learning. http://www.linezine.com/2.1/features/cqmmwiyp.htm. Accessed on 31 May 2018
Reeves D (2010) A framework for assessing 21st century skills. In: 21st century skills: rethinking how students learn. Solution Tree Press, pp 305–325
Ridgeway CL, Smith-Lovin L (1999) The gender system and interaction. Ann Rev Sociol 25(1):191–216. https://doi.org/10.1146/annurev.soc.25.1.191
Ryan RM, Deci EL (2002) Overview of self-determination theory: an organismic dialectical perspective. In: Handbook of self-determination research. University of Rochester Press, pp 3–33
Sanchez-Gordon S, Lujn-Mora S (2017) Technological innovations in large-scale teaching: five roots of massive open online courses. J Educ Comput Res. https://doi.org/10.1177/0735633117727597
Seale JK (2014) E-learning and disability in higher education accessibility research and practice. Routledge, London
Stahl G, Koschmann T, Suthers D (2006) Computer-supported collaborative learning: an historical perspective. In: Sawyer RK (ed) Cambridge handbook of the learning sciences. Cambridge University Press, pp 409–426. http://www.cis.drexel.edu/faculty/gerry/cscl/CSCL_English.pdf
Stracke CM (2017) The quality of MOOCs: how to improve the design of open education and online courses for learners? In: Zaphiris P, Ioannou A (eds) Learning and collaboration technologies. Springer International Publishing, Cham, Novel learning ecosystems, pp 285–293
Traxler J (2010) Distance education and mobile learning: catching up, taking stock. Distance Educ 31(2):129–138. https://doi.org/10.1080/01587919.2010.503362
Voogt J, Roblin NP (2012) A comparative analysis of international frameworks for 21st century competences: implications for national curriculum policies. J Curric Stud 44(3):299–321. https://doi.org/10.1080/00220272.2012.668938
Zyngier D (2008) (Re)conceptualising student engagement: doing education not doing time. Teach Teach Educ 24(7):1765–1776. http://www.sciencedirect.com/science/article/pii/S0742051X07001102. https://doi.org/10.1016/j.tate.2007.09.004

Part I
Foundations, Frameworks, Principles

Chapter 2
Education, Technology and Design: A Much Needed Interdisciplinary Collaboration

Muriel Garreta-Domingo, Davinia Hernández-Leo and Peter B. Sloep

Abstract In this chapter we defend and underpin our claim that, to improve and innovate education, a novel conception of the role of design in education is needed. What this conception is we will elaborate on, specifically on how it affects design in education as it is customarily practiced. We will translate this conception to the context of technology-enhanced learning (TEL). Because of its potential to have an impact on education, TEL more than any other form of learning demands consciously devised learning designs. Thus, our proposal addresses both the design of learning, in particular learning activities, and the design of educational technology. We focus on human-centred design (HCD), a problem-solving framework underpinned by user involvement in all stages of the process. HCD provides professional designers with a mindset and a toolbox that includes both process and methods. It is multidisciplinary by default and also practice-oriented, context-aware, empathetic and incremental. As such it naturally fits many of educators' everyday realities. Leveraging human-centred design theories and practices will greatly benefit educational design and give it the push it has been missing, we argue. Our proposal focuses on how HCD can enhance and facilitate technology-enhanced learning by (1) focussing on the design of learning activities, (2) involving all its actors in a timely and meaningful way; and (3) affecting its micro, meso and macro levels.

M. Garreta-Domingo (✉) · D. Hernández-Leo
ICT Department, Universitat Pompeu Fabra, Roc Boronat 138, 08018 Barcelona, Spain
e-mail: murielgd@gmail.com

D. Hernández-Leo
e-mail: davinia.hernandez@upf.edu

P. B. Sloep
Open University of the Netherlands, Heerlen, The Netherlands
e-mail: Peter.Sloep@ou.nl

E. Kapros and M. Koutsombogera (eds.), *Designing for the User Experience in Learning Systems*, Human–Computer Interaction Series,
https://doi.org/10.1007/978-3-319-94794-5_2

2.1 Introduction

The notion that education 'lives' in a designed environment hardly becomes apparent in the classroom or lecture room. Although in the early days of the industrial revolution, lecturing (instead of one-on-one teaching) was invented, it now is so much part and parcel of our everyday experience we barely notice education's designed character anymore (Bates 2015). The advent of technology-enhanced learning changed that, for now conscious decisions had to be made on what technologies to include and how to apply them. However, there is a tendency to shun innovations through the application of learning technologies, in particular those that may disrupt existing practice (Flavin and Quintero 2018). In our view this results from a lack of conscious acknowledgement that teaching and learning are essentially designed activities. By focussing on technology-enhanced learning, we aim to show how a conscious design stance may improve education and indeed educational technology as well.

Whereas most physical classrooms layouts and models resemble those of decades ago, the tasks of educators have been deeply affected by the changes in society. We might still encounter that odd educator who just uses a paper textbook for her teaching or keeps using the same written notes year after year to address her students. However, such educators now can only be the exception as the pressure from society on education is mounting and the adoption of technology has become unavoidable. It is our conviction that this push towards change in education—not only incremental but also disruptive—has mostly been done without adequate support. Instead, educators are being asked to take on so many more roles representing equally many different specialities that it is impossible for them—as individuals—to master them all.

Psychologist, conflict mediator, actor, counsellor, coach, technologist, diversity expert, individual empowerment expert, and many other "hats" are pushed on educators. Networked learning is even pushing on more hats, as authors have identified roles such as "the collector", "the curator", "the alchemist", "the programmer", "the concierge", to mention just a few of them (Downes 2010; Siemens 2008). These many roles have then to be interpreted within an increasingly complex classroom orchestration (Dillenbourg 2011), that includes a number of tools and meso and macro levels requirements. Our claim is that this constant push to bring change through the micro-level of the teacher is unrealistic.

Technology is sometimes seen to form the core of online learning, a complement in blended learning and tangential to face-to-face learning. However, this is hardly true anymore, technology is pervasive and its effects are expansive: technology is a constant part of the lives of educators and students; whether it has an "educational" origin or not. Thus, questions such as which technology to incorporate, how to integrate it, when to deploy it, how to assess the results, and what to do next, call for conscious decisions. Such decisions are seldom made (Kirkwood and Price 2016). To remedy this situation we suggest that the integration of technology in education needs to be 'designed' from the ground up, with the support of experts from other disciplines, but with educators leading these design tasks. Furthermore, a human-centred design approach will make a key difference to such design efforts.

Thus, our focus is on the activity of designing technology-enhanced learning. Admittedly, this is also the focus of the Learning Design field (Dalziel et al. 2012; Laurillard 2012), but the term wrongly suggest that learning can be designed. At best the conditions for it can (see also Carvalho and Goodyear 2014; Goodyear 2015). This notwithstanding, we conceptualize Learning Design as a specialisation of human-centred design. Matching the goals of Learning Design, we believe that human-centred design can bring more coherence to the current, rather loosely organised and individually-oriented task of design for learning with Information and Communication Technologies (ICT) tools. To accomplish this, three intertwined aspects need to be addressed: (1) how to incorporate the human-centred design *mindset* in the design of technology-enhanced learning, (2) how to bring the human-centred design *process* in the design of ICT-based activities and educational technology, and (3) how to bring in human-centred design *methods* to the design for learning.

The present chapter elaborates on these three aspects. It is structured as follows. We start with an overview of the two key ingredients of our argument: human-centred design as well as current trends in technology-enhanced learning. Then follows a survey of what is known of educators as designers and an overview of a real intervention that was aimed to guide educators through the design of an ICT-based learning activity. Drawing on our desk research and our own experiences with said intervention, we conclude with a proposal on how, through the incorporation of human-centred design, teams could design more relevant technology-enhanced learning.

2.2 An Exploration of Human-Centred Design and Technology-Enhanced Learning

Many educators pride themselves on being pedagogically (as opposed to technologically) driven in their teaching and learning designs (Anderson and Dron 2011). Without delving into the many possible reasons, we do acknowledge that there are still tensions when it comes to incorporating technology in education. Terry Anderson (2009) uses the metaphor of a *dance* to explain how technology and pedagogy intertwine: technology sets the beat and creates the music, while pedagogy defines the moves. Pursuing this metaphor, we can view Jonassen and Reeves' categories (1996) of how students interact with technologies as three different types of dances, scripted by educators. Their categorial system differentiates between *learning about technology* (technology as a subject), *learning from technology* (technology as a delivery tool) and *learning with technology* (technology as a cognitive partner). When we described earlier the use of technology in education as either incremental or disruptive, it is only the third option—technology as a cognitive partner—that holds promises for educational innovation; whether incremental or disruptive.

2.2.1 *Human-Centred Design*

With Herbert Simon, we believe that design is a problem-solving, process-oriented activity and we subscribe to his idea that: "everyone designs who devises courses of action aimed at changing existing situations into preferred ones" (Simon 1996, p. 111). This quote captures the essence of our point of view: not only designers design but everyone does at some point of time. Nevertheless, we also consider design to be a specialist undertaking. As such, its results profit from a specific mindset, a set of methods and a defined process.

As we already announced our theoretical approach is aligned with the notion of human-centred design (HCD), as it provides this specific mindset, toolbox of methods, and process. Some of these are clearly defined by the six key *principles* that guide the implementation of HCD from the ISO 9241-210 'Ergonomics of human-centred system interaction' (ISO 2009):

1. the design should be based upon an explicit understanding of users, tasks, and environments;
2. users should be involved throughout the design;
3. the design should be driven by user-centred evaluation;
4. the process should be iterative;
5. the design should address the whole user experience; and
6. the design team should be multidisciplinary in terms of skills and perspectives.

We strongly believe that these principles should also guide the conceptualization, implementation, integration and refinement of technology-enhanced learning and educational technology.

As per the first principle, HCD is a design philosophy that incorporates the end user's' perspective at each step of the product or service development. This way both the design process and its results become humanized in a two-way process of information exchange (Norman 2013; Cooper 2004). This is linked with the concept of iteration (principle 4) and fits with current HCD developments such as the idea of "sense and respond" (Gothelf and Seiden 2017), which we will explain later. Crucially, humans are a prominent part of the equation and so we also embrace a bidirectional relationship between users and designers.

In education, there are two main groups of users: educators and students. Note, however, that our focus lies with the meta-level of the design of learning. That is, we do not focus on how learning design affects the learners but rather on the question of how to support educators in their design activities. In our view, the realm of the design for learning—that is, the design of technology-enhanced learning activities—ought to be governed by educators. Thus, in this layered environment that is education, educators are our key target users. Educators—forming education's micro-level—also become the "bridge" with other stakeholders—such as learning technologists or instructional designers—who contribute to the creation of technology-enhanced learning activities and educational technologies per se.

In a HCD process, users are continuously involved in service or product development (principle 2). The ways in which this is done vary depending on the development stage and of course the resources available, both in time and budget. It is key to define evaluative "checkpoints" in order to integrate the users' feedback into the development of the designs (principle 3). This evaluation process also needs to be designed: how will the integration of that specific ICT tool be assessed? Which inputs will the educator use to decide what to do next?

The fifth principle demands that the effects and, thus, the evaluation of technology-enhanced learning be analysed at the system level. It is not just the tool per se that counts but also how it supports the learning activity, how it is perceived and grasped by the students, how the educator can follow what is going on, etc. The field of Teachers Inquiry into Student Learning (TISL) (Wasson et al. 2016) promotes the idea that the usage of student data is a skill that teachers must develop in order to teach in the information and technology-rich classroom (data literacy).

This proposal, however, takes us back to our previous claim: individual educators themselves cannot be expected to master and orchestrate the increasingly complex and diverse array of tools, resources, activities, data and people that make up learning ecosystems. This is why, distancing ourselves from fields such as TISL or Teachers as Designers (Kali et al. 2015), we bring in principle 6: educators should be surrounded by multidisciplinary teams in terms of skills and perspectives.

To sum up our design stance, we adopt human-centred design as our lens and baseline because:

1. It is a mindset, one that entails a specific and guided approach to problem-solving.
2. It acknowledges the role of humans both as designers and users of design processes, services and artefacts.
3. It is system-aware, it does not take technology or the users out of their context. It concerns itself with the many forces that interact and collide.
4. It is process-oriented and provides a set of methods to address design as a continuous activity based on learning from and improvement of the designed artefacts.

These characteristics, we propose, should provide the guiding principles for the processes of conceptualization, implementation, evaluation and improvement of technology-enhanced learning. Although the design stance we advocate does not restrict its use to technology-enhanced learning contexts in education, it best shows its strength there.

With the growing intricacy and pervasiveness of technology, human-centred design has evolved and branched off into different fields; in spite of their different approaches and names, they all share a focus on the end user of a product or service. Thus, whether one calls it "user experience" (UX), "design thinking", "service design" or "lean UX", all are still following the same human-centred design principles.

Whereas in academia, human-computer interaction is the common term for the same concept, user experience (UX) (Kuniavsky 2003) is the most widespread name in the industry and less formal training settings. Design thinking (Buchanan 1992, to cite just one) is also well-known and promotes an empathic, empirical and iterative approach, again very similar to human-centred design.

Service design (Stickdorn and Schneider 2012) openly acknowledged the idea that user experience is holistic and encompasses all moments and levels of a user interacting with a service and not just with the product itself. Thus, the design needs to encompass people, infrastructure, communication and material components of a service. Carvalho and Goodyear (2017) advocate the application of service design ideas and methods in the realm of education since "design for learning is hybrid, involving mixtures of service, product and space design. This hybridity is accompanied by a need for a more complex knowledge-base for design than is sometimes found in discussions of knowledge for university teaching" (Goodyear 2015).

The design of technology-enhanced learning should not only learn from service design but also incorporate more "agile" and novel approaches which—again based on the same HCD principles—call for faster cycles of design to constantly learn from users and, thus, reduce uncertainty (Gothelf and Seiden 2017). As is characteristic of the social realm, educators cannot know beforehand the impact and effects that a given learning activity will have. The Lean UX approach focuses on how to learn about this impact as early as possible to make the necessary adjustments to the designed service or product.

In Lean UX (Gothelf and Seiden 2016) as in the Lean Startup movement (Ries 2011), the design cycles consist of three phases: learn, build and measure. The main difference with HCD—besides the focus on short cycles—is that the process starts with a solution (normally called a 'Minimum Viable Product') as opposed to an initial period of investigating the target users. The goal of the minimum viable product is to put the product in the hands of users as soon as possible to gather feedback and improve subsequent product iterations.

Thus, as Gothelf and Seiden (2017) state, any company needs to establish a continuous conversation with its users in order to learn from them and include these learnings in the product development. This approach also involves a shift in focus: instead of working to get "outputs", teams should aim to get "outcomes". This is best done through cross-functional and autonomous teams, whose main goal is to learn about the interaction between the users and the designed product or service. These newer HCD approaches have also incorporated the scientific method to guide the validation of assumptions and hypotheses, all aimed at reducing uncertainty.

There have been attempts to strengthen collaboration and combine perspectives of designers, educators and educational technologists, but research on how to organize this is still limited. Researchers have tested the integration of educators in the design processes: research for practice (Shrader et al. 2001); design-based implementation research (Penuel et al. 2011); teachers as collaborative designers (Cviko et al. 2014; Svihla et al. 2015; Voogt et al. 2015); teachers as participatory designers (Cober et al. 2015); or through partnerships (Matuk et al. 2015). Although these initiatives go a long way, they still fail to properly empower educators.

2.2.2 Technology-Enhanced Learning (TEL)

Within technology-enhanced learning, *technology as a delivery tool* is the mainstream mode of adoption of educational technology nowadays. However, *technology as a cognitive partner* is what we strive for. This is true for both educational researchers (Jonassen and Reeves 1996; Ertmer and Ottenbreit-Leftwich 2012; Ertmer et al. 2012) and educational technologists (Brown et al. 2015; Merriman et al. 2016; Dron and Anderson 2016). Thus, these often siloed and tensioned disciplines seem to have a common goal: integrate technology to allow students to do real work and, therefore, facilitate authentic student learning (see also Sloep 2013).

With this aim in mind, several institutions have already worked on the development of post-Learning Management Systems (LMS) solutions. This is the case of the OUNL and Athabasca University, for example. The former, under the name of OpenU, has created a learning system with four distinct environments: the Personal Learning Network, the Course Learning Network; the Professional Development Network and the topic/research networks (Hermans et al. 2014). Similarly, to support the need for social learning, Athabasca University has developed the "Athabasca Landing", an Elgg-based beyond-the-LMS social system (Rahman and Dron 2012). These solutions are part of what Anderson and Dron (Anderson and Dron 2011; Dron and Anderson 2016) define as the "fourth or holistic generation" of educational technology; one that will be deeply integrated within learners' whole lives and those of others.

These new environments respond to the increasing unease with existing LMSs (Kop and Fournier 2013) and the need for more social-oriented, not course-limited environments. About ten years ago, the limitations and constraints of mainstream LMSs gave birth to the Personal Learning Environments (PLEs) concept (Wilson et al. 2007). Whereas the LMS is built around the course concept and intended for formal instruction in particular, the idea behind the Personal Learning Environment is that it is governed solely by the learner. Essentially, PLEs aim to facilitate students' use of technology as a cognitive partner (Rajagopal et al. 2017).

The current state of the TEL art is that there are a myriad of technology tools and devices that currently support technology-enhanced learning, which can be integrated through a "Lego-approach", already foreseen in the PLE literature and now apparent in the Next Generation of Digital Learning Environments (NGDLE) reports (Table 2.1). This next generation is closer to a learning ecosystem: a learning environment consisting of learning tools and components that adhere to common standards and enable different and diverse pedagogies.

This flexibility, disaggregation, modularity, Lego-structure of the upcoming educational-technology environments is extremely challenging from the designers' and users' perspectives since it places the focus on their activities. The underlying characteristic of NGDLE is that learners and educators will be able to shape and customize their learning environments to support their needs and objectives. Yet, still most educational technology is developed without the inputs from educators or educational sciences (Könings et al. 2007, 2014).

Table 2.1 Characteristics of the next generation of digital learning environments

The NDGLE: a component infrastructure to leverage technology for teaching and learning	
The Next Generation Digital Learning Environment: A Report on Research—EDUCAUSE 2015 (Brown et al. 2015)	Next-generation environments must address five dimensions: interoperability and integration; personalization; analytics, advising, and learning assessment; collaboration and accessibility and universal design
The Next Generation Learning Architecture—(Merriman et al. 2016)	The next generation of digital learning environments consists of a marketplace of Enterprise Infrastructure Services and a marketplace of educational applications, of various types or classes, which consume Enterprise Infrastructure Services A new class of applications, the Learning Method eXperience (LMX) provides the context and overall user experience required for a particular educational methodology or pedagogical model
Educational Provisioning System (EPS)—(Hermans et al. 2015)	Rather than implementing provisioning rules directly in an online learning system, the EPS allows for managing provisioning rules independent of the learning application(s) in use. This EPS allows for both managing and processing provisioning rules in order to meet the demands of new online educational formats

On the other hand, due to its component-based architecture grounded in standards and best practices, the NGDLE brings the opportunity to explore new approaches and develop new tools. The success of these learning ecosystems is highly dependant on the processes and activities that actually involve learning science knowledge as well as educators (and at a later stage, students) in the conceptualization and refinement of the educational technologies' features. Without this involvement, *learning* will still not be part of the environment and it will be yet another technology limited to the status of delivery tool at best.

As a result, technology-enhanced learning is at a paradoxical stage. On the one hand, practitioners of all related disciplines—educational researchers, educators, learning technologists—agree on the essentials: (1) learning with technology has yet to mature; (2) technology in education should become a cognitive tool. On the other hand, the means to make this happen have not yet been established.

Our proposal is that HCD provides these means to purposely implement TEL and impact the three levels of learning and teaching—micro, meso and macro. HCD will facilitate the "conversations" between these levels and related stakeholders by providing, first of all, a shared mindset: all work for the end users' (students') needs; and secondly, by establishing a process and the tools that allow one to integrate these needs and context into TEL designs and also the educational technology involved.

In fact, following the NGDLE metaphor of Lego pieces, our approach also puts into play the human pieces. Only with an interplay of disciplines will education include technology as a cognitive tool, will educational technology be designed for its users, and will learning environments be designed for learning. We will do so by screening off a precious yet battered resource: educators. Then, we will see the same evolution as professional designers will soon have to embrace (Manzini 2015; Sanders 2006): both educators and designers will be *enablers*, facilitators and process managers for others to learn and design, respectively.

2.3 Educators as Designers

In the HCD sense, educators are our target users. They are ultimately responsible for the design, enactment and development of TEL activities. They also liaise with their students and with the educational institution they work for. Thus, their role is pivotal in any effort to incorporate the HCD mindset, process and methods in education.

We start by providing an overview of what is known of how educators design and then we introduce the results of an intervention. It was designed to guide educators through a HCD process which was meant to facilitate educators to design technology-enhanced learning activities.

2.3.1 Teachers as Designers, What We Know

By now it should not come as a surprise that we claim designing to be a complex and intricate task. It demands of the designer to take into account and integrate many different and diverse elements. It also requires her to consider the problem and the solution from many different perspectives. This description of design deeply resonates with an educator's work. Teachers must perceive, interpret and enact existing resources, evaluate the constraints of the classroom setting, balance trade-offs and devise strategies—all in the pursuit of their instructional goals (Brown and Edelson 2003). As in design, educators create, adapt and try out resources to fit their specific needs and contexts.

Many researchers such as Brown and Edelson (2003) emphasize this situated and practice-oriented design work that educators accomplish. This pragmatic approach to design means that educators privilege practicality and feasibility (McKenney et al. 2015) and leverage practice-based experiences to make decisions (Roschelle and Penuel 2006). As a result, much relevant teacher design expertise comes intuitively, is acquired on a daily basis and congruent with the teacher's beliefs and convictions.

Schön (1983) defined this kind of intuited expertise as "designerly ways of knowing", which are learned through direct and indirect engagement in authentic design practices, rather than an explicit, formally-represented body of knowledge and skills. According to Schön, professionalism is gained by *reflection-in-action*, which enables the practitioner to think deeply about situations while they are happening, interpret and frame them in particular ways and adapt his/her actions accordingly, as opposed to *reflection-on-action*, which is done after the fact, much as an afterthought.

Extending the research on how educators actually design, according to Matuk et al. (2015) teachers' decisions in customizing technology-enhanced learning materials are the result of interactions between knowledge of their students and the subject matter, beliefs about teaching and learning, and orientations toward technology and their roles as designers. The authors conclude: "Research also indicates that whereas attendance to students' ideas can result in customizations that greatly benefit learning, *issues of practicality primarily drive teachers' intuitive customizations*" (italics ours).

Similarly, Bennett et al. (2015) observed that Higher Education teachers' perceptions of student characteristics, their own beliefs and experiences, and contextual factors are key influences on design decisions. In another study, Boschman et al. (2014) found that the considerations Kindergarten teachers entertained during design were influenced mostly by practical concerns, although their pedagogical orientation, beliefs about how children learn, and convictions of how learning should be supported by teachers also played a role.

So, there can be little doubt that the praxis of teachers involves design:

- As in design, teaching is a highly complex activity that draws on many kinds of knowledge (Mishra and Koehler 2006).
- As with the problem spaces in design, teaching occurs in ill-structured, dynamic environments and, therefore, teaching also deals with what are known in design as wicked problems (Rittel and Weber 1973; Opfer and Pedder 2011; Sloep 2013).
- As in design, teaching is iterative: it seldom happens just once; there is a continuous enactment and tweaking of activities and resources (Pardo et al. 2015; Bates 2015).

While we can see some patterns emerging from existing research—that we further analyse below—some authors (Agostinho et al. 2011; McKenney et al. 2015) also point out how more empirical research is needed to better understand teachers' design practices so as to achieve closer alignment between teachers' needs and their design initiatives.

However, the way in which educators design, also reveals a number of idiosyncrasies:

1. **Teacher designs are experience-shaped**. Kali et al. (2011) talk about "folk pedagogy" (in an apparent analogy to folk psychology), that is, how an individual teacher's ways of teaching are strongly shaped by his/her personal experience of having been taught themselves. Educators can discuss sophisticated ideas of instruction in the abstract, for example on how to incorporate educational technology. And yet, specific design situations activate experiential knowledge, which more often than not leads to traditional forms of instruction.
2. **Teacher designs are underpinned by beliefs**. In 1999, Ertmer (1999) distinguished between two types of barriers that impact teachers' uses of technology in the classroom:

   a. First-order barriers are defined as those that are external to the teacher and include resources (both hardware and software), training, and support.
   b. Second-order barriers comprise those that are internal to the teacher and include teachers' confidence, beliefs about how students learn, as well as the perceived value of technology to the teaching/learning process.

   Although first-order barriers pose significant obstacles to achieving technology integration, the underlying, unconscious second-order barriers have proved to pose the greater challenge (see also Kreijns et al. 2013).
3. **Teacher designs are learner-adapted**. Stark (2000) reported how educators' design decisions were strongly influenced by the perceived characteristics of their students. Bennett et al. (2015) confirm this influence and suggest that these judgements are currently reliant on recollections and impressions built up over time and through contact with students.
4. **Teacher designs are practice-driven and practice-oriented** (Doyle and Ponder 1977; Ertmer 1999; Janssen et al. 2013; Boschman et al. 2014; Matuk et al. 2015). Practicality and feasibility is the key driver of educators when designing: teachers must ensure that the enactment with the students fulfils the learning outcomes and, for that reason, possible barriers have to be reduced to a minimum.
5. **Teacher designs are context-shaped**. As part of the practice-driven component but relevant to take into account as a separate factor, many authors have stated the relevance of context [Bennett et al. (2015) and McKenney et al. (2015), for example]. Context needs to be understood not as the immediate physical space of the classroom but in a broader sense, as encompassing all factors and constraints impinging on the educator. These include the customary meso level of the school and the macro level of national educational policies and whatever bodies oversee and monitor the operation of schools.

From this set of factors, it is relevant to notice that almost all of them operate very much at an unconscious level, are deeply rooted in the experiences and beliefs of educators, and are grouped in what Ertmer (1999) defined as second-order barriers (Kreijns et al. 2013).

Kali et al. (2011) also explored how novices carry out design activities. They report how they exhibit a lack of Schön's reflection-in-action, which derives from experience. Using HCD terms, in their 'rush to implementation" (Goodyear 2015, p. 31) novices skip two key phases of the design process: the exploration phase and the analysis/reflection phase (Hoogveld et al. 2001; O'Neill 2010). They ignore the "fuzzy front end" (Sanders and Stappers 2008) of exploration. But this is a critical phase, one that determines what is to be designed and sometimes what should not be designed; in it designers take into account considerations of many different natures. As such it is a divergent phase. Similarly, novices also often ignore the reflection phase. However, it is an essential step for continuous improvement, like learning by doing. Here too, novices fail to take the opportunity to use the enactment of the learning activities as a source for learning and enhancing their practices.

But what then is it that teachers do know and how does this knowledge affect their design activities? Teaching requires a complex set of knowledges, as illustrated by the Technological Pedagogical and Content Knowledge framework. This conceptual framework (Magnusson et al. 1999) for educational technology builds on Shulman's formulation of "pedagogical content knowledge" (Shulman 1986) and incorporates the role of technology in education.

The relationships between content (the actual subject matter that is to be learned and taught), pedagogy (the process and practice or methods of teaching and learning), and technology (both commonplace, like chalkboards, and advanced, such as digital computers) are complex and nuanced (Mishra and Koehler 2006). The analysis of the interplay needs to consider these components as a whole, in pairs, but also in isolation.

Here, we focus on the pedagogical knowledge only. For a teacher to have this type of knowledge she should understand how students construct knowledge, acquire skills, and develop habits of mind and positive dispositions toward learning. As such, pedagogical knowledge requires an understanding of cognitive, social, and developmental theories of learning and how they apply to students in their classroom (Mishra and Koehler 2006). This is the type of knowledge that one expects educators to master.

Yet, many educators lack this "deep pedagogical knowledge". In the terms of Kali et al. (2011), the pedagogical knowledge of educators often takes the form of 'folk' beliefs. While it is true that educators think in terms of learning outcomes and the change they want to promote, they seldom ground their praxis in theories (Bennett et al. 2015).

This does not mean that educators are not concerned with pedagogy but that, rather than having a coherent and consistent theory of teaching and learning, teachers apply a loose collection of practice-oriented strategies, each one locally coherent, although not necessarily systematically validated. Kali et al. (2011) call this notion "pedagogical knowledge in pieces".

This "pedagogical knowledge in pieces" is adequate for the praxis of teaching. However, it hampers the systematization of learning designs and the conversation with other disciplines. It actually clashes with the idea that one has about what educators know. For an outsider, educators know about pedagogy. It is assumed that they ground their practice in validated theories of learning. This turns out not to be the case. We believe that this gap between how educators operate in actual fact and what other disciplines expect from them is at the core of many problems of the implementation of educational technology.

In summary, teachers are designers of learning, there can be little doubt about that. However, they design in an intuitive fashion, with a focus on direct educational practice, making use of an eclectic collection of pedagogical insights that are more informed by their own practice and perhaps those of others they know about than by theoretical insights. Various authors discussed in the above have argued this position. Many also have wondered how the design abilities of teachers could be improved upon. In an experimental intervention, in the guise of a Massive Online Open Course, we made an attempt to improve teachers' design abilities. We summarise our key learnings in the next section. Details on the experience and its results can be found in Garreta-Domingo et al. (2015, 2017, 2018, accepted for publication).

2.3.2 Teachers as Designers, an Intervention

Earlier we introduced the notion that educators design with a particular mental model of who and what their learners are. Taking into account the characteristics of the students is key to good design; even if this raises the question of the quality of the information that educators have about their students (Bennett et al. 2015).

Research shows that teachers' student-centred beliefs tend to result in more authentic uses of technology while traditional beliefs tend to have a negative impact on the integrated use of computers (Hermans et al. 2008). And, at a broader level, Bennett et al. (2015) reported how many authors have concluded that student-focused approaches to teaching encourage deep approaches to learning, that result in high quality learning outcomes.

These beliefs not only affect the conceptualization of the learning activities but are beneficial also during their implementation and evaluation. A student-focused approach allows a teacher to be responsive to student needs and interests during the enactment of the activities (Postareff et al. 2008).

As Ertmer et al. (2012) confirm, research results suggest close alignment; that is, student-centred beliefs undergird student-centred practices (authenticity, student choice, collaboration). But despite such beliefs there are also constraints that prevent student-centred practices to blossom to the full. In fact, teachers with student-centred beliefs do not necessarily translate those beliefs into learning activities that use technology as a cognitive partner or indeed in activities that use technology at all. Educational practitioners often see technology as a burden, an imposition (Kreijns et al. 2013; OECD 2015). How come? Is education different, are educational practitioners different, or is there an issue with the way technology affects education?

To tackle these issues, we advocate a shift of focus, away from the technology and also, in some sense, away from the students. Educators and educational designers, developers and researchers should primarily focus on the design of learning activities and on how to enhance them through technology. This shift of focus has dramatic consequences. It implies designing *for use* rather than *for users* (Williams 2009). Following the Activity-Centred Design approach (Gay and Hembrooke 2004; Gifford and Enyedy 1995), designers should focus on the activity in order to deliver tools that effectively support users in real-world contexts (Norman 2005; Hoekman 2010). In the educational research realm, the Activity-Centred Analysis and Design (ACAD) framework (Goodyear and Carvalho 2014; Carvalho and Goodyear 2017) advocates the same shift.

The ACAD framework places the learning activity at the centre of the design process and differentiates between three different dimensions: epistemic, set and social (Table 2.2). Like HCD, the ACAD framework acknowledges the interplay of the different components in a system. It is our belief that we need this holistic perspective to build the next generation of digital learning environments and pedagogies and, as a consequence, the next generation of educators and learners (Sloep 2013).

Despite their differentiation between these three design dimensions, Goodyear and Carvalho (2014, p. 57) emphasize the importance to carefully distinguish between

Table 2.2 Learning design dimensions according to Goodyear and Carvalho (2014) and how they were designed in our intervention

Dimensions	Short description	Our intervention
Task structure and **epistemic design**	Epistemic design refers to the knowledge-oriented structure of a network; the activity is goal-oriented and facilitates learning and knowledge creation	A Massive Open Online Course (MOOC) that walks educators through the design process of an ICT-based learning activity of their own making
Structures of place and **set design**	The activity is also shaped by the physical/digital setting in which it unfolds. Thus, the relations between place, tools and activity are key to both analysis and design	A combination of online tools chosen to provide the necessary learning and design support to the design efforts of the MOOC participants
Organizational forms and **social design**	What people do is often influenced by the actions of other people around them, including the instructions, advice, encouragement and warnings they give At a broader level, social norms, rules and habits tend to have an effect, even if other people are not physically around	A set of facilitators to guide participant educators through their design processes; together with the comments and feedback from their peers. And of course the set of norms, rules, etc. that each participant brings along, which are outside of intervention control

what can be designed and what cannot: "We *may* be able to design the thing that is experienced, but we cannot design the experience itself" (italics theirs). The context, the tasks and the tools can be designed; however at learn time learners are likely to reconfigure what has been proposed in new ways (see also Goodyear 2015). As we have seen earlier, this difference between what a designer intends and what actually happens is acknowledged by HCD approaches. It is through a continuous and iterative approach to design that we learn and reduce uncertainty; at each iteration, the team analyses what happened and takes action according to it with the aim of improving the design for the forthcoming iteration and bringing that what happens closer to that which is intended.

Thus, to reiterate a point made earlier, to implement HCD in TEL three intertwined aspects need to be addressed: (1) how to incorporate the HCD *mindset* in the design of TEL, (2) how to bring the HCD *process* in the design of ICT-based activities and educational technology; and (3) how to bring in HCD *methods* to the design for learning. To gather insights into the relative importance of these three aspects, we designed an intervention along the lines of the ACAD model. After briefly introducing the context of our intervention, we explain next its 'set', 'social' and 'epistemic' design dimensions.

The context of our intervention is a Massive Open Online Course (MOOC) on a topic that—as we have seen—many teachers struggle with: the inclusion of ICT in education (OECD 2015). It was intended to offer a genuine professional development opportunity for educators of all educational levels (Garreta-Domingo et al. 2018; Stoyanov et al. 2014). The HANDSON MOOC—implemented under a Lifelong Learning Programme project (http://www.handsonict.eu/)—was open and free. Based on HCD methods and process, the course guided educators through the design of their own TEL activity.

The *set design* of the MOOC included Moodle, for the first edition, and Canvas, for the second one, as the course platform; Moodle/Canvas contained the syllabus, the design tasks as well as the discussion forums. The Integrated Learning Design Environment (ILDE) was the design platform on both occasions; this web platform allows communities of educational designers to co-create and share learning designs both from scratch or by using templates provided (Asensio-Pérez et al. 2017).

The MOOC's *social design* comprised interaction with facilitators and peers in the forums and through weekly synchronous sessions. The first iteration of the MOOC featured three facilitators, experts in Learning Design and HCD. The second iteration was offered in seven languages in parallel, thus there were 15 facilitators who addressed the students in their native language. These facilitators were all volunteers; they had no formal HCD expertise, but were trained to act as process managers for the participants. English was used for instructions and general communications only.

The *epistemic design* was grounded in the idea of studio-based teaching (Mor and Mogilevsky 2013; Reimer and Douglas 2003; Winograd 1990). In this online studio, participants designed a TEL activity that by the end of the course was intended to be ready for enactment in their respective teaching settings. The epistemic design concerns the tasks learners (in our case, educators as lifelong learners) carry out in order to acquire new knowledge. Following our focus on human-centred design to empower educators as designers, our epistemic design mimics a HCD process from considering the user requirements, to conceptualising the solution and, then, testing it on each iteration (Fig. 2.1).

It is not the focus of the present chapter to analyse the results from these two interventions, interested readers are referred to the following papers: set design (Garreta-Domingo et al. 2015), social design (Garreta-Domingo et al. 2017), epistemic design (Garreta-Domingo et al. 2018 and Garreta-Domingo et al. under review). We summarize here what we learned from our inclusion of HCD in technology-enhanced learning:

1. **Incorporating the HCD *mindset* in the design of TEL**
   As "amateur" designers, participant educators showed some designerly concerns and tasks. Interestingly, more pedagogically-savvy educators tended to place the focus on the ICT-tool as opposed to the activity; but educators with little familiarity with pedagogical models and trends, were able to act according to the HCD mindset that was "transmitted" to them through the design tasks (epistemic design) and in the conversations in the forums (social design).

Design Studio for ICT-based Learning Activities - HANDSON MOOC (2)

Week 1: Initiate **Learning goals:** Get acquainted with LDS and define an initial version of the educational challenge.	A1: Introduction to the Design Studio for ICT-based Learning Activities! A2: Set up your Design Studio Journal. It is a tool for you! A3: ILDE Account and Dream Bazaar A4: Peer-mentoring - your dream!
Week 2: Investigate **Learning goal:** Get acquainted and apply HCD methods for user needs analysis. Review educational challenge based on peer feedback.	A5: Get familiar with the persona concept A6: Create your own persona A7: Analyzing context, factors and concerns A8: The objectives of your ICT-based learning activity A9: Revisit your dream and update it A10: Peer-mentoring - Your personas!
Week 3: Inspire & Ideate **Learning goal:** Continue user needs analysis and shaping the learning activity. Start thinking on monitoring the experience.	A11: Define the heuristics for your design project A12: Search for existing ICT-based learning activities A13: Learn about user scenarios A14: Ideate through writing a user scenario A15: Peer-mentoring - The objectives
Week 4: Prototype **Learning goal:** Translate the results of previous tasks into a prototype and assess it with a user or peer.	A16: Prototype your artifact A17: Revisit and update your evaluation heuristics A18: Test your prototype *Advanced authoring and implementation* A19: Consolidate your prototype A20: Peer-mentoring - Consolidate your prototype
Week 5: Evaluate & Reflect **Learning goal:** Receive peer feedback on the design activity. Reflect on the course.	A21: Publish your learning activity A22: Peer-mentoring - Your learning activity A23: Your design studio report A24: Reflect and share your thoughts!

Fig. 2.1 The HANDSON MOOC's (2nd edition) course activities (see also Garreta-Domingo et al. under authors' revision)

2. **Including the HCD *process* in the design of ICT-based activities and educational technology**
   Our intervention also aimed at solving several of the shortcomings that many professional development activities have: our focus was not on the theory or the technology but on a personal educational challenge that each educator wanted to address through the design of an ICT-based learning activity. This made the process much more relevant and meaningful to each participant and, therefore, useful for the desired outcome: to have an activity ready to implement.
3. **Including HCD *methods* in the design for learning**
   Participant educators had a hard time comprehending and actioning some of the HCD methods. The general trend was to assimilate the method to what was already known to them. Thus, we see how many "personas" were just a description

of a real student rather than archetypical ones, and how many "heuristics" were turned into student evaluation rubrics rather than means to evaluate their design.

Taking Carvalho and Goodyear's (2017) service design lens to analyse the insights we gained from the intervention, at the base level of learning (what educators did according to themselves) our interventions were valued very positively and participants would both repeat and recommend the experience (Garreta-Domingo et al. 2015). Nevertheless, at the superposed level of managing their own learning, participating educators did not have the necessary context nor the scaffolding to understand what was expected from them in the case of some HCD methods. We concluded that more introductory tasks as well as a less domain-specific vocabulary would facilitate the of HCD to educators (Garreta-Domingo et al. under authors' revision). Moreover, in line with HCD, educators should be able to practice this new framework as an iterative, in-context and applied activity.

2.4 Conclusions: Empowering Educators as Designers and Team Members

This chapter has explored the design as undertaken by teachers through the juxtaposition of human-centred design and technology-enhanced learning. The relevance of design for education is widely acknowledged. However, in line with the key ideas of HCD, our position stands out in that we emphasize that only *through its related mindset, processes and methods* design can play a key role in the creation of learning activities and of educational technology. We believe that only then design can integrate currently scattered but strongly interrelated activities. What does this imply for teachers?

Traditionally, educators have worked almost always singly. Admittedly, they have to follow curriculum programmes and abide by both educational and institutional guidelines. However, they have mostly operated on their own in their daily practices. Moreover, the traditional tensions between education and technology are still present. Still many educators and educational researchers pride themselves on being pedagogically (as opposed to technologically) driven in their teaching and learning research and designs. Still most educational technology is developed without sufficient inputs from educators or educational sciences.

We have seen how educators approach the design of learning activities and lesson plans. Their practice-oriented, experience-based and mostly intuitive design activities call for a more systematic and professional approach. We have also seen how properly designed interventions can empower teachers as HCD designers. Our empirical research has provided insights in how educators can acquire a design mindset, follow a design process and apply HCD methods, albeit that they need support through an applied learning process.

So, our answer to the question '*how can HCD bring coherence to the currently loosely organised and individually-oriented task of design for learning with ICT tools?*' would be the following. Given that educators accomplish design tasks almost on a daily basis, they could—like many designers—benefit from a hands-on, multidisciplinary, collaborative and iterative approach, as advocated by the field of human-centred design. In fact, all actors in technology-enhanced learning design would benefit from such an approach. They may not approach design in the same way, some may not even call it design, but willy-nilly they all abide by Simon's (1996) maxim to *devise courses of action aimed at changing existing situations into preferred ones*.

That said, the design of technology-enhanced learning activities is strongly related to the affordances and features of (educational) technologies. Some, erroneously, still claim technology to be 'just a tool'; but technologies also influence and define their usage, something which is even more relevant if one wants these tools to become cognitive tools. The near future holds promises: thanks to the flexibility, interoperability and distributed nature of the next generation of digital learning environments any learning design could be supported. For this to happen, we first need to design them. The foreseen software architecture allows for a Lego approach, but *someone* needs to decide which are the bricks and how they are to be put together.

As advocated by a human-centred design approach, this *someone* should be a multidisciplinary team. We cannot expect a single individual to master all components, that is, expect teachers to be jacks of all trade. It is the hands-on collaboration among disciplines that will allow for qualitatively high ranking and innovative learning designs, pedagogies and technologies. Educators, instructional designers and educational technologists need to find a common language and common processes. Heeding the maxims of human-centred design will facilitate the emergence of genuine technology-enhanced learning.

We envision, then, how a human-centred design approach will not only impact the design for learning but also the design of educational technology. The learning ecosystem is expected to be in continuous evolution and it is up to the *learning* processes and activities to guide this development. Educators, designers and technologists need to leverage data-driven (qualitative and quantitative) approaches to enhance, inform and intertwine their design spaces.

Indeed, looking further forward we see how the design for learning and the design of educational technology go hand in hand. To make this become a reality, silos need to be broken down and all actors involved need to embrace multidisciplinarity. This can only be achieved if processes, tools and language are shared. It is our belief that human-centred design as a philosophy and process facilitates these two essential changes.

Multidisciplinarity is a cornerstone of HCD in all its different representations and evolutions. For example, the idea of "sense and respond" (based on the Lean startup and Lean UX approaches, as discussed) is based on the existence of small and autonomous teams that have the capacity to learn—build—measure, thanks to a constant "conversation" with users.

Let's then imagine a scenario, one in which cross-functional teams define the design of technology-enhanced learning as well of educational technologies. The educator is the expert on her topic as well as on the classroom orchestration, but she works closely with expert instructional designers, UX designers and educational technology developers. The instructional designers contribute their expertise as pedagogical models. The UX designers are process facilitators, design enablers; they know the methods and they ensure that the user involvement is present at all project stages, they ensure a good user experience by having a holistic view of the different elements at play. The educational technologists are the experts on ICT tools or on the next generation digital learning environment; they are key in making the necessary changes in the technology.

These self-contained teams operate at a micro-level. For them to be successful, a shared mindset and common language, processes and tools are needed. HCD is an iterative process; through complete design lifecycles, solutions are conceptualized, defined, tested and improved. These lifecycles vary in complexity and length. In a lean UX setting, the cycles are fast, we need to learn—build—measure in short periods of time because we're also working in self-contained problems. In a more traditional HCD process, the problems we address have a larger scope and weeks become months. In both cases, the results of the design lifecycles percolate through at the meso-level and progressively the same process, methods and mindset is applied for institution-wide aspects. And this, in turn, impacts the macro-level.

We can also expect another outcome to result from applying human-centred learning design with technology. Through the HCD processes and activities, teachers will learn differently and from these new collaborative, hands-on and iterative experiences they will be able to design new learning activities. As we have seen, educators design based on their beliefs and experiences and tend to fail in the initial and final analysis stages. Providing them with a context that allows them to learn differently, explore before designing and analyse the results before implementing, will have a rippling effect on their learning designs, educational technology and students. As opposed to asking them to become "jacks of all trades", educators would be surrounded by specialists that bring in new perspectives as well as empower them as the designers of learning.

Acknowledgements We gratefully acknowledge the help of the HANDSON Consortium partners. Special thanks go to the UOC team for the HANDSON project without whom this chapter would not exist: Francesc Santanach, Israel Conejero, Mireia Garcia, Gemma Aguado, Toni Mangas, Xavi Aracil, Jorge Ferrera and Jean-François Colas.

References

Agostinho S et al (2011) The future of learning design. Learn Media Technol 36(2):97–99

Anderson T (2009) The dance of technology and pedagogy in self-paced distance education. Athabasca University, Canada, pp 1–7

Anderson T, Dron J (2011) Three generations of distance education pedagogy. Int Rev Res Open Distance Learn 12(3):80–97

Asensio-Pérez JI et al (2017) Towards teaching as design: exploring the interplay between full-lifecycle learning design tooling and teacher professional development. Comput Educ 114:92–116

Bates T (2015) Teaching in a digital age: guidelines for designing teaching and learning. Tony Bates Associates Ltd., Vancouver, BC. http://opentextbc.ca/teachinginadigitalage/

Bennett S, Agostinho S, Lockyer L (2015) Technology tools to support learning design: implications derived from an investigation of university teachers' design practices. Comput Educ 81:211–220
Boschman F, McKenney S, Voogt J (2014) Understanding decision making in teachers' curriculum design approaches. Educ Tech Res Dev 62(4):393–416
Brown M, Edelson DC (2003) Teaching as design: can we better understand the ways in which teachers use materials so we can better design materials to support their changes in practice?. Evanston, IL
Brown M, Dehoney J, Millichap N (2015) The next generation digital learning environment: a report on research, p 11
Buchanan R (1992) Wicked problems in design thinking. Des Iss 8(2):5–21
Carvalho L, Goodyear PM (2014) The architecture of productive learning networks. Routledge Falmer, New York, London
Carvalho L, Goodyear P (2017) Design, learning networks and service innovation. Des Stud 1–27. http://linkinghub.elsevier.com/retrieve/pii/S0142694X17300649
Cober R et al (2015) Teachers as participatory designers: two case studies with technology-enhanced learning environments. Instr Sci 43(2):203–228
Cooper A (2004) The inmates are running the asylum: why high-tech products drive us crazy and how to restore the sanity, 1st edn. Sams-Pearson Education, Indianapolis, IN, USA
Cviko A, McKenney S, Voogt J (2014) Teacher roles in designing technology-rich learning activities for early literacy: a cross-case analysis. Comput Educ 72:68–79. http://dx.doi.org/10.1016/j.compedu.2013.10.014
Dalziel J et al (2012) The Larnaca declaration on learning design. http://www.larnacadeclaration.org/
Dillenbourg P et al (2011) Classroom orchestration: the third circle of usability—why is paper highly usable in classrooms ? In: CSCL 2011 proceeding, I, pp 510–517. http://infoscience.epfl.ch/record/168741/files/ClassroomOrchestration:TheThirdCircleofUsability.pdf?version=1
Downes S (2010) The role of the educator. http://www.downes.ca/post/54312
Doyle W, Ponder GA (1977) The practicality ethic in teacher decision-making. Interchange 8(3):1–12
Dron J, Anderson T (2016) The future of E-learning. In: Haythornthwaite C et al (eds) SAGE handbook of E-learning research. Sage, pp 1–32
Ertmer P (1999) Addressing first- and second-order barriers to change: strategies for technology integration. Educ Tech Res Dev 47(4):47–61
Ertmer P et al (2012) Teacher beliefs and technology integration practices: a critical relationship. Comput Educ 59(2):423–435. http://dx.doi.org/10.1016/j.compedu.2012.02.001
Ertmer P, Ottenbreit-Leftwich AT (2012) Removing obstacles to the pedagogical changes required by Jonassen's vision of authentic technology-enabled learning. Comput Educ 64:175–182. http://dx.doi.org/10.1016/j.compedu.2012.10.008
Flavin M, Quintero V (2018) UK higher education institutions' technology-enhanced learning strategies from the perspective of disruptive innovation. Res Learn Technol 26(1063519):632–637. https://journal.alt.ac.uk/index.php/rlt/article/view/1987/
Garreta-Domingo M et al (2015) Teachers' perceptions about the HANDSON MOOC: a learning design studio case. In: Proceedings of the European conference on technology enhanced learning (EC-TEL). Springer, pp 420–427. https://link.springer.com/chapter/10.1007%2F978-3-319-24258-3_34
Garreta-Domingo M et al (2017) Design for collective intelligence: pop-up communities in MOOCs. AI Soc 33(1):91–100
Garreta-Domingo M, Hernández-Leo D, Sloep PB (2018) Evaluation to support learning design: lessons learned in a teacher training MOOC. Australas J Educ Technol 33(1). https://ajet.org.au/index.php/AJET/article/view/3768
Gay G, Hembrooke H (2004) Activity-centered design: an ecological approach to designing smart tools and usable systems (acting with technology). MIT Press
Gifford BR, Enyedy ND (1995) Activity centered design: towards a theoretical framework for CSCL

Goodyear P (2015) Teaching as design. HERDSA Rev High Educ 2:27–50. http://www.herdsa.org.au/wp-content/uploads/HERDSARHE2015v02p27.pdf
Goodyear P, Carvalho L (2014) Framing the analysis of learning network architectures. In: The architecture of productive learning networks, pp 48–70
Gothelf J, Seiden J (2016) Lean UX: designing great products with agile teams. O'Reilly Media
Gothelf J, Seiden J (2017) Sense and respond: how successful organizations listen to customers and create new products continuously. Harvard Business Review Press
Hermans R et al (2008) The impact of primary school teachers' educational beliefs on the classroom use of computers. Comput Educ 51(4):1499–1509
Hermans H, Kalz M, Koper R (2014) Towards a learner-centred system for adult learning. Campus-Wide Inf Syst 31:2–13
Hermans H et al (2015) Flexible provisioning for adult learners. J Univ Comput Sci 21(2):206–222
Hoekman R (2010) Designing the obvious: a common sense approach to web application design, 2nd ed. New Riders
Hoogveld AWM et al (2001) The effects of a web-based training in an instructional systems design approach on teachers' instructional design behavior. Comput Human Behav 17(4):363–371
ISO (2009) Ergonomics of human system interaction—Part 210: Human-centred design for interactive systems (ISO 9241-210:2010; formerly known as 13407). International Organization for Standardization
Janssen F et al (2013) How to make innovations practical. Teach Coll Rec 115(7):1–42
Jonassen DH, Reeves TC (1996) Learning wth technology: using computers as cognitive tools. In: Handbook of research for educational communications and technology, pp 694–719
Kali Y, Goodyear P, Markauskaite L (2011) Researching design practices and design cognition: contexts, experiences and pedagogical knowledge-in-pieces. Learn Media Technol 36(2):129–149
Kali Y, McKenney S, Sagy O (2015) Teachers as designers of technology enhanced learning. Instr Sci 43(2):173–179
Kirkwood A, Price L (2016) Technology-enhanced learning and teaching in higher education: what is "enhanced" and how do we know ? A critical literature review, vol 9884(May), pp 1–44
Könings KD, Brand-Gruwel S, van Merriënboer JJG (2007) Teachers' perspectives on innovations: Implications for educational design. Teach Teach Educ 23(6):985–997
Könings KD, Seidel T, van Merriënboer JJG (2014) Participatory design of learning environments: integrating perspectives of students, teachers, and designers. Instr Sci 42(1):1–9
Kop R, Fournier H (2013) Developing a framework for research on personal learning environments. eLearning Papers 35(November):1–16
Kreijns K et al (2013) What stimulates teachers to integrate ICT in their pedagogical practices? The use of digital learning materials in education. Comput Hum Behav 29(1):217–225
Kuniavsky M (2003) Observing the user experience: a practitioner's guide to user research, 1st edn. Morgan Kaufman Publishers, Elsevier
Laurillard D (2012) Teaching as a design science: building pedagogical patterns for learning and technology. Routledge, New York and London
Magnusson S, Krajcik J, Borko H (1999) Nature, sources and development of pedagogical content knowledge for science teaching. In: Gess-Newsome J, Lederman NG (eds) Examining pedagogical content knowledge: the construct and its implications for science education. Kluwer Academic Publishers, New York, Boston, London, Dordrecht, Moscow, pp 95–132
Manzini E (2015) Design, when everybody designs: an introduction to design for social innovation. The MIT Press, Cambridge MA
Matuk CF, Linn MC, Eylon BS (2015) Technology to support teachers using evidence from student work to customize technology-enhanced inquiry units. Instr Sci 43(2):229–257
McKenney S et al (2015) Teacher design knowledge for technology enhanced learning: an ecological framework for investigating assets and needs. Instr Sci 43(2):181–202
Merriman J et al (2016) Next generation learning architecture. http://hdl.handle.net/10609/47481
Mishra P, Koehler MJ (2006) Technological pedagogical content knowledge: a framework for teacher knowledge. Teach Coll Rec 108(6):1017–1054

Mor Y, Mogilevsky O (2013) The learning design studio: collaborative design inquiry as teachers' professional development. Res Learn Technol 21(1):1–15
Norman DA (2005) Human-centered design considered to be harmful. Interactions - Ambient intelligence: exploring our living environment 12(4):14–19
Norman DA (2013) The design of everyday things: revised and expanded edition. Basic Books
O'Neill G (2010) Initiating curriculum revision: exploring the practices of educational developers. Int J Acad Dev 15:61–71
OECD (2015) Students, computers and learning; making the connection
Opfer VD, Pedder D (2011) Conceptualizing teacher professional learning. Rev Educ Res 81(3):376–407. http://rer.sagepub.com/cgi/doi/10.3102/0034654311413609
Pardo A, Ellis RA, Calvo RA (2015) Combining observational and experiential data to inform the redesign of learning activities. In; Proceedings of the fifth international conference on learning analytics and knowledge—LAK '15, pp 305–309. http://dl.acm.org/citation.cfm?id=2723576.2723625
Penuel WR et al (2011) Organizing research and development at the intersection of learning, implementation, and design. Educ Res 40(7):331–337
Postareff L et al (2008) Consonance and dissonance in descriptions of teaching of university teachers. Stud High Educ 33(1):49–61. http://dx.doi.org/10.1080/03075070701794809
Rahman N, Dron J (2012) Challenges and opportunities for learning analytics when formal teaching meets social spaces. In: Proceedings of the 2nd international conference on learning analytics and knowledge—LAK '12. ACM Press, New York, New York, USA, pp 54–58
Rajagopal K, Van Bruggen JM, Sloep PB (2017) Recommending peers for learning: matching on dissimilarity in interpretations to provoke breakdown. Educ Technol 48(2):385–406
Reimer YJ, Douglas SA (2003) Teaching HCI design with the studio approach. Comput Sci Educ 13(3):191–205
Ries E (2011) The lean startup: how today's entrepreneurs use continuous innovation to create radically successful businesses. Currency
Rittel HWJ, Webber MM (1973) Dilemmas in a general theory of planning. Policy Sci 4(2):155–169
Roschelle J, Penuel WR (2006) Co-design of innovations with teachers: definition and dynamics. In: Proceedings of the 7th international conference of the learning sciences, pp 606–612. http://dl.acm.org/citation.cfm?id=1150122
Sanders EB-N (2006) Scaffolds for building everyday creativity. In: Frascara J (ed) Designing effective communications: creating contexts for clarity and meaning. Allworth Press, New York, New York, USA, pp 65–77
Sanders EB-N, Stappers PJ (2008) Co-creation and the new landscapes of design. CoDesign 4(1):5–18
Schön DA (1983) The reflective practitioner; how professionals think in action. Basic Books, USA
Shrader G et al (2001) Participatory design of science curricula: the case for research for practice. In: Annual meeting of the American Educational Research Association, Seattle, WA
Shulman LS (1986) Those who understand: knowledge growth in teaching. Educ Res 15(2):4–14
Siemens G (2008) Learning and knowing in networks: changing roles for educators and designers. http://www.academia.edu/2857165/Learning_and_knowing_in_networks_Changing_roles_for_educators_and_designers
Simon HA (1996) The sciences of the artificial, 3rd edn. MIT Press, Cambridge, MA
Sloep PB (2013) Networked professional learning. In: Littlejohn A, Margaryan A (eds) Technology-enhanced professional learning: processes, practices and tools. Routledge, London, pp 97–108. http://hdl.handle.net/1820/5215
Stark JS (2000) Planning introductory college courses: content, context and form. Instr Sci 28:413–438
Stickdorn M, Schneider J (2012) This is service design thinking: basics, tools, cases. Wiley
Stoyanov S et al (2014) Teacher-training, ICT, creativity, MOOC, Moodle—what pedagogy? In: Gómez Chova L, López Martínez A, Candel Torres I (eds) Proceedings of Edulearn 14, the sixth international conference on education and new learning technologies (EDULEARN 14). IATED

Academy, IATED Digital Library, Barcelona, Spain, pp 5678–5686. http://hdl.handle.net/1820/5463
Svihla V et al (2015) A fingerprint pattern of supports for teachers' designing of technology-enhanced learning. Instr Sci 43(2):283–307
Voogt J et al (2015) Collaborative design as a form of professional development. Instr Sci 43(2):259–282
Wasson B, Hansen CJ, Netteland G (2016) Data literacy and use for learning when using learning analytics for learners. In: LAK 2016, Edinburgh. http://ceur-ws.org/Vol-1596/paper6.pdf
Williams A (2009) User-centered design, activity-centered design, and goal-directed design. In: Proceedings of the 27th ACM international conference on design of communication—SIGDOC '09, pp 1–8
Wilson S, Johnson M, Sharples P (2007) Personal learning environments: challenging the dominant design of educational systems. Je-LKS J e-Learn Knowl Soc 3(2):27–38. http://ubir.bolton.ac.uk/index.php?action=fileDownload&resourceId=289&hash=0382c207c66a9834d4390e0f2be6ed3c52e718e5&filename=iec_journalspr-9.pdf
Winograd T (1990) What can we teach about human-computer interaction. In: CHI'90 proceedings, New York, NY, pp 443–449

Chapter 3
A Universally Accessible Self-assessment Gamified Framework and Software Application to Capture 21st Century Skills

Kathy Kipp, Evangelos Kapros and Ian O'Keeffe

Abstract In our increasingly complex lives, 21st Century or Transversal Skills such as collaboration, communication, problem solving, and critical thinking are seen as key to the development of successful individuals. In response to the changing needs and expectations of industry, this focus on 21st Century Skills has begun to filter down into universities and other higher and further educational institutions and is now becoming an important factor in the K-12 educational sector. These skills are often implicit in lessons and so can be difficult for students to identify and express. Their implicit nature also means that they are not traditionally taught to students and so measuring or assessing the development of these skills can be problematic. Furthermore, the development of these skills is not constrained to the classroom environment but occurs in many different contexts and environments. Additionally, the recognition of these individual student learning needs in and around these skills along with the ability of these skills to assist in the accessibility of the classroom is a challenge to be met. To address these challenges we have developed SkillTrack! framework and learning application for mobile devices such as tablets that brings together innovative pedagogy and supportive technology to promote the practice, development and self-assessment of 21st Century Skills in the K-12 space. The effectiveness of SkillTrack! as a teaching and learning tool for 21st Century Skills has been evaluated in an authentic classroom context; the final evaluation of the application validates not only the concept and design premises but also the need for such an application.

K. Kipp
Endurae, Aurora, IL, USA
e-mail: kkipp@tcd.ie

E. Kapros (✉)
Science Gallery, Trinity College Dublin, Dublin, Ireland
e-mail: ekapros@tcd.ie

I. O'Keeffe
Learnovate, Trinity College Dublin, Dublin, Ireland
e-mail: ian.okeeffe@learnovatecentre.org

E. Kapros and M. Koutsombogera (eds.), *Designing for the User Experience in Learning Systems*, Human–Computer Interaction Series,
https://doi.org/10.1007/978-3-319-94794-5_3

3.1 Introduction

21st Century Skills have been identified as key to the development of successful individuals. In implementing new business models focused increasingly on competitiveness and productivity, industry has driven the movement towards identifying and developing these skills. Already in 1999, there was a realisation that the workforce and the workplace landscape was changing rapidly, and training would need to reflect these changes, in what was called "21st Century Skills for 21st Century Jobs" (Stuart 1999). Despite the initial focus on the workplace, and the recognition that competency-based-education is not a new concept[1] (Spady 1977), opportunities to shift educational systems and priorities, and re-surface desirable student-centred pedagogies and alternative assessment methods were also recognised (Reeves 2010). In response to the changing needs and expectations of industry, this focus on 21st century Skills has begun to filter down into our universities and other higher and further educational institutions and is now becoming an important factor in the K-12 educational sector.

In regards to what is meant by 21st century skills (or competencies) in the K-12 context and for the purposes of this paper, 21st century skills are: skills that are considered transversal, having mobility, adaptability, and accessibility across subject matter without being directly linked to a content base; they are inclusive of attitudes, behaviours, knowledge, skills; and they are higher order in their nature (Voogt 2012; OECD 2005; Griffin 2012; Dede 2010). With this in mind, multiple frameworks have been put forward internationally in an attempt to define, clarify and shape these skills, and while there are great differences in categorisation, qualification and semantics, generally and generically, these skills include, but are not limited to: Citizenship, Collaboration, Communication, Creativity, Critical Thinking, Global Awareness, ICT literacy, Personal and Social Responsibility, and Problem Solving (Binkley 2012; SRI 2016; ATC21S 2012; European Parliament 2007; OECD 2005; P21 2009; NCCA 2009).

With the shift towards promotion and valuation of these 21st century skills, a natural counterpart has been the desire to capture and assess ability in and around these skills, as assessment provides insight into both teaching and learning. As the skills are increasingly complex and inherently individual, assessment in the traditional standardised fashion is not possible nor is it desirable (Reeves 2010). This then has provided the opportunity for the development of more appropriate and innovative tools within the assessment space to help articulate where an individual is, such as criterion-referencing (Griffin 2013), and has led to a global initiative.

With regard to the development of assessment frameworks for 21st century skills in the K-12 space, one well-known approach in K-12 is the Programme for International Student Assessment (PISA), developed by the Organisation for Economic Co-operation and Development (OECD), where computer-based collaborative problem-solving was introduced in part for the 2015 exam (OECD 2013). Other

---

[1]Papers from the 70s go so far as mapping U.S. efforts to capture competencies during the 20s and 30s back to the operationalisation of WWI (Callaghan 1962; Davies 1976; Neumann 1979).

attempts include the Assessment and Teaching of 21st Century Skills (ATC21S) project and the Collaborative Assessment Alliance (CAA) (CAA 2016). However, these attempts have been challenged by a number of arguments (Murphy 2010). One aspect that was of special interest to us was that current approaches seem to be tightly-coupled to specific tasks or contexts and treat skills as independent of each other. Thus, it can be the case that the obtained results are a matter of task-design as much as they are the result of the students' skills.

There are also a number of challenges when integrating the development of 21st Century Skills into teaching and learning in schools. These skills are often implicit in lessons and so can be difficult for students to identify and express. Their implicit nature also means that they are not formally taught to students and so measuring or assessing the development of these skills can be problematic.

Furthermore, the individual experiences of students can play a significant role in their skills development especially as the development of these skills is not constrained to the classroom environment but occurs in many different contexts and environments. Any approach that aims to capture these experiences can benefit from thinking in broader terms than "traditional" accessibility; that is, in terms of Inclusive Design (IDRC 2016), so as to ensure true universal access in doing so.

SkillTrack! is a learning application for mobile devices such as tablets that brings together innovative pedagogy and supportive technology to promote the practice, development and self-assessment of 21st Century Skills in the K-12 space. SkillTrack! is intended to act as both an individualised skills literacy tool that allows each student to progress along their own personal path while also supporting students in developing metacognitive skills through the use of reflection.

In contrast to many of the existing approaches, we set out to develop a skill and task-independent approach that would create a common framework for 21st century skills assessment as well as have the ability to assess informal learning and social activity while being able to scale and maintain its flexibility at the same time. Additionally, as a student-led curricular experience that incorporated self-assessment, this task-independent approach allowed for accessibility through this flexibility as well as a foundational want for student ownership of app interaction and classroom integration. Our intention then was to develop a pedagogical design, see Sect. 3.3, which would be implemented as a software tool to be deployed at institutions of primarily K-12 Education. While K-12 is our initial focus, the design has no component that explicitly excludes informal education settings or other educational sections such as higher/further education or corporate learning. To this end, we designed a gamified pedagogical framework to capture 21st century skills in K-12 Education. Then, we designed and built a tablet software application as one of the many ways to implement our framework (see Sect. 3.4). As part of the design process, we sense-checked our approach with teachers and students in preparation for a user trial.

The effectiveness of SkillTrack! as a teaching and learning tool for 21st Century Skills has been evaluated in an authentic classroom context through the use of the app as part of day-to-day classroom activities over two trialling periods, one a one month period and an additional three month period. The methodology used as part of this evaluation is described in Sect. A.1 while the qualitative and quantitative results from the evaluation are explored in Sects. A.3 and A.4.

3.2 Related Work

In considering the research questions and objectives, a small review was undertaken. The purpose of this research was to establish an understanding of how the challenge of 21st century skill assessment in the schools' setting was being approached internationally. Reading was done with the intent of informing the pedagogical design by identifying the trends in development from a pedagogical perspective as well as the related pedagogical discussions, extensions, and innovations within this context. This research then helped to establish a base of knowledge from which spaces for innovation were identified and pedagogical recommendation and design features emerged.

There were two strands to the related-work review. The first part looked into the various skill frameworks (Binkley 2012; Voogt 2012), the problematic nature of assessing the highly complex, multifaceted and ill-defined 21st century skills (Griffin 2012, 2013), the link between technological assessment and 21st century skills assessment (Redecker 2013), and the link between pedagogy and the integration of technology in the classroom (Puentedura 2014).

The second strand of research considered existing solutions and developments in and around the area of 21st Century Skills, their assessment and the promotion of personal reflection around them. In the K-12 space, work of interest in the area included that of 21CLD (2016), P21 (2009), ATC21S (2012), CAA (2016), PISA (2009), The European Commission (2007), and the GRASS project (2016) along with many other smaller incubator projects. From this, one research organisations' attempt in the area, namely ATC21S, will be looked at as a representative sample of our findings around what the 21st century skills assessment landscape looked like at the time this research took place. ATC21S is a particularly strong example for consideration as they worked with those in OECD/PISA on the development of this international wide-scaling and innovative frame and had the backing of Cisco, Intel, and Microsoft.

The ATC21S project was a large scale international research collaboration between industry, academics, governments and schools aimed at accelerating global education reform by mobilizing those communities to help transform the teaching, learning and measurement of 21st century skills (ATC21S 2012; Griffin 2013). In terms of reaching this goal, the project focused on the development of an assessment framework around two 'soft skills', collaborative problem solving and ICT. In terms of collaborative problem solving, ATC21S developed hypothesis and determined a framework for the assessment. Within these, cognitive and social sub-skills were articulated along with performance indicators and developmental progressions. Based on this work, assessment tasks were designed and piloted first within cognitive laboratories and then within schools. Resources were refined based on the testing and put in to the public domain for international use and development.

Specifically, the assessment tasks designed for ATC21S took a single-person, problem-solving task design and structured it so that it was a computerised collaborative effort. In the collaborative task, each partner received different, yet complementary, information and needed to communicate and engage with each other to complete the task's objective. Each partner's actions were captured and the data was mapped to and scored on the developed framework. Due to the complexity of collaborative problem solving, and the multiple sub-skills and strands, no one task fully addresses the skill as a whole and ATC21S developed a series of tasks bundled together to offer a more accurate picture of a student's competency in the skill.

In terms of offering perspective on where global research was at the time this project commenced, the ATC21S project is an exemplar, explicitly in terms of the specific features of:

1. Focusing on a single skill or skill set,
2. Developing a deep exemplar framework for assessment based on the complexity of the skill as attitudinal, behavioural, cognitive, etc.,
3. Creating a specific task for the purpose of assessment,
4. Creating a curriculum independent task,
5. Supporting the task content with subject material, and
6. Utilising data to offer benchmarks for skill measurement.

A goal of ATC21S' work was to inform development in and around conceptual, methodological and technological advances in assessment in the the 21st century skill arena; their work, and the similar work of others in the field, informed our research direction.

3.3 Framework and Application Design

This section looks into the pedagogical and user experience (UX) frameworks we designed for a self-assessment, gamified experience to capture and assess 21st century skills. We have designed both frameworks as complementary to each other and interweaved, as opposed to parallel processes that run independently.

3.3.1 Pedagogical Design Features

In addressing the challenge of supporting the teaching and learning of 21st century skills in K-12 and based on the review in 21st century skills, their assessment, and the pedagogical design surrounding these areas, we identified a number of pedagogical recommendations—which would become design features within the actual application—based on the findings of the review, and in regards to where gaps in innovation exist within the space:

Vertical and horizontal mobility: The developed SkillTrack! model and user application should be able to cross grade/age levels and content areas as opposed to being grade level or subject specific.

Not activity specific: The SkillTrack! model should be more than a 'once-off' activity and have longevity and breadth to it as opposed to being a singular activity that a student/teacher only interacts with once.

Authentic classroom dynamic: SkillTrack! should fit within the authentic classroom dynamic and become an extension of regular classroom practice, inclusive of all students, as opposed to being something that interferes, prohibits or breaks up the standard rhythm of instruction or targets specific student groups.

Activate student skill literacy: Student understanding of the skills is not being addressed—global focus seems to have jumped straight to the assessment of the skills without focusing on the 'teaching' and 'learning' of the skills.

Be based in experiential learning: As opposed to forcing a context for the skill if possible the pedagogy should be rooted in a naturally occurring learning experience and work to make these implicit skills explicit.

Offer formative assessment for learning: Currently assessment activities in this area are summative, ending in nature; there should be a more streamlined approach that utilises continuous formative, continuous assessment to promote true and deep learning.

And lastly, the premise was established that within the SkillTrack! app:

The design be flexible: as it is clear that this is not a well defined space the SkillTrack! app should be flexible and dynamic offering many options for future design and extension of the original frame. For example supporting different 21st century skills models.

Transform the relationship student-teacher-knowledge: The design look to transform the relationship among student-teacher-knowledge. Using the SAMR model of technological integration in the teaching and learning setting, the technology should offer more than a Substitution to or Augmentation of typical classroom practice but work towards Modifying and/or Redefining it (Puentedura 2014).

Data be viewed as baseline: that the data generated from the SkillTrack! experience be something that is not limiting and can be used to establish a baseline for future development.

With these design features, it was established that the best direction for innovative and accessible development was in the self-assessment space. Self-assessment allowed for the needed flexibility established within the recommendations, was not a path being pursued by most researchers at that moment and had the potential for more innovation. Additionally, a self-assessment format would:

1. Activate student understanding of 21st century skills, providing knowledge base and literacy as well as 'direct' instruction for what is traditionally considered implicit

2. Allow for a student owned experience that leveraged personal goal setting, continuous feedback, strength and deficit identification and formative assessment
3. Allow for metacognitive awareness to increase student ownership and responsibility for skill development
4. Inform classroom choices and is universally applicable in all three realms of the educative relationship (student-teacher-knowledge).

The decision was then made to create a 21st century skills self-assessment app, SkillTrack! With the knowledge that this app would be trialled in Ireland, the framework that was chosen for the 21st century skills was that used by the Irish National Council for Curriculum and Assessment (NCCA) for the Junior Cycle (see below). It should be noted that while informed by and trialled within this context, the pedagogical frame and the gamification framework are not limited to the Irish setting and have been designed to be as generic and extensible as possible. At the time of app creation, these skills included Being Creative, Working With Others, Communicating, Managing Myself and Managing Information.

3.3.2 Context to Inform Design Recommendations

With the research being trialled within the Irish context, the defined setting for the design in the K-12 setting was the secondary school. In Ireland, K-12 education is divided into primary (ages 4–5/5–6 until the ages of 11–12/12–13) and secondary (ages 11–12/12–13 until the ages of 16–18/17–19). Within the secondary system, there is a division between Junior Cycle (ages 12–14/14–16) and Senior Cycle (ages 14–16/17–19) with an exam marking the end of each cycle. Based on the nature of the research objectives as well as the background of the researchers, the Senior Cycle within the secondary setting was initially defined as an appropriate context for design and trialling: specifically, the 4th year cohort (ages 14–16), as this is considered a transition year between the two exam cycles and offers more classroom flexibility. However, due to certain practical trial limitations (e.g., the ability of 1:1 devices in schools), it should be noted that the application was trialled within the 1st and 2nd year cohorts (ages 11–14, inclusive) of the Junior Cycle setting.

3.3.3 Pedagogical Frame

Building on the above design recommendations, the pedagogical frame created for this use case was based on assessment strategies for self-directed learning and utilised the conceptual design of manage, monitor and modify in regards to student behaviour around 21st century skills. Specifically, the model of reference is (Costa and Kallick 2008) model of self-directed learning and their process design model for feedback and continuous learning.

Generally, the pedagogical frame consists of a the learner working through a *phased* experience which:

1. Starts with an identification of an experiential learning instances (a tagging of one of the identified 21st century skills on the home page),
2. Continues with multiple benchmarked experiences (an answering of either a quick answer multiple choice or free text question to activate student literacy and learning within the tagged skill),
3. Ends with the selection of an exemplar (student uploading of personal evidence of work in the skill) and a self-assessment (self-rating based on reflection).

At the completion of one phase, the learner enter into the next phase. To support this, a frame was selected with the steps of each phase being built using a blend of feedback spirals and metacognitively scaffolded benchmark prompts that are designed to activate experiential learning (using Bloom and Krathwohl 2000's revised taxonomy, Wiggins 2005's '6 Facets of Understanding', Kolb's learning cycle Kolb 1975, 1976; Zimmerman 2013's 'Phases and Sub-process of Self-Regulation').

Considering the specific self-assessment activities, benchmark activities within each phase are based on Rolheiser (1996)'s growth scheme for teacher implementation of stages of student self-assessment and student self-rating is done using a modified version of Marzano (2006)'s 4-Point Self-Assessment Scale. Additionally, Ross (2006) on how self-assessment contributes to learning was referenced.

In regards to the specific creation and scaffolding of content within the onboarding, benchmarked experiences and exemplar questions and tasks, Blooms revised taxonomy (Bloom and Krathwohl 2000) was used to formulate questions and tasks as was the concept of knowledge acquisition needing to occur prior to knowledge application.

3.3.4 Gamification Framework

This section describes and explains a gamified system for the aforementioned pedagogical design, mainly focusing on a proof-of-concept tablet app. The system consists of a tablet app, and a group of players who are students. The way the system will be designed and deployed is explained below, using the 6D Gamification Design Framework (Werbach 2012) (each sub-heading in the section below is one of the Ds of the framework).

3.3.4.1 Description of the Gamified System

The system consists of a tablet app, a website, and players who meet in real life to participate in class activities. The players with the role of a student will be using the tablet app. The setting is a physical and synchronous classroom environment for the majority of the game tasks, and other environments for a few tasks. No asynchronous teaching or learning is assumed, but is not prohibited either.

The students will use the tablet app to identify when in class they are active in one of the 21st century skills defined by the NCCA. The home screen provides the students with the identified skills and they have to tap the appropriate choice each time they have used a skill in the classroom (e.g., Alice taps "Creativity" after solving a new problem in Mathematics). To qualify this input without interrupting the class, the app will occasionally ask the student to perform short benchmark tasks after they have tapped a skill. However, these benchmark tasks will not appear each and every time the student has selected a skill. These skills-literacy and contextualisation tasks activities are organised in levels (phases) of increasing difficulty and are rewarded as described in the following sections. A preliminary on-boarding phase has been designed in a way that it can be delivered by the teacher in class without consuming too much class time. Moreover, to clear a phase the student will have to upload an exemplar of an achievement of theirs that reflects each skill.

This gamified self-assessment process is suitable for both the Junior and the Senior Cycle and is not affected by pedagogical decisions with regard to the language of the assessment. Thus, it can facilitate multiple models of 21st century skills, multiple education systems, curricula, age groups, taught modules, or languages. Many of these benefits derive from the curriculum-independent nature of the self-assessment pedagogy itself, and not specifically from the gamification process.

The role of other stakeholders such as the teachers and parents is beyond the scope of this paper.

3.3.4.2 Define Business Objectives

One main reason why a design decision was made to gamify the process is that the self-assessment process is a continuous one. Indeed, the pedagogy is based on the continuous feedback spiral described in Costa and Kallick (2008).

Since self-assessment is an iterative process, it is only safe to assume that initial iterations will produce poorer results than subsequent ones. Competence in self-assessment depends greatly on familiarisation with the assessment language. Thus, it is important to keep motivation among students high until they reach a stage where they will produce rich self-assessment material.

Gamification can facilitate getting the best out of students' self-assessments by keeping them in a mental state of flow (Csíkszentmihályi 1990). A state of flow is one where the students immerse into their tasks and thus they are more likely to respond in a qualitatively appropriate way.

3.3.4.3 Delineate Target Behaviours

The target behaviours are the following. Firstly, tagging. That is, a player is expected to use the system to digitally tag a physical activity. That is, a key performance indi-

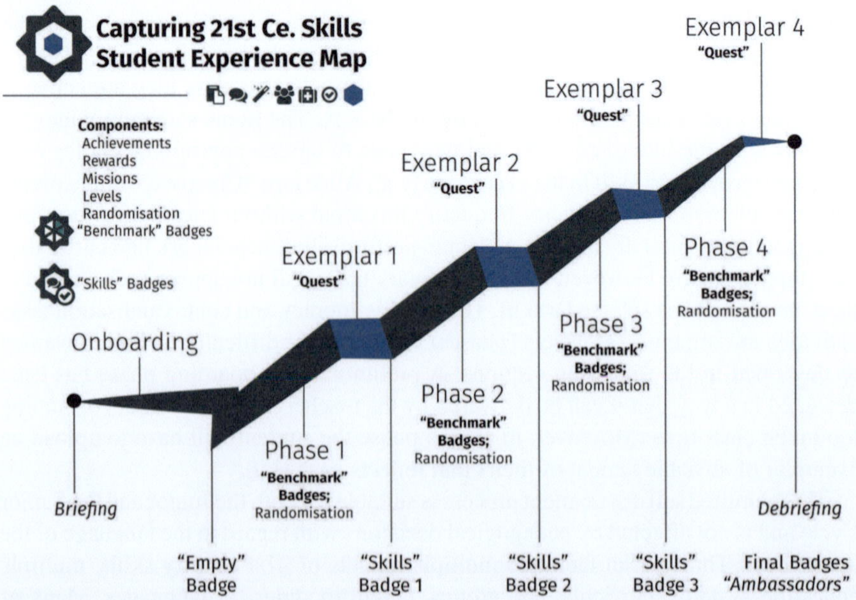

Fig. 3.1 The student user-experience map for the capturing of the 21st Ce. skills. A 'Hero's Journey' experience is designed by phases of increasing difficulty, micro-credentials as rewards, and personalised solutions (exemplars) to 'quests'

cator (KPI) of the system will be the amount of user activity related with identifying that they have used a 21st century skill in the classroom.

Secondly, a target behaviour is for the player to explain their involvement with the skills. That is, a KPI of the system is the amount and the quality of user activity around the benchmark tasks during the phases, and the uploaded exemplars at the end of each phase (see Fig. 3.1).

3.3.4.4 Describe Your Players

The players are young, and relatively tech savvy (as we assume that their schools has provided them with tablet devices). While the pedagogical design and the overall gamification framework (phases, exemplars, etc.) have nothing that absolutely prescribes a tablet app and could be used with paper-based forms, the age of the players favours a digital solution.

The players, depending on their exact age, could have a varying level of workload and this could affect the use of the system. New students could use the system more due to excitement about its novelty, while near-graduation students could be affected by the current Irish educational system's high appreciation of examination results and focus on those rather than on 21st century skills.

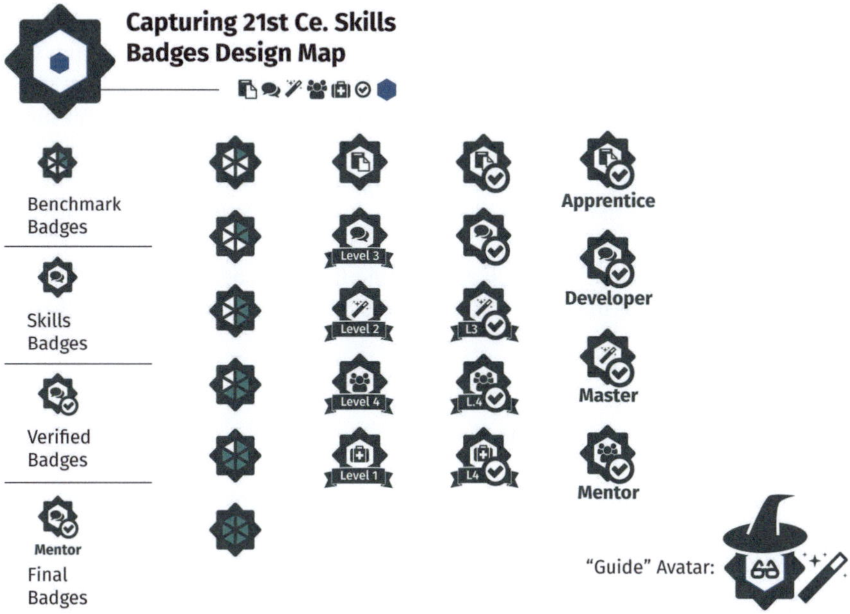

Fig. 3.2 Various designs for badges for the system. Benchmark badges also function as a progress indicator within a phase, while skills badges can indicate both progress across all phases and Marzano scale. Badges can be verified—but not evaluated—by teachers. A 'guide' avatar is designed to provide guidance to the students

3.3.4.5 Devise Activity Loops

The main activity loop will be to tag classroom activities in the system/app. Moreover, if the user has tagged a skill a set number of times they will be asked to complete a short benchmark task. Finally, the users get to upload an exemplar work of theirs for each skill that represents their best example of what each skill looks like in practice. For the main activity, the feedback is a simple notification that they have performed the tagging (see about microinteractions at the section below). For the benchmark and the exemplar tasks, the users will receive digital badges within the system (see Fig. 3.2). These badges were designed so as to assign a status to users depending on their self-assessment and include some teacher validation (not evaluation, rather validation in the sense of avoiding plagiarism etc.).

3.3.4.6 Don't Forget the Fun!

All the points said above, it is expected that satisfaction, within-school civic-duty-like fun, not necessarily playful fun is going to be the key motivator for players to participate in the system. Fun is sought by expanding intrinsic motivation, it is not the goal that the aforementioned badges will be a major motivation force. Rather, extrinsic motivations will provide moments of instant gratification for sticking with the system, while, using again the examples of Alice tagging "Creativity" in a Mathematics activity, the Mathematics activity itself is supposed to be the playful fun of the system.[2] This can be conveyed to the users via the app's visual design and text. However, various benchmark tasks can be designed so as to have playful elements. A "guide" avatar, designed to provide guidance to the students, can also consist as an element of playful behaviour.

Due to practical limitations, such as changing the target age group and, thus, the visual design, not all of these fun elements were eventually implemented in the app (i.e., the "guide").

3.3.4.7 Deploy the Appropriate Tools

The appropriate tool here is a tablet app. The tablet app is intended to capture skills on the spot. Moreover, one can see their badges and previous exemplars.

A tablet is preferred since it is a mobile device which is less cumbersome for text input than a mobile phone. It allows on-the-spot capturing of skills and also to complete benchmark tasks that would require text input (e.g., "What does it mean to be excellent at Collaboration?"). Larger screen real-estate at tablets also means that browsing history or an overview of exemplars is better than using a mobile device. Furthermore, tablets are increasingly being adopted as one-to-one devices in schools.

As the players are young and tech savvy, they shouldn't have any difficulty in using this technology.

Overall, our gamification framework suggests the design of a finite game, where

(i) mastery, ownership, and identity are the chief motivators,
(ii) there are clear checkpoints as victory conditions,
(iii) levels of difficulty, levels, rewards (badges), reinforcement through teacher validation of the badges, and quests (exemplars) are the game mechanics,
(iv) and status, achievement, and feedback by the teacher are the social interactions.

3.4 Application Experience

This section describes the functionality of SkillTrack!, a learning application for tablet devices that brings together innovative pedagogy and supportive technology by implementing the aforementioned pedagogy and gamification framework, to make learning more relevant and effective for students by supporting their practice, development, and self-review of 21st century skills.

[2]There is lack of evidence to suggest that it is even feasible to substitute most fun in-class activities with a piece of software.

3.4.1 Functionality

Generally, SkillTrack! is a student-led curricular app that runs simultaneously to teacher instruction (and includes a Teacher Dashboard component). While in class, students have the app up and running and when they think they have used one of the pre-identified set of 21st century skills to complete a classroom task, they hit that skill's button on the homepage (see Fig. 3.3). This may be done during classroom transitions or at the end of class. In response to the student hitting the skill, the app acknowledges the student's input with a thumbs up or a quick answer question appears regarding why the student has just hit that skill. After the question is answered, the student returns to the homepage to continue tracking skill usage throughout the class and their school day. This structure allows for the app to be used throughout the user's day irrespective of the activities that they engage in as well as providing a frame that can be adapted based on age and ability.

To familiarise students with the skills and the type of self-reflection that the app requires, the app has an onboarding phase that is teacher-led and comes before the students begin tracking their skill usage. This onboarding phase reviews the skills, asks for the students to think about what the skill is, when they use it, what being excellent in it looks like, how they would define it and how they would rate themselves in their ability to do it. Once onboarding has been completed for each skill (either in class or at home—the recommendation is for the teacher to model at least one of the skills), the app is active for tracking.

In tracking, students encounter up to four phases. A phase consists of a series of tags or tracks by the student, the answering of intermediate quick answer questions, and an outside of class exemplar stage. Once the student has completed the interactive classroom portion of the phase (which can be tracked by the filling up of the badge

Fig. 3.3 The microinteraction for the capturing of the 21st century skills. A user performs some activity in the classroom and then in the app they tag it by tapping the respective option. The system gives them feedback about the success of the microinteraction. Two possible designs for different tablet platforms are presented

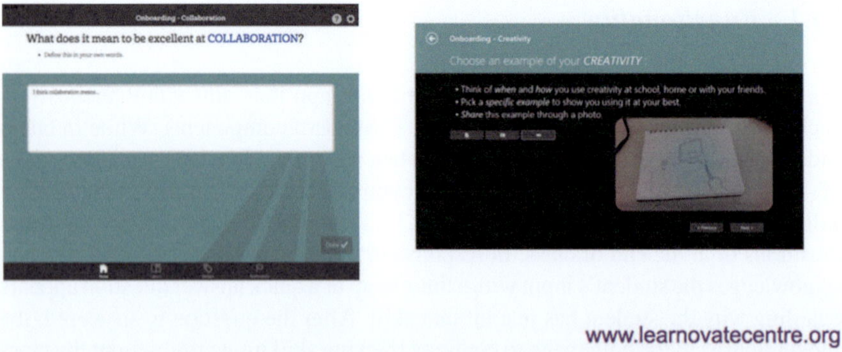

Fig. 3.4 Extension loops of the tagging microinteraction for the capturing of the 21st century skills. After a user taps a skill for a certain number of times (as in Fig. 3.3) they are prompted to perform a benchmark task (left). After they have performed all the benchmark tasks of a phase they are asked to upload an exemplar of the skill to move to the next phase (right)

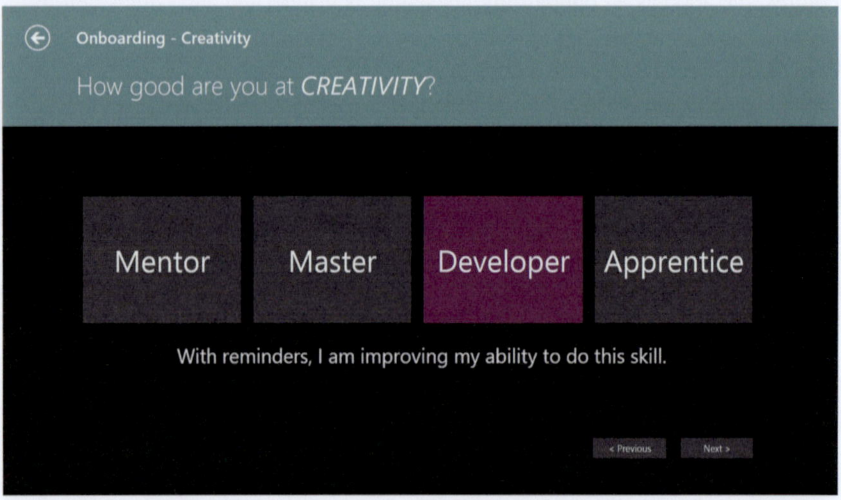

Fig. 3.5 Selection of self-assessment ratings. Descriptions of each rating help contextualise them

next to the skill on the homepage) the button for the skill will change to notify them that they are entering the exemplar stage. This stage of the phase is done outside of class and is where the students reflect on their work and ability, providing and qualifying an example of evidence of their work in the skill (see Fig. 3.4 left) as well giving a self-assessment rating (see Fig. 3.5). At the end of the exemplar stage, the student receives a badge (upon teacher approval via the accompanying teacher dashboard where student progress is being recorded and can be monitored by the teacher). A student is unable to move on to the next phase until every skill in the previous phase has been completed.

3.4.2 User Experience Design

The pedagogical design and the gamification framework described above can result in many different implementations, but they all require a single interaction: to digitally tag the physical activity of the skill by tapping the appropriate choice each time they have used a skill in the classroom (e.g., Alice taps "Creativity" after solving a new problem in Mathematics). This interaction is a microinteraction: microinteractions are "contained product moments that revolve around a single use casethey have one main task" (Saffer 2014) and they consist of four parts.

3.4.2.1 Triggers

The trigger (see Fig. 3.3) that initiates the microinteraction is the user. The user performs some activity in the classroom and then in the app they tag it by tapping the respective option.

3.4.2.2 Rules

The rules for tagging are explained during an onboarding phase to the students, and also by the teachers. It is anticipated that teachers would adapt the use of the tool to their teaching style. From the systems point of view, the rule is that the microinteraction needs to be triggered and then it will give feedback to the user or will initiate a loop (see the fourth part of microinteractions below).

3.4.2.3 Feedback

Feedback needs to be kept to a minimum in order to avoid interruptions of teaching in the classroom. A "thumbs up" icon with an informative text about which skill has been tagged should appear (see Fig. 3.3).

3.4.2.4 Modes and Loops

Two extension loops of the tagging microinteraction for the capturing of the 21st Ce. skills are based on user behaviour as described below:

- After a user taps a skill for a certain number of times (as in Fig. 3.3) they are prompted to perform a benchmark task (see Fig. 3.4 left).
- After they have performed all the benchmark tasks for a phase, they are asked to upload an exemplar of the skill to move to the next phase (see Fig. 3.4 right).
- After the user has completed either a benchmark task or an exemplar, they receive their respective badge (see Fig. 3.2).

Overall, the aforementioned microinteraction design has a twofold intention. Its simplicity aims to enhance the usability and the user experience of the system. Moreover, the interaction design needs to facilitate the use in an authentic classroom environment and not interrupt teaching.

3.5 Implementation

3.5.1 Conceptual Framework

Figure 3.6 provides a high level overview of the SkillTrack! Framework illustrating how the SkillTrack! application fits into the wider context of use. The 'user' at the heart of the framework is the student that wants to engage in continuous self assessment of 21st century skills. As illustrated the framework includes a feedback cycle in which the student engages in their day to day activities, attending classes, completing assignments, etc. and tags when they use any of the skills available to them using the SkillTrack! app. The feedback loop is completed through positive motivational mechanisms such as badges. The exact nature of the skills assessed through SkillTrack! is dependent on the needs of the organisation and can be tailored to best fit those needs.

The students' interactions with SkillTrack! can be through any medium that best suits their day to day environment. For example an app for tablet devices in schools

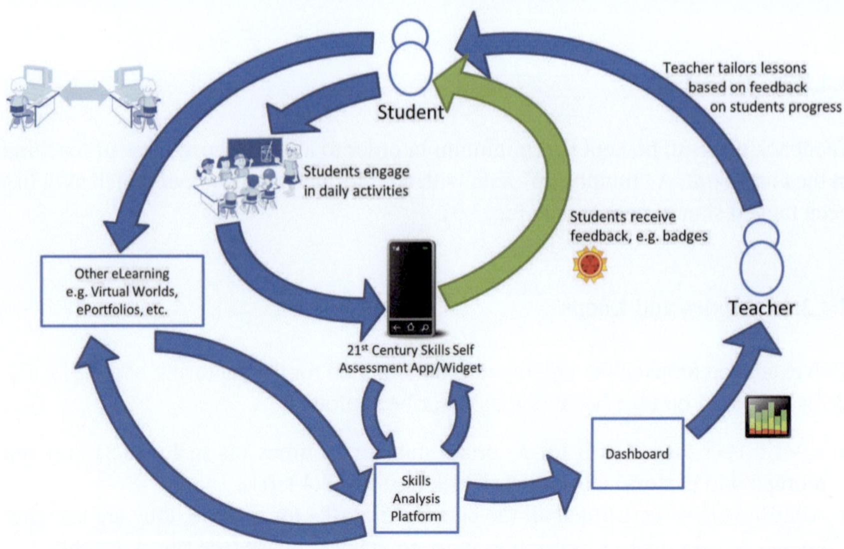

Fig. 3.6 SkillTrack! framework

with one to one devices, a mobile phone app or a widget built into an existing platform or service such as MS Office 365 or even an immersive virtual environment. The widget or plugin based implementation is an interesting mode of use as many different digital environments require the use of 21st century skills (e.g. communication and collaboration in virtual environments, information management and critical thinking in productivity tools). A widget embedded into such an environment allows these skills that are implicit in the use of that tool to be made explicit for the learning turning that tool into a 21st century skills platform.

The students interactions with SkillTrack! are analysed using a centralised Skills Analysis Platform, this allows observations about the student's use and application of the skills tracked by SkillTrack! to be presented back to the student in ways that help them to better understand their use and application of skills and to understand better their strengths and weaknesses when it comes to 21st century skills. This information is also used to provide others within the organisation with a view of how the organisation as a whole is performing with respect to 21st century skills, for example a teacher or principal in a K-12 context. Depending on specific needs this dashboard can provide information on individual students or it can provide an anonymised, aggregated view that can be used to better understand the skills across the school structure (classes, years, etc.).

The final component of the SkillTrack! Framework is the integration of skills evidence from sources other than the SkillTrack! application. The SkillTrack! application provides a holistic baseline of all of the skills that an organisation is interested in developing amongst their students and does so in a way that is agnostic to the actual context in which those skills are applied. This feature of SkillTrack! provides the opportunity to incorporate more specific or contextual information about how an individual applies or utilises 21st century skills. For example information from an activity in an virtual world activity can be fed into the Skills Analysis Platform in order to enhance or bolster the evidence of a specific skill. This element of the framework is beyond the scope of this paper.

3.5.2 *Software Architecture*

The SkillTrack! tablet app is a key component of a wider architecture designed to support multiple stakeholders (students, teachers, etc.) in the assessment of 21st century skills. A component based approach was used for SkillTrack! allowing features to be added to the system with little or no impact on the existing client applications. Additionally, this approach makes as much of the architecture as possible agnostic to the specific application domain in which SkillTrack! might be applied. Although the initial use case that SkillTrack! has been evaluated in on focuses on 21st century skills for 12–15 year-old students in Irish secondary schools (Junior Cycle) it was realised very early on that the approach should be and indeed is more broadly applicable. As such, it was important that the architecture could easily facilitate its application in other use cases, e.g., 21st century skills for a different age range and

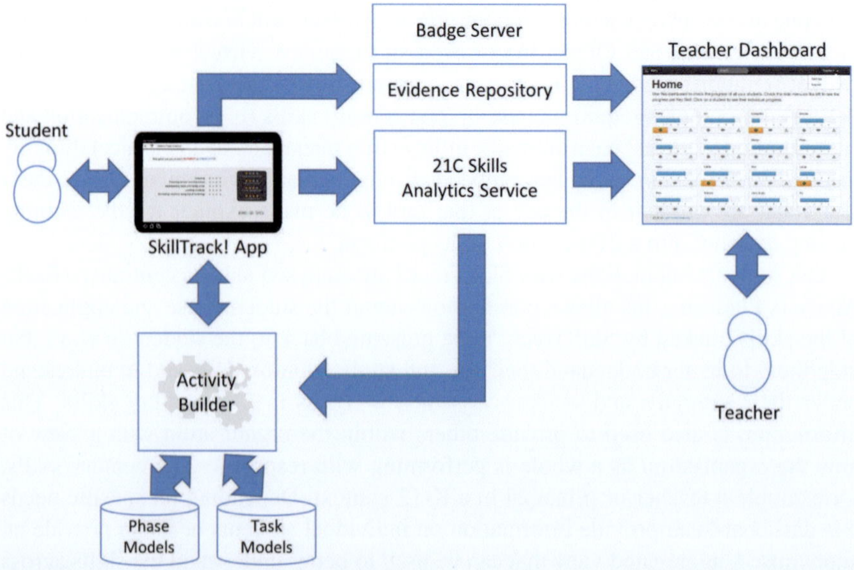

Fig. 3.7 SkillTrack! architecture as implemented

or different domain or in a different context altogether such as corporate business competencies. The component based approach helps in this case as the use case specific aspects of the system (the activities that the user engages in) are independent of the client application, which can be reused across multiple use cases with minimal modification.

Figure 3.7 provides a high level overview or the SkillTrack! architecture, which consists of two client components designed to addressing the needs of the primary stakeholders in the SkillTrack! use case, namely the student and the teacher. Students use the SkillTrack! app on their personal device (e.g., tablet) or alternatively on their PC providing them with a self-paced, self-assessed experience. Other stakeholders such as teachers are provided with a web based dashboard that provides them with an overview of how specific groups of users are utilising the SkillTrack! app, giving them insights into the skills that students feel they are using in their day to day activities both as part of their school day and beyond. The Dashboard allows teachers to gain insight into the progress of individual students both in terms of their general engagement and use of the app and based on individual skills.

The experience itself is generated by the Activity Builder, which reconciles a set of models to generate the activity model that the tablet app instantiates in order to deliver the desired activity (sequence of tagging, benchmark and exemplar tasks). The Activity Builder is implemented as a web service, which is accessed by the app in order to retrieve dynamically generated models for each skill/phase combination. This approach has been taken to allow for the activity to be adapted based on the student's engagement with the system allowing for a more dynamic and open ended

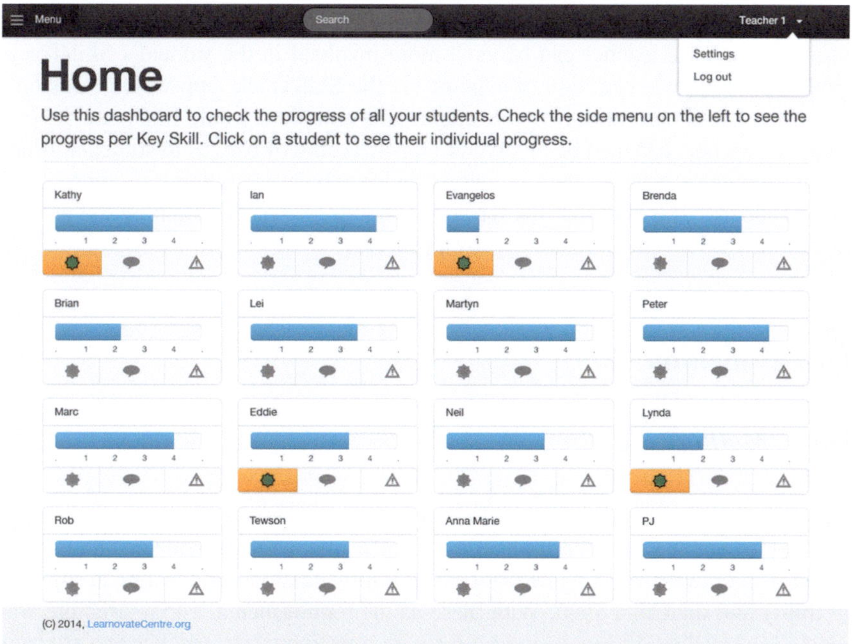

Fig. 3.8 Screenshot of the SkillTrack! teacher dashboard class overview page

experience that is less predictable. However, a prebuilt SkillTrack! experience can be bundled with the app itself removing the need for the Activity Builder if desirable. This comes at the cost of the dynamic, adaptive experience.

The student's interactions with the SkillTrack! app are logged with the Analytics Service, a web service that supports the logging and analysis of the student's interactions. The Analytics Service supports the logging of student actions such as the tagging of skills, completion of benchmark tasks (rating, ranking, etc.) and submitting exemplars. The Analytics Service is responsible for the analytical functions of the SkillTrack! architecture, both for the generation of basic usage statistics and the more advanced analytics such as the use of Natural Language Processing (NLP) based analytics. These NLP based analytical functions include sentiment analysis of the free text entries submitted by the users, analysis of the lexical complexity of submitted text and a measure of the 'coverage" or alignment of the language used by the students with the language used to define those skills in the underlying skills rubric upon which the SkillTrack! activities are based. The role of these more advanced analytical functions is to provide a deeper insight into the usage and understanding of the 21st century skills beyond simple usage based statistics.

The Dashboard, Fig. 3.8, is a web, browser-based application that allows teachers to gain an insight into the progress of relevant groups of students as well as to delve deeper into the use of SkillTrack! by individual students. It interacts with the Analytics Service through a web service API to retrieve the relevant information which can then be visualised. The Dashboard also provides several mechanisms through which the teacher can become more involved in the student's SkillTrack! experience. Students can request support via the SkillTrack! app which turns on a flag in the Dashboard notifying the teacher that a student would like some help or support. Teachers can also be involved in the awarding of badges to students. When a user completes a phase they request a badge which a Teacher can approve via the Dashboard. This provides the teacher with a degree of oversight on the process though their involvement in the approval process.

3.6 Evaluation

3.6.1 Methodology

In regards to evaluating SkillTrack! and the SkillTrack! Teacher Dashboard, the main goal was to be able to test the application in a way that would provide insight into the research objectives, resulting pedagogical recommendations, and technical supports (usability and data analytics). With these as the requirements, a trial structure was selected for evaluating the design in use with questionnaires, teacher and students interviews, providing end-of-use evaluation and overall triangulation.

The trial and its specifics are presented at Appendix A. A summarised version is offered here.

3.6.2 Overview of the Results

An interesting observation that was made about the usage of the SkillTrack! app by students was the time of day at which it was used. As might be expected, the majority of the usage of the SkillTrack! app was during the school day between 9am and 4pm. However, a significant proportion of the observed interactions (22% or 1436 interactions) were outside of this time period. This can be seen as indicative of the students being motivated to engage with the SkillTrack! app.

Interviewed students did not associate SkillTrack! with any specific activity, nor did they comment negatively about integrating it into the authentic classroom experience.

One of the underpinning pedagogical premises of SkillTrack! was in creating an app experience that addressed student understanding, experience, practice and development, or overall literacy, of the 21st century/Key skills. With students commenting specifically on this pedagogical design element, and in a unprompted and generally positive strain, a preliminary finding can be made around the app successfully activating student literacy and creating informal learning opportunities around the skills.

In regards to designing an app that would be based in experiential learning, the pedagogical design of SkillTrack! was interested in students utilising their own naturally occurring learning experiences to anchor the app experience and bring about the explicit recognition of the implicit. Student comments, while referring to the metacognitive experience of linking the skills to personal experience, offer no conclusive finding on this design element.

The badging feature was considered to be a strong feedback mechanism to the students and that it could be expanded; additionally, with greater development the badges could have greater worth in providing feedback on practice and development.

In summary, generally in regards to the pedagogical portion of the app, from the student users point of view, the pedagogical design and activities accomplished what they intended to (with certain noted reservations).

In all of the evaluated areas, the strongest feedback given was in support of use of the app activating student literacy of the skills. The strongest drawbacks within the app design were around the language and the difficulty in using the app without teacher support.

In summary, the teacher's response paralleled those of the students, with the pedagogical design and activities accomplishing what they intended to.

In all of the evaluated areas, the strongest feedback given was in the design areas of integrating into the authentic classroom dynamic, activating student literacy and experiential learning. In regards to the pedagogical activities, the onboarding received strong praise as did the exemplar and self-assessment portion, validating both the choice and design of them. The strongest drawbacks within the app design were around, as in the student feedback, the use of age appropriate language as well as the ability of students to remember to use the app.

3.7 Conclusions

When considering both (Trial 1 and Trial 2) qualitative data sets, and the findings and conclusions from both students and teacher, there are some clear parallels that allow for conclusions in regards to both the pedagogical design elements and activities.

The design element with the strongest support from both the students and the teacher was that of Activating Student Literacy with both groups providing unsolicited positive comments around their experience of this element.

Other design elements to receive favourable comments included those of Experiential Learning, Formative Assessment. Additionally, the Exemplar activity was viewed as a strong element by both the students and the teacher. The teacher also felt quite strongly about the Onboarding activity, and while no students commented on this activity, the teacher feedback was enough to view this activity as favourable (especially as it is the one activity within the app specifically designed for the teacher). Additionally, the teacher confirmed the choice of Self-Assessment for the purpose of 21st century skills assessment.

This qualitative data then would preliminarily affirm and support the effectiveness of the following pedagogical design choices:

- Activating Student Literacy
- Experiential Learning
- Formative Assessment
- Exemplar Activity
- Self-Assessment Activity
- Onboarding Activity.

Two pedagogical design choices that would have received both positive and negative comments were the Integration into Authentic Classroom Dynamic and Benchmarking Tasks.

In regards to Integration into Authentic Classroom Dynamic, while the teacher spoke favourably about SkillTrack!'s ability to integrate into the class without interfering or interrupting, this statement was also qualified with the comments by both the students and the teachers on the need for teacher support of the app as well as a notification system to remind students to engage with the student-led curriculum.

Additionally, the design activity of the Benchmarking Tasks received qualified positive feedback, with both students and teacher commenting favourably on the concept but qualifying the comments with mention of the language used within the questions being too sophisticated for this age group.

Two pedagogical choices that received mostly negative comments were those around Vertical and Horizontal Mobility and Transformative Technology. It should be noted, as in the above, the negative comments were not due to the design premise but due to the execution of the design premise. In the case of these two elements, however, this execution prohibited the overall experience.

Specifically, in regards to the Vertical and Horizontal Mobility, both students and the teacher focused quite specifically on the language used within the app being pitched above the user group, meaning that in regards to vertically mobility and SkillTrack! being used at various age/grade/year levels, considerable thought would need to be put into the language (and design) choices to make it appropriate. This is not an unexpected preliminary finding as the original pedagogical script was written for the 3 age/year levels above the final user group.

A finding then around the design premises of Vertical and Horizontal Mobility can be made in regards to how these concepts are articulated within the app itself as well as how the app is used.

In regards to the design element of Not Activity Specific and the design activities of Skill Tagging, none of the qualitative data by either the students or the teacher spoke to these. This is an understandable finding concerning Not Activity Specific as there would be no need to comment on this (unless the feeling was that it should be activity specific). With regard to Skill Tagging, while this is the main pedagogical activity (through which many of the design elements are articulated) no specific comments may be seen to mean that this was an effective activity that was both easy to understand and not problematic enough to note.

In conclusion, concerning Universal Access to self-assessment for 21st century skills, we identified several factors towards this direction (such as experiential learning, formative assessment), while others (vertical and horizontal mobility) require further experimentation. Overall, the framework was enhanced by the parallel pedagogical and UX design, as shown by the positive reception of processes such as the onboarding and the gamification.

Acknowledgements This research is supported by the Learnovate Centre at Trinity College, the University of Dublin. The Learnovate Centre is funded under the Technology Centre Programme through the Government of Ireland's state agencies Enterprise Ireland and IDA Ireland.

References

Ananiadou K, Claro M (2009) 21st century skills and competences for new millennium learners in OECD countries. OECD Education Working Papers, No. 41, OECD Publishing
Assessment and teaching of 21st century skills (ATC21S) (2012)
Binkley M, Erstad O, Herman J, Raizen S, Ripley M, Miller-Ricci M, Rumble M (2012) Defining twenty-first century skills. In: Griffin P, McGaw B, Care E (eds) Assessment and teaching of 21st century skills. Springer
Bloom BS, Krathwohl D (2000) Taxonomy for learning, teaching, and assessing: a revision of Bloom's taxonomy of educational objectives
Callaghan RE (1962) Education and the cult of efficiency. Chicago University
Collaborative assessment alliance. Janison. Case study (2016)
Costa AL, Kallick B (2008) Learning and leading with habits of mind: 16 essential characteristics for success. Association for Supervision and Curriculum Development
Csíkszentmihályi M (1990) Flow: the psychology of optimal experience. Harper & Row
Davies I (1976) Objectives in curriculum design. McGraw Hill
Dede C (2010) Comparing frameworks for 21st century skills. In: Bellanca J (ed) 21st century skills: rethinking how studens learn. Solution Tree Press, pp 51–76
European Parliament (2007) Key competences for lifelong learning: a european reference framework. Annex of a recommendation of the European Parliament and of the Council of 18 December 2006 on key competences for lifelong learning, Official Journal of the European Union, 30.12.2006/L394
Grading Soft Skills (GRASS) Project. European Commission (2016)
Griffin P, Care E (Oct 2013) Methodological approach underlying the scoring of a 21st century skill. 12 the National Convention on Statistics (NCS) EDSA
Griffin P, McGaw B, Care E (eds) (2012) Assessment and teaching of 21st century skills. Springer
Inclusive design research centre: what it inclusive design. OCAD University (2016)
Kolb DA (1976) The learning style inventory: technical manual. McBer
Kolb DA, Fry R (1975) Toward an applied theory of experiential learning. In: Cooper C (ed) Theories of group process. Wiley, London
Marzano RJ (2006) Classroom assessment and grading that work. Association for Supervision and Curriculum Development
Murphy S (2010) The pull of PISA: uncertainty, influence, and ignorance. Inter-Am J Educ Democr 3(1):27–44
National Council for Curriculum and Assessment: Key Skills framework. NCCA (2009)
Neumann W (1979) Educational responses to the concern of proficiency. In: Grant G (ed) On competence: a critical analysis of competence based reform in higher education. Jossey Bass

Organization for Economic Cooperation and Development (OECD) (2005) The definition and selection of key competencies: Executive summary. OECD
Organization for Economic Cooperation and Development (OECD) (2013) Pisa 2015 Draft Collaborative Problem Solving Framework. OECD
Partnership For 21st century skills (P21): framework definitions (2009)
Puentedura R (2014) Building transformation: an introduction to the SAMR model [Blog post]
Redecker C (2013) The Use of ICT for the assessment of key competences. Publications Office of the European Union, European Commission Joint Research Centre for Prospective Technological Studies
Reeves D (2010) A framework for assessing 21st century skills. In: Bellanca J (ed) 21st century skills: rethinking how studens learn. Solution Tree Press, pp 305–325
Rolheiser C (1996) Self-evaluation... helping students get better at it! a teachers resource book. Cooperative Learning Evaluation Assessment Research Group
Ross JA (2006) The reliability, validity, and utility of self-assessment
Rotherham AJ, Willingham D (2009) 21st century skills the challenges ahead. Educ. Leadersh. (ASCD) 67(1):16–21
Saffer D (2014) Microinteractions. O'Reilly Media
Spady WG (1977) Competency based education: a bandwagon in search of a definition. Educ Res 6(1):9–14
SRI International (2016) 21st century learning design: 21CLD learning design rubrics
Stuart L (1999) 21st century skills for 21st century jobs. A Report of the U.S. Department of Commerce, U.S. Department of Education, U.S. Department of Labor, National Institute for Literacy and Small Business Administration. U.S. Government Printing Office
Voogt J, Pareja Roblin N (2012) A comparative analysis of international frameworks for 21st century competences: implications for national curriculum policies. J Curric Stud 44(3):299–321
Werbach K, Hunter D (2012) For the win: how game thinking can revolutionize your business. Wharton Digital Press
Wiggins G, McTighe J (2005) Understanding by design (expanded 2nd edn). ASCD
Zimmerman BJ (2013) From cognitive modeling to self-regulation: a social cognitive career path. Educ Psychol 48(3):135–147

Chapter 4
Designing Pedagogy for Virtual Worlds in Multicultural Environments

Elaine Hoter and Manal Yazbak Abu Ahmad

Abstract This position paper looks at the design and pedagogical model for using virtual worlds in a collaborative multicultural learning environment. Virtual worlds are gradually becoming an integral part of education and this paper discusses the place of virtual worlds to connect between learners and cultures. The paper presents different pedagogical designs, perspectives, projects and models, stressing the need for incorporating design theory with collaborative learning and multicultural considerations. It shows the development of these pedagogies and how these can be integrated within virtual worlds. The paper shows the need for the design of a new pedagogical working model, TEC Town, for working in virtual worlds allowing for collaborative online learning between groups from different cultures. This model is a combination of previous models for virtual worlds; social, gaming, building and collaborative models. In the new model, the participants share a virtual apartment in a virtual world and working in diverse cultural groups, they design and build the interior. They add games according to the class topic together with children from conflicting cultures.

4.1 Introduction

This position paper looks closely at the design of virtual reality for connecting between students from different backgrounds. In order to understand how virtual worlds can be used for developing empathy through collaborative online multicultural, there will first be a discussion which deals with research in a number of related fields including motivation, multiculturalism, collaborative learning environments, and then the combinations of these areas of research to multicultural collaborations

---

E. Hoter (✉)
Talpiot College of Education, Holon, Israel
e-mail: ehoter@gmail.com

M. Yazbak Abu Ahmad
Sakhnin College for Teacher Education, Sakhnin, Israel
e-mail: manalyazbak@gmail.com

E. Kapros and M. Koutsombogera (eds.), *Designing for the User Experience in Learning Systems*, Human–Computer Interaction Series,
https://doi.org/10.1007/978-3-319-94794-5_4

in virtual worlds. The paper will relate to the TEC Model (Technology, Education and Cultural diversity) where technology is used to bring an understanding between people from different cultures through a gradual process of collaborative learning (Hoter et al. 2012).

4.2 Motivation

Even though modern technology allows us to be in contact with almost anyone, most people choose to stay in their own safe environments and don't reach out to people from other cultures. They prefer to converse in their own language with people with similar ideas, interests and beliefs. It is true that in the business world, people work together online, but they are task oriented. They do not share interests or cultures. Fortunately, technology has invaded the education field and now it is possible to bring together students from diverse cultural background and even cultures in conflict to be in a place where the participants learn to collaborate, respect and understand one another.

International and intercultural connections help develop understanding of those different to ourselves. Connections under specific conditions over a period of time can change attitudes and help build empathy towards the other (Allport 1954; Pettigrew 1998; Walther et al. 2015). It is the role of educators to supply the opportunities and frameworks to allow their students to meet with other cultures in a safe environment. However, percentage wise, not many students get to participate in intercultural experiences.

4.3 Multiculturalism

Due to the rapid global changes in this century, multiculturalism with all its complications has become a major issue that needs to be dealt with on the educational and the national level. The massive amount of migration from the Middle East and growth in foreign workers have changed European countries to become nations containing many diverse cultures. Xenophobia and Islamophobia are on the rise and the European countries in particular need to find a way to combat the prejudice and stereotypes (Helbling 2010). On the other hand, most immigrants are afraid to assimilate with the host cultures because they wish to preserve their own cultures and religions (Van Driel et al. 2016).

4.4 Collaborative Learning Environments

Collaborative/cooperative learning theories have been prevalent in the field of education for the last 60 years. Since the 1990s, this has been adapted to collaborative online learning and is being used to bring together people from different parts of the globe (Hoter 2018; Sharan 2010; Slavin 1985). Multicultural connections have always existed through pen pals and in the 1980s through email and later the Internet. Originally these encounters were text based, but with all the added advantages of instant communication and media these encounters can be richer.

Numerous projects have been developed to bring cultures together ranging from single encounters to short term projects over a few weeks to long term connections (Publish 1995). All these projects involve some level of collaboration between the teachers themselves and the participants. The types of online collaborations that have a lasting impact are those designed pedagogically for the pupils to be actively involved in areas that interest them. An example for a single virtual encounter could be meeting an expert or a well-known sports personality or writer in an online synchronous session. Another option is the popular 'mystery hangouts' sessions. Classes join online for a hangout session where the children do not know the location of the other school and have to try and guess where the other class is from. These types of exchanges are often whole class based and the individual often does not get to interact on a more personal level.

Short term virtual projects (4–6 weeks) could be in projects such as iEARN (http://www.us.iearn.org/) or Kidlinks (https://www.kidlink.org/) where classes are connected over a few weeks to learn a specific topic together for example learning about and making kites (Talking Kites). There are many examples of this in higher education where classes join for a unit of studies across the globe, for example the European Virtual Seminar (http://www.ou.nl/evs) Some topics are more successful than others due to the learners' ages and interests in the class. Another example of a short term project is being virtually part of an event or journey. For example 'discovery education' 'Google Expeditions' 'Skype virtual field trips', where you can join experts and go on virtual field trips. The children ask questions and follow the event.

Longer term (6 months and more) virtual projects allow for gradual development and understanding between the students. Students can gradually get to know one another and the collaborative demands can be raised over time for the assignments. Learning in pairs or small groups with students from other societies allows for more personal connections (Walther 2005; Hoter 2009; Hoter et al. 2012). Examples for long term virtual projects include projects connecting different communities for a semester or year where the students/pupils study together for at least an hour a week such as "Deaf and Hearing" (Hoter 2006).

Some projects are designed to involve higher levels of collaboration than others. The more collaboration there is on an individual basis with students from other cultures, the more deeply you get to know people from other cultures and thus you become more empathetic. Some are around projects and themes and others are around problems (Shapira 2016).

4.5 Virtual Worlds

Virtual online worlds developed with the introduction of the internet. These worlds allow participants from different locations to meet through their avatars and interact through voice, gestures and text. Virtual worlds are part of virtual reality. They are 3D worlds where the avatar participants feel that they are present in the virtual world. These worlds are categorised in the 2017 Horizon Report under social media technologies and are considered as one of the important developments in educational technology (Freeman et al. 2017). Our guiding question was can this environment be used not just to bring together students from diverse cultural background and even cultures in conflict but to be a place where the participants learn to collaborate, respect and understand one another? Second Life, the most popular 3D virtual world, started in 2003. This world is open to and free for adults and has been used successfully for various online learning and collaborative ventures. However, by 2007, the idea of an open simulator began and in the last few years numerous private worlds have been made using the OpenSim for educational purposes. These environments can be protected for the learners and they allow the young learner to participate as well as form a closed and safe environment for students.

When choosing or designing your virtual learning environment, as in the real world. It is crucial to identifying the desired learning outcomes to shape effective learning designs for virtual spaces, whether they utilise autonomous learning activities, teacher led activities or participatory group experiences (Gregory et al. 2015). Virtual worlds are realised in various forms or combinations. The first type is "Social Virtual worlds" (SVWs) where the stress is on engaging in social interaction (Vrellis et al. 2016). 'Edorble' is an example of a very accessible SVW Virtual world. The world is designed as a virtual campus where the students as avatars can meet socially, attend online classes and also watch live presentations. This environment facilitates blended and online learning between the students. Teachers can request to have their own campus specifically for their own students. The design of this world does not allow users to build and develop in the environment, but be participants in the activities and social interactions.

The second type of virtual worlds is "Gaming Virtual Worlds" (GVWs) which are 3D environments which normally involve clearly defined quests such as The World of Warcraft (Nardi 2006). Gaming is today understood as a cause of motivating learners. The challenges to get to higher levels motivate the learner to continue. Research has shown that a game-based learning approach might be effective in facilitating students' 21st century skill development (Qian and Clark 2016).

The third category is "Collaborative Virtual Learning Worlds" (CVLWs). In the educational world, CVLWs are used for blended (mixed online and face to face courses) or online instructional formats. Spatially or temporally separated students can work collaboratively in teams by co-existing in a common virtual environment and interacting through synchronous communication tools. Active Worlds, Quest Atlantis, Multiverse and Aeroquest (Pellas 2017) are examples of CVLWs.

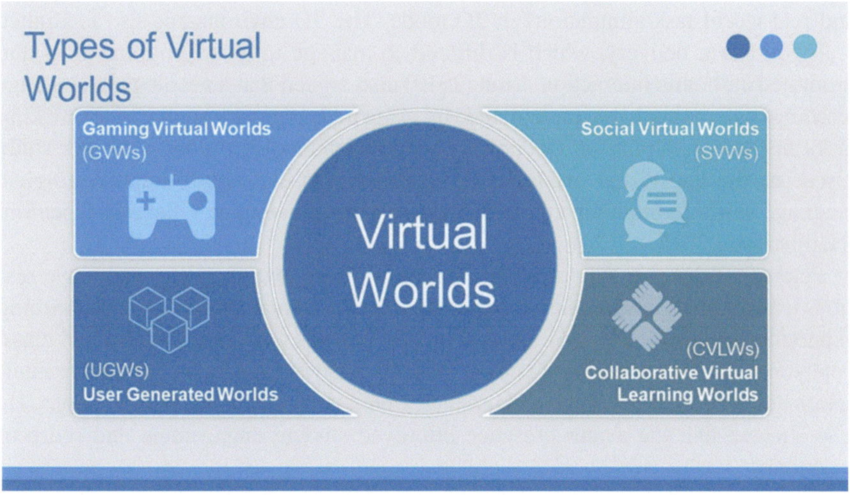

Fig. 4.1 Types of virtual worlds

The last category is "User Generated Worlds" (UGWs) which have an open-ended technological infrastructure and can be in different server modes (networked or standalone). In these worlds users interact and can, if permitted by the owner, create their own virtual environment (grids). In this case, users can be involved alone or with others in co-creating or coordinating their activities, using programming scripting languages 'open' to all users without financial cost for constructing a virtual environment. The most well-known open source virtual worlds are Open Simulator (or Open Sim) and Open Wonderland and the new technology and spaces called High Fidelity.

One of the most popular virtual worlds today is Minecraft which according to 'Business Insider' has 74 million monthly players (2018). In Minecraft participants build using cubes, activities include exploration, resource gathering, crafting, and combat. This environment has been used for a pilot project to bring youth from different cultures together to work on collaborative gaming challenges (Games for Peace, http://gamesforpeace.org/). In their extensive review and assessment of the use of virtual worlds in the teaching of STEM, Pellas (2017) present the results of various studies that show the tremendous effect of working in Virtual Worlds on students' learning results including knowledge transfer, higher-order thinking, problem solving and social skills. They also show a big progress in student interaction referred to as the affective learning experience (Fig. 4.1).

Liou (2012) explored EFL (English as a foreign language) college students' attitudes toward a computer-assisted language learning course conducted in SL (Second Life). The research emphasised the advantages of virtual worlds for language competence and collaboration. Thus, the students perceived SL as an optimal virtual environment for language learning due to its features, such as immersive collaboration and real-world task simulations in 3D mode. The 3D environment also facilitated real-world task delivery, which is difficult to manage in a conventional class and promoted authentic interaction. Liou (2012) also argued that an ecological language learning system should be implemented by using pedagogically sound, sense-making tasks instead of relying on the novelty value of technology alone. Another study discussed the quests and mysteries in virtual worlds that aim to improve English language skills through Chatterdale Mystery virtual language village in OpenSim (Hadjistassou 2016).

Peterson (2016), in his numerous studies on using text chats for interactive sessions using Active Worlds and SL, shows that the EFL students saw their SL learning experience as beneficial, more enjoyable, and less stressful than a traditional class. Peterson's findings show that the EFL students were engaged in collaborative interaction and also used different social management strategies to their interactions. He also showed that the avatar presence improved student engagement and sense of autonomy.

With advanced scripting and the use of HUDS (Head-ups display), it is now possible to make simulations in the virtual worlds. NPCs, non playing characters, can speak and interact with the other players. This has further enhanced the possibilities for using virtual worlds for educational experiences. In the near future, we will see more educational uses combining VR headsets with advanced graphics for example 'high fidelity' where participant presence is felt considerably more than on the low tech graphic platforms. Various headsets and equipment can be connected to enable a complete feeling of presence in the virtual world where the avatar can mimic reflect and mirror the real actions of the participant (Cooper et al. 2018).

4.6 Multicultural Collaboration in Virtual Worlds

When students from diverse cultures meet, the issue of intercultural literacy needs to be addressed. Hasler (2011) uses Heyward's Model of Intercultural Literacy (Heyward 2002) together with the Cultural Historical Activity Theory and claims that Intercultural learning environments need to be designed so that students from different cultures will be able to participate equally. The students need to be aware of their own culture and of other foreign cultures so as to increase their understanding, develop their competencies, increase their language proficiencies, and ultimately to form transcultural or global identities. Hasler's research using SL shows that although the cross-cultural exchanges in SL do not guarantee intercultural literacy, they provide participants with opportunities to move in that direction.

Firstly, it should be noticed that there is a great difference between presence and collaboration in a virtual world. Working together is not necessarily collaboration. Many practitioners and researchers have concluded that totally free, unguided or unstructured collaboration does not necessarily result in productive activity or learning (Kreijns et al. 2003). Some see the establishment of rules to be an important feature to support cooperation (Owens et al. 2009).

Most of the existing virtual worlds tend to be individualistic or competitive in nature which doesn't help to make bonds with other cultures. According to the contact hypothesis, competition is seen as destructive in trying to reduce bias between groups in conflict (Allport 1954). Therefore, if there is gaming and competition it should be in virtual teams where the participants come from different cultures and through the assignment or quest are forced to collaborate.

According to the ample practice and research for the last 60 years in Collaborative Learning (CL), students benefit from learning this way (Slavin 2016). However, CL's effect is not automatic. Placing students in groups, in any context, does not assure that they will work easily together especially when there is a potential gap between teachers and students' expectations and behaviours in the classroom (Sharan 2010).

Sociable computer-supported collaborative learning (CSCL) environments focus on the social (emotional) facets of group learning. Sociability is defined by Kreijns et al. (2003) as the extent to which a CSCL environment is seen to facilitate a social space with attributes as trust and belonging, and where there is a strong sense of community, and good working relationships.

CSCL can be combined with the "Big Five" components for teamwork (Salas et al. 2005) which are:

- Team Leadership: this is ability to direct and coordinate the activities of other team members, assign tasks, develop team knowledge, skills and abilities, assess team performance, plan and organise, motivate team members and establish a positive atmosphere.
- Mutual performance monitoring: The ability to develop common understandings of the team environment and apply appropriate task strategies to accurately monitor teammate performance.
- Backup behaviour: Ability to anticipate other team members' needs through accurate knowledge about their responsibilities. This includes the ability to shift workload among members to achieve balance during high periods of workload or pressure.
- Adaptability: Ability to adjust strategies based on information gathered from the environment through the use of backup behaviour and reallocation of intra-team resources. Altering a course of action or team repertoire in response to changing conditions (internal or external).
- Team orientation: Propensity to take other's behaviour into account during group interaction and the belief in the importance of team goals over individual members' goals. Together we have the requirements to be able to build collaborative activities in a virtual world and the criteria for making this effective.

A six-stage model (Lim 2009) is suggested for working in virtual worlds with children. Lim termed it six learnings where the stages are not necessarily hierarchical or mutually exclusive, but they present the range of pedagogies that can be used while using the island as a learning experience. He recommends that interventions should target one or two of these "learnings".

- Learning by exploring within the virtual island
- Learning by collaborating with others on different tasks
- Learning by being through understanding self and role-playing
- Learning by building through designing and building on the island
- Learning by championing; By this Lim means to "adopt, champion, and evangelise causes from Real Life" (P.8)
- Learning by expressing this would include explaining to the "outside world" what is going on in the world using different forms of media and genres.

4.7 The TEC Model

The TEC (Technology, Education and Cultural Diversity) model is a collaborative online learning framework for small groups that comprise students from different cultures (Hoter 2009; Hoter et al. 2012). The TEC model enables students from different cultures and religions, often in conflict, to work together online. It has been fully explained elsewhere (https://youtu.be/haqc8rNa7I8). It is sufficient to say that the model moves from a low level of collaboration to higher levels, from low technology use, to high technology use and from written text to hearing to verbally communicating online to actual face to face meetings. The rationale is to first get to know the person before meeting face to face in order to decrease prejudice and bias.

4.7.1 TEC4 Schools

The largest project for online collaborative learning in Israel is called TEC4 Schools. This is one of the programs offered by the TEC Center (center for technology, education and cultural diversity). In the TEC4 Schools project, teachers and pupils from 3 different schools and cultures take part in a year long program where for one hour a week the pupils work in small groups (6 students) with the children from the other two schools. They work through the internet and carry out assignments which gradually demand higher levels of collaboration. They work in accordance with the TEC Model (Hoter et al. 2012) About 3000 children from 100 schools take part each year in the program. Results and feedback from this year of collaboration show the students improve their intercultural competencies. However, the most prevalent complaint about the year is that it finishes and the pupils want to continue studying together. Some teachers and pupils would also like to use more virtual environments to collaborate.

4.7.2 The Process

According to the TEC Model students gradually get to know one another through tasks demanding more collaboration. The environment chosen for this is a social network developed specifically for the population in three languages. This allows the pupils to work in small groups. Initial communication is intentionally text based so the students do not know how the others look (just seeing clothes, hijab, skull caps etc. cause bias before they have even met). The problems we have previously faced using the social network was the difficulty to create a sense of belonging to the small group and develop interdependence within the small group. With all the advantages for using virtual worlds to enhance collaboration and intercultural competence we built a social virtual world (SVW) called TEC Island as a meeting place to understand other cultures.

The TEC island includes 4 places of worship: a Mosque, a Synagogue, a Church and a Khilwah (place of worship for the Druze religion). The Island is a place for the children and students to meet virtually and carry out joint assignments. The Island has a storytelling corner, a "dabuka" drum circle, a place to learn languages: Hebrew, Arabic and English as well as games about festivals connected to the other religions (Fig. 4.2).

As creative and fun this world might be, there were a number of drawbacks. Not enough teachers used the world and aside from technical considerations we realised that many of the teachers, despite in-service training, were not confident in themselves when using the island. To overcome these issues, we made a training Island for everyone as a precondition to being on the TEC Island where the participants need

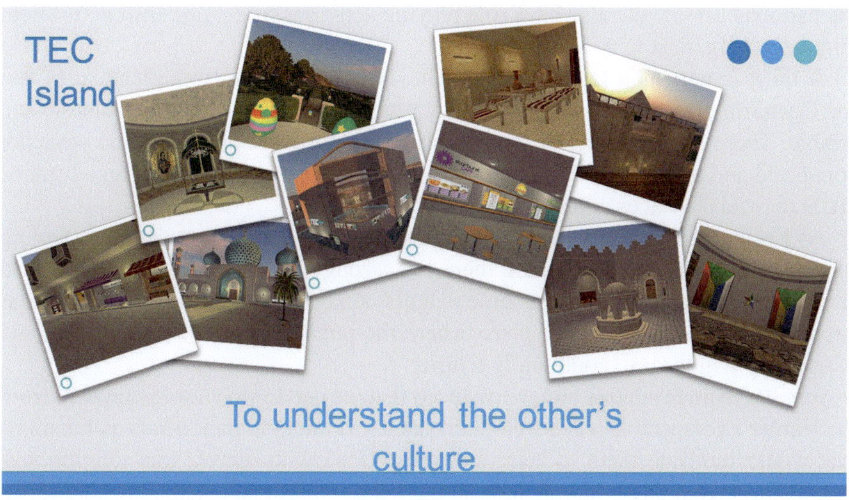

Fig. 4.2 TEC Island introduction

Fig. 4.3 The fruit market

to go through 14 stations and then they earn their wings and can proceed to the TEC Island.

Another issue was that most of the activities, unless set specifically by the teachers, are individualised experience and children don't want to return to the island unless there they have new activities. We started to develop more collaborative activities in the Island. For example, in the virtual Jerusalem area, you can add a prayer for Jerusalem onto a balloon and only when three different people write a prayer do the balloons lift off. We also have role playing activities for buying fruit in different languages (Fig. 4.3).

A third issue was a language one. The TEC Island is in three languages and the OpenSim environment does not allow typing from right to left for Hebrew and Arabic. There are programs to correct this issue but the letters in Arabic were not connected and it was very difficult to read. Solutions were found using an advanced HUD to receive notices and messages.

As Kreijns et al. (2003) stated, we needed a social space where there is a feeling of trust and belonging, and where there is a strong sense of community and good working relationships. This takes time to build and can't be done through a one hour session. We needed to build a place where the pupils feel they really belong and where they will want to continually return.

In order to do reach this aim, we realised that we needed to view the process from the learner's perspective and develop an island according to their needs and features that would motivate them to learn and collaborate with others. Our solution was to build an Island that would belong to the learners. As explained above, there are islands where the participants can jointly build the Island, but this is specialised work belonging to a different course on building virtual worlds with different pedagogical

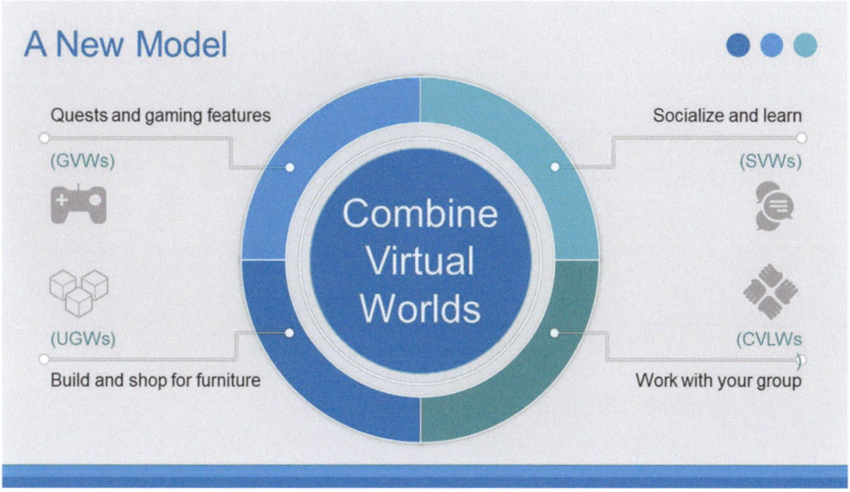

Fig. 4.4 A new model for virtual worlds

aims. Not everyone likes to build, and we can't make an Island just for the techno-minded students. As in life, there are people who prefer to buy ready-made items and not DIY (Do It Yourself)! We wanted the students to work truly collaboratively and learn from one another.

The solution we came up with was to form a new model for interactive learning in virtual worlds that combine building and shopping as well as gaming and socialising (Fig. 4.4).

We built a new virtual world to be used for continuing pupils and classes whose teachers felt confident with using the technology. The world is divided into areas, each area for a different cluster of schools (three classes work together) in accordance with the TEC Model (Fig. 4.5).

Each area consists of residential areas with beautiful modern houses. The small group of six pupils (two from each class) get an empty house with the number of their small group on the door. They get to live in their house throughout the year and design the interior of their home. Many items they can get from the various shops on the Island and adapt and some they learn to build. The world is designed so that each student can only build within his own group house and garden (Figs. 4.6, 4.7 and 4.8).

The project has been enhanced by having a face to face session early on in the project with the pupils from the other schools and cultures so they can discuss the designs and activities. After this meeting it was easier for the children to collaborate. We hope that the world and activities will encourage the students to join from home and feel this is a home away from home. This is surely the highest level of collaboration that comes the closest to actually living together.

Fig. 4.5 TEC town

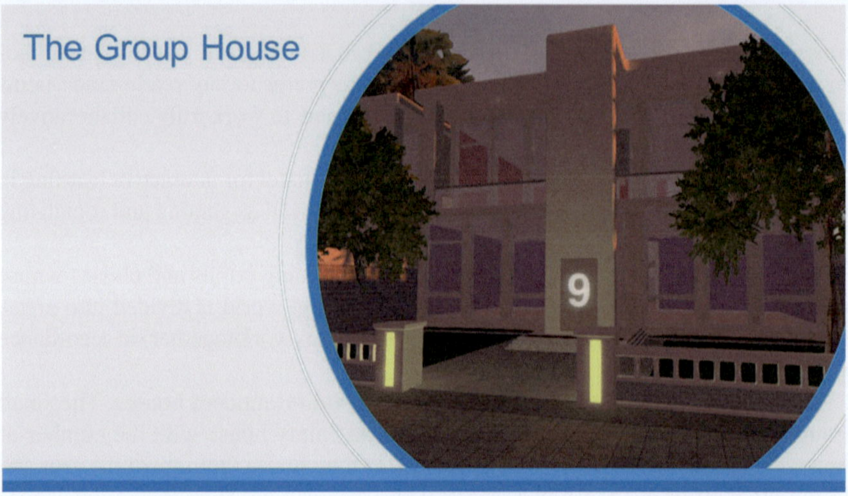

Fig. 4.6 The group house

Fig. 4.7 A group of participants inside the virtual world

Fig. 4.8 The home store

4.8 Challenges

The reticence to using virtual worlds to improve language skills and collaboration in the classroom is not just because of issues of technophobia for some of the teachers, but based on real technical issues. These include lack of the minimal technical requirements to use virtual worlds in many schools (bandwidth, compatible graphic cards etc.). The system often crashes, and there is still an issue of platform stability. Users also need to invest time to master the skills required to work in a virtual world (Dawley and Chris 2014; Liou 2012). Taking into account these drawbacks (Cooke-Plagwitz 2008) argue that there is great potential for integrating SL to promote authentic target language learning and simulating real-world language immersion when the use of SL is planned and constructed within the language curricula (Chen 2016).

Despite the technological challenges, virtual worlds are being integrated into education (Jarmon 2010). In the near future we will see improved graphics and animations as well as more usage of appliances to make the experience more real. Virtual worlds offer a way of involving and motivating the pupils because they can be learner centred enabling the student to take part in the building process, the gaming the collaborative and the social elements.

References

Allport G (1954) The nature of prejudice. Addison-Wesley, Cambridge, MA

Business Insider, http://www.businessinsider.com/minecraft-has-74-million-monthly-players-2018-1

Chen JCC (2016) The crossroads of English language learners, task-based instruction, and 3D multi-user virtual learning in second life. Comput Educ 102:152–171

Cooke-Plagwitz J (2008) New directions in CALL: an objective introduction to second life. CALICo J 25(3):547–557

Cooper N, Milella F, Pinto C, Cant I, White M et al (2018) The effects of substitute multisensory feedback on task performance and the sense of presence in a virtual reality environment. PLOS ONE 13(2):e0191846. https://doi.org/10.1371/journal.pone.0191846

Dawley L, Dede C (2014) Situated learning in virtual worlds and immersive simulations. In: Spector M, Merrill D, Elen J, Bishop MJ (eds) The handbook of research for educational communications and technology. Springer, New York, NY, pp 723–734

Edorble. https://www.edorble.com

Freeman A, Adams Becker S, Cummins M, Davis A, Hall Giesinger C (2017) NMC/CoSN horizon report: 2017 K-12 edition. The New Media Consortium, Austin, Texas

Games for peace. http://gamesforpeace.org/

Google Expeditions. https://edu.google.com/expeditions/ar/

Gregory S, Gregory B, Wood D, O'Connell J, Grant S, Hillier M, Nikolic S (2015) New applications, new global audiences: educators repurposing and reusing 3D virtual and immersive learning resources. In: Australasian society for computers in learning and tertiary education (ascilite), pp. 121–133

Hadjistassou S, Molka-Danielsen J (2016) Designing alien mysteries in chatterdale: an instructor's perspective. In: Handbook of research on gaming trends in P-12 education. IGI Global, pp 222–236

Hasler B (2011) Intercultural collaborative learning in virtual worlds. Cutting-edge Technol High Educ 4:265–304

Helbling M (2010) Islamophobia in Switzerland: a new phenomenon or a new name for Xenophobia? In: Paper prepared for Annual Conference of the Midwest Political Science Association (MPSA), Chicago

Heyward M (2002) From international to intercultural. Redefining the international school for a globalized world. J Res Int Educ 1:9–32

High fidelity. http://highfidelity.com

Hoter E (2006) Building community or a collaborative project? Connecting the hearing and non-hearing communities. Inf Technol Educ Soc 7(1):45–58

Hoter E, Shonfeld M, Ganayim A (2009) Information and communication technology (ICT) in the service of multiculturalism. Int Rev Res Open Distrib Learn 10(2):

Hoter E, Shonfeld M (2012) Ganayem A (2012) TEC Center: linking technology, education and cultural diversity. I-Manag J Educ Technol 9(1):15

Hoter E (2018) Developing a model for online collaborative learning. In: Shonfeld M, Gibson D (eds) Collaborative learning in a global world. Information Age Publishing, In print

iEARN Collaboration Centre. https://iearn.org/

Jarmon L (2010) Homo virtualis: virtual worlds, learning, and anecology of embodied interaction. Int J Virtualand Pers Learn Environ (IJVPLE) 1(1):

Kidlink Global Education Projects. https://www.kidlink.org/

Kreijns K, Kirschner P, Jochems W (2003) Identifying the pitfalls of social interaction in computer-supported collaborative learning environments: a review of the research. Comput Human Behav 19(3):335–353

Lim K (2009) The six learnings of second life. J Virtual Worlds Res 2(1):3–11

Liou H-C (2012) The roles of second life in a college computer assisted language learning (CALL) course in Taiwan. ROC. Comput Assist Lang Learn 25(4):365–382

Minecraft Official Site. https://minecraft.net/

Mystery Hangout. https://plus.google.com/communities/110369120141935358658

Nardi B, Harris J (2006) Strangers and friends: collaborative play in world of warcraft. In: Proceedings of the 2006 20th anniversary conference on computer supported cooperative work. ACM, pp 149–158

OpenSim. https://plus.google.com/communities/116284417302234467612

Owens D, Davies A, Murphy J, Khazanchi D, Zigurs I (2009) Real-world. IT Pro. IEEE, pp 34-41

Pellas N, Kazanidis I, Konstantinou N, Georgiou G (2017) Exploring the educational potential of three-dimensional multi-user virtual worlds for STEM education: a mixed-method systematic literature review. Educ Inf Technol 22(5):2235–2279

Peterson M (2016) Virtual worlds and language learning. In: The routledge handbook of language learning and technology, p 308

Pettigrew T (1998) Intergroup contact theory. Ann Rev Psychol 49:65–85

Publish W, Harris J (1995) College of William and Mary organizing and facilitating telecollaborative projects. Comput Teach 22(5):66–69. http://publish.wm.edu/educationpubs

Qian M, Clark Karen R (2016) Game-based learning and 21st century skills: a review of recent research. Comput Human Behav 63:50–58

Salas E, Sims DE, Shawn Burke C (2005) Is there a "big five" in teamwork? Small Group Res 36(5):555–599

Sharan Y (2010) Cooperative learning for academic and social gains: valued pedagogy, problematic practice. Eur J Educ 45:300–313

Shapira N, Kupermintz H, Kali Y (2016) Design principles for promoting intergroup empathy in online environments. Interdiscip J e-Skills Life Long Learn 12(12):225–246. http://www.informingscience.org/Publications/3605

Skype Virtual Field Trips. https://education.microsoft.com/skype-in-the-classroom/virtual-field-trips
Slavin R (1985) Cooperative learning: applying contact theory in desegregated schools. J Soc Issues 41(3):45–62
Slavin R (2016) Instruction based on cooperative learning. In: Mayer RE, Alexander PA (eds) Handbook of research on learning and instruction. Taylor & Francis, pp 344–360
Van Driel B, Darmody M, Kerzil J (2016) Education policies and practices to foster tolerance, respect for diversity and civic responsibility in children and young people in the EU. Publications Office of the European Union, NESET II Report, Luxembourg. https://doi.org/10.2766/46172
Vrellis I, Avouris N, Mikropoulos T (2016) Learning outcome, presence and satisfaction from a science activity in second life. Australas J Educ Technol 32(1):59–77
Walther JB, Bunz U (2005) The rules of virtual groups: trust, liking, and performance in computer-mediated communication. J Commun 828–846
Walther JB, Hoter E, Ganayem A, Shonfeld M (2015) Computer-mediated communication and the reduction of prejudice: a controlled longitudinal field experiment among Jews and Arabs in Israel. Comput Human Behav 52:550–558

Chapter 5
The CHI of Teaching Online: Blurring the Lines Between User Interfaces and Learner Interfaces

David Joyner

Abstract The growing prevalence of online education has led to an increase in user interface design for educational contexts, and especially an increase in user interfaces that serve a central role in the learning process. While much of this is straightforward user interface design, there are places where the line between interface design and learning design blur in significant ways. In this analysis, we perform a case study on a graduate-level human-computer interaction class delivered as part of an accredited online program. To evaluate the class, we borrow design principles from the HCI literature and examine how the class's design implements usability principles like equity, flexibility, and consistency. Through this, we illustrate the unique intersection of interface design and learning design, with an emphasis on decisions that are not clearly in one design area or the other. Finally, we provide a brief evaluation of the class to endorse the class's value for such an analysis.

5.1 Introduction

The rising role of technology in education has led to a blurring of the lines between user interface design and learning design. The requirements of teachers, students, administrators, and parents dictates elements of the design of user interfaces used in educational contexts, but the design of those interfaces in turn fundamentally alters the learning process. At times, specific design decisions or elements of instruction cannot solely be attributed to learning design or user interface design.

This trend has existed for decades, from classic interfaces for correspondence learning to more modern learning management systems, but it has taken on a new significance with the advent of entirely online learning environments. While in some ways these learning environments are a natural evolution of these prior interfaces, the fundamental change that has occurred is the placement of the user interface as

D. Joyner (✉)
College of Computing, Georgia Institute of Technology, 801 Atlantic Drive NW, 30084 Atlanta, GA, Georgia
e-mail: david.joyner@gatech.edu

E. Kapros and M. Koutsombogera (eds.), *Designing for the User Experience in Learning Systems*, Human–Computer Interaction Series,
https://doi.org/10.1007/978-3-319-94794-5_5

the core of the class experience. Rather than complementing traditional classroom experiences with learning management systems or in-classroom technologies, these online learning environments *are* the classroom.

As a result, for perhaps the first time, the classroom itself is a user interface. This can be taken very literally, as with synchronous virtual classroom environments (Koppelman and Vranken 2008; Martin et al. 2012; McBrien et al. 2009), or it can be taken more figuratively, where user interfaces can serve the same functional roles as traditional classrooms while eschewing the typical requirements of synchronicity and telepresence (Hiltz and Wellman 1997; Joyner et al. 2016; Swan et al. 2000). These latter classrooms are particularly notable because the interface changes the interaction more fundamentally; whereas synchronous virtual classrooms may aim to recreate in-person interactions as completely as possible, asynchronous learning environments must use these computational interfaces to create the same effects through different mechanisms. Significant work has been devoted to investigating how these interfaces may replicate components of traditional learning environments, such as peer-to-peer learning (Boud et al. 2014), peer assessment (Kulkarni et al. 2015), social presence (Tu and McIsaac 2002), laboratory activities (O'Malley et al. 2015), and academic integrity (Li et al. 2015; Northcutt et al. 2016).

This trend toward interfaces *as* classrooms brings new emphasis to the intersection between learning design and user interface design. The two are highly compatible: principles like rapid feedback are comparably valued in user interface design (Nielsen 1995) and learning design (Chandler 2003; Kulkarni et al. 2015). However, it is also important to understand the nature of desirable difficulties (Bjork 2013; McDaniel and Butler 2011) within the material, as an interface designer may inadvertently undermine the learning experience in pursuit of higher user satisfaction (Fishwick 2004; Norman 2013). For this reason, we must carefully prescribe principles and guidelines for designing learning interfaces that emphasize when the roles of student and user are compatible.

Thus, due to both the advent of fully online learning environments and the underlying similarities between user interface design and learning design, there is tremendous opportunity to examine the user experience in learning systems from the perspectives of both interface design and learning design. However, the different objectives of the two design paradigms—one to support immediate interaction, the other to support long-term learning gains—mean that the application of one paradigm's heuristics and guidelines to the other must be performed carefully. Toward this end, some work has already been performed evaluating user interface design specifically within the realm of digital learning environments (Cho et al. 2009; Jones and Farquhar 1997; Najjar 1998), but relatively little work has been done on specifically the user interface design of fully online learning environments.

In this analysis we perform a case study on a graduate-level class offered as part of an online Master of Science in Computer Science program at a major public university. Both the program and the class are delivered asynchronously and online, with no requirement for synchronous activities or in-person attendance. While considerable attention could be paid to evaluating the specific user interfaces that deliver the program, this case study instead focuses on higher-level design decisions. Specifically, we are interested in transferring principles of human-computer interaction into the realm of learning design, especially insofar as their application is facilitated by the online nature of the program.

To do this, we first provide some necessary background on the nature and structure of the program and this class, and then move through four prominent principles from the human-computer interaction literature: flexibility, equity, consistency, and distributed cognition. For each topic, we examine how it transfers into this online learning environment as a principle of both interface design and learning design. We also look at a smaller number of additional principles with narrower applications in this course, and then evaluate the course based on student surveys.

5.2 Background

While this case study focuses specifically on a single class, that class exists in the context of a broader online Master of Science program at a major public university in the United States. Several of the principles we observe in this class are actually derived from the broader principles of the program, especially as it relates to equity. Thus, we begin by giving a brief background on the program, and then focus more specifically on the course under evaluation in this case study.

5.2.1 Program Background

The course under evaluation in this case study is part of an online Master of Science in Computer Science program launched by a major public university in the United States in 2014. The program merges recent MOOC-based initiatives with more classical principles and approaches to distance learning. The goal is to create an online program whose learning outcomes and student experience are equivalent or comparable to the in-person experience; as such, the program carries equal accreditation to the traditional on-campus degree.

In drawing inspiration from MOOC initiatives over the past several years, however, the program emphasizes low cost and high flexibility. On the cost side, the cost of attendance is $170 per credit hour plus $200 in fees per semester of attendance. Thirty credit hours are required to graduate, and thus, the total degree costs between $6100 and $7100, a small fraction of comparable programs or the university's own on-campus program. These costs are digestible because each class draws dramatically higher enrolment than their on-campus counterparts: as of Spring 2018, the program enrolls over 6,500 total students taking an average of 1.4 classes per semester, with individual courses enrolling as many as 600 students.

On the flexibility side, the program emphasizes that it requires no synchronous or collocated activities: students are never required to attend a virtual lecture at a specific time or visit campus, a testing center, or a remote lab for a course activity.

Proctored and timed exams are typically open for three to four days at a time, while lecture material is pre-produced and assignments are published well in advance of the due date.

The program thus captures an audience for whom a Master of Science in Computer Science is otherwise inaccessible, either due to high costs, geographic immobility, or scheduling constraints. Evaluations have shown that as a result, the program draws a dramatically different demographic of student from the university's on-campus program: online students tend to be older, are more likely to be employed, have more significant prior education and professional experience, and are more likely to be from the United States (Goel and Joyner 2016; Joyner 2017). The program is forecast to increase the annual output of MSCS graduates in the United States by 8% (Goodman et al. 2016).

5.2.2 *Course Background*

This case study focuses on one specific course in this broader program. Fitting this analysis's contribution, the course is on human-computer interaction, and covers HCI principles, the design life cycle, and modern applications such as virtual reality and wearable computing. At time of writing, the course has been offered four complete times, including three 17-week full semesters and one 12-week summer semester.

Each week, students watch a series of custom-produced lecture videos, complete a written assignment, and participate in peer review and forum discussions. Participation is mandated by the course's grading policy, but students have multiple pathways to earning participation credit to fit their personalities and routines. Students also complete two projects—one individual, one group—and take two timed, proctored, open-book, open-note multiple choice exams. Proctoring is supplied by a digital proctoring solution, allowing students to take the exam on their own computer.

Aside from the exams, all work is manually graded by human teaching assistants. One teaching assistant is hired for approximately every 40 enrollees in the course, and teaching assistants are solely responsible for grading assignments: course administration, announcements, Q&A, office hours, etc. are all handled by the course instructor.

The course generally enrolls 200–250 students per semester, supported by 5–6 teaching assistants. Its completion rate is 92%, ranking slightly higher than the program's overall average of approximately 85%. To date, 708 students have completed the course across four semesters, with 205 more on track to complete the course this semester.

To explore the crossover between interface design principles and learning design, we take four common design principles or theories from the HCI literature—flexibility, equity, consistency, and distributed cognition—and examine their applications to the design of this online course. In some ways, these principles are applied by analogy: flexibility, for example, traditionally refers to flexible interactions with a specific interface, but in our case, refers to flexible interactions with course material. In others, the application is more literal: equity, for example, refers in part to accommodating individuals with disabilities, which is more directly supported by the course and program structure.

5.3 Flexibility

For flexibility, we apply the Principle of Flexibility from Story, Mueller and Mace's Principles of Universal Design, which they define as, "The design accommodates a wide range of individual preferences and abilities" (Story et al. 1998). We also inject the heuristic of Flexibility and Efficiency of Use from Jakob Nielsen's ten heuristics, where he writes, "Allow users to tailor frequent actions" (Nielsen 1995). The flexibility of the course generally flows from the inherent properties of the online program, although the course design takes care to preserve and accentuate this flexibility. Most importantly, these applications of the principle of flexibility support the subsequent applications of the principle of equity.

5.3.1 Geographic Flexibility

Geographic flexibility refers to the online program's ability to accept students regardless of their geographic location. At a trivial level, this relates to the program's ability to accept students who do not live within range of campus. As it pertains to flexibility as a usability guideline, however, this flexibility relates more to accommodating individual preferences for where they complete their work. This relates in part to individual circumstantial constraints, such as the need for working professionals to be able to take course material with them during work trips. It has more significant implications, however, especially as flexibility ties into equity: for example, individuals with disabilities that deter them from leaving the house may participate in a program that offers true geographic flexibility. In a computer science program, several of the abilities required for in-person attendance (e.g. walking, driving to campus, relocating to campus) are largely unrelated to the material itself, and thus this geographic flexibility resolves individual characteristics that pose threats to a student's participation in the field that are unrelated to the content.

It is worth noting that geographic flexibility is inherent in distance learning as a whole; this class's instantiation of geographic flexibility is not unique except insofar as an identically-accredited distance learning program at a major public institution is still somewhat novel.

Table 5.1 Enrollment and number of instructor and student forum contributions by semester

Statistic	Fall 2016	Spring 2017	Summer 2017	Fall 2017
Enrollment	83	231	183	211
Student contributions	3,477	9,147	7,970	9,381
Instructor contributions	785	1,768	1,143	1,265

5.3.2 *Temporal Flexibility*

Temporal flexibility refers to flexibility of the student's time, allowing them to work on the class not only wherever they want, but whenever they want. Temporal flexibility offers a greater difference between this program and traditional distance learning as the presence of live interaction has typically differentiated distance learning from correspondence learning. Given the program's goals of equality with the on-campus program, however, simplifying delivery to correspondence education would be insufficient; requiring live interaction, however, would challenge temporal flexibility.

The class achieves balances these competing needs by maximizing the usage of asynchronous communication tools in course delivery. Most course forums garner over ten thousand posts per semester, with approximately 80% coming from students and 20% coming from the instructor. Table 5.1 shows the class's enrollment and contribution statistics by semester. In addition to forum participation, the class also leverages asynchronous tools for peer review and instructor feedback, as well as an asynchronous video-based method for disseminating pre-recorded custom-produced lecture videos.

This temporal flexibility refers strictly to those activities that are typically synchronous in traditional course delivery. Other activities, such as completing homework, are usually somewhat asynchronous. As a result, the design of this course accommodates individual students with a wide range of preferences or constraints on when they work on course material. We will discuss the impacts of this more in the section below on equity.

5.3.3 *Preference Flexibility*

The geographic and temporal flexibility described above give way to an abundance of flexible accommodations for individual students' preferences and abilities. For example, as a product of being able to watch and re-watch lectures at any pace and in any setting, students may choose to watch lectures while actively working on the assignment they target; to attempt an assignment prior to watching the lecture videos in order to pre-load questions to consider while watching; or to only watch the videos as needed knowing that lecture material cannot be permanently missed the way a single in-person class may be missed.

For this course, flexibility is extended through the course's participation policy as well. It is common for online courses to attempt to capture in-person participation by requiring forum participation, but most research instead focuses on incentivizing or encouraging it more authentically [e.g. Kizilcec et al. (2014)]. There are multiple reasons to focus on more organic discussion stimulation, not least among them that requiring such participation does not address recognized gender issues in forum communication (Freeman and Bamford 2004). To accommodate a greater range of student preferences, this course instead offers multiple routes to earning participation credit: students may contribute to the forums, complete peer reviews of their classmates' work, give instructors feedback on the course, or participate in their classmates' need finding or evaluation studies as part of their coursework. These different activities fit with different student preferences and behaviors; for instance, it is easier to set aside a block of time for peer reviews, whereas it is easier to participate in a course forum in several short moments of time.

5.4 Equity

In defining equity as a design principle, we borrow in particular the Principle of Equitable Use from Story, Mueller, and Mace, which they define as "The design is useful and marketable to people with diverse abilities" (Story et al. 1998). In particularly, we note the sub-guidelines, "Provide the same means of use for all users: identical whenever possible, equivalent when not" and "Avoid segregating or stigmatizing any users" (Story et al. 1998).

Our application of equity begins with the natural consequences of the flexibility described above; flexibility focuses on what students within the program can do, but equity focuses on what students can participate due to that flexibility. We then examine equity as well as facilitated by the program's admissions structure and pseudo-anonymity in course delivery.

5.4.1 Equity Through Flexibility

In many ways, the greatest advantage of the geographic and temporal flexibility referenced above is not in the experience of students in the program, but rather in what students may enter the program in the first place. A traditional graduate program draws from a very narrow population: individuals (a) who either live near the university or have the financial or lifestyle flexibility to relocate, and (b) have the scheduling flexibility to attend classes during the day or pre-selected evenings. Financial flexibility plays into this as well: a traditional graduate program is only available to those who have or can secure (through loans or employer reimbursement) the funds to pay high tuition rates.

Because this program is available to students regardless of location or specific scheduling availability, it is equally available to students who otherwise would lack the ability to participate in such a program. The requirements are distilled down to only those that are inherently required for the content: a significant time commitment (albeit flexible to the student's own schedule) and sufficient prior background. The cost supports this equity as well: while still expensive, the program does not demand access to an exorbitant amount of funds. As noted previously, these factors directly correspond to the unique demographics the program draws (Goel and Joyner 2016; Joyner 2017).

It is worth noting that this audience is not one for which we might stress equity: students entering the program must have a bachelor's in computer science or a similar field with a strong GPA (or equivalent work experience); these criteria generally mean the students are advantaged in the first place. Thus, one takeaway of this program's application of the principle of equity comes instead in how similar models may be extended to otherwise-disadvantaged populations. However, another application comes in expanding the view of the program's audience from geographically dispersed mid-career working professionals and considering also individuals with chronic illnesses, caretakers for others with illnesses, expecting parents, and others for whom obstacles to participation exist.

5.4.2 *Equity Through Admissions*

One component discussed above is the program's size: at 6,500 students, it is believed to be the largest program of its kind in the world (Goodman et al. 2016; Joyner 2018). While this is often discussed as part of counterbalancing the low tuition rate, it has a profound effect on equity as well. While the program's on-campus analogue sets a minimum bar for acceptance, it draws far more qualified applicants than it has capacity to handle. As a result, the top few percent are admitted, leaving out many students who meet the minimum requirements but are not competitive with the most-decorated applicants.

As the online program lacks a set capacity, however, any student who meets the minimum requirements is admitted. This expands access to students who otherwise would be uncompetitive, typically due to a more meager prior background. These students meet the minimum requirements and stand a strong chance of succeeding, but they would not be in the top percentile of applicants typically accepted to a limited-capacity program. Thus, the limitless capacity supports the principle of equity by accepting students with the potential to succeed who may not otherwise have the opportunity.

5.4.3 Equity Through Anonymity

A classic internet aphorism states, "On the internet, no one knows you're a dog." In some ways, the principle applies to this program: although students are identified by name and work is tied to their real identity (unlike MOOCs, where a username may supplant a true name), students have considerable control over what portions of their identity they reveal to classmates and instructors. To classmates, students have the option to reveal essentially no personal information: they may select the name that is shown in discussion posts and peer review, which typically are the only communications inherently surfaced to classmates. Even to instructors, students reveal little about their personal selves.

While a systematic study of this dynamic is still in the works, we have anecdotally observed several applications. At a broad level, it is known that there are issues with perceived identity mismatches between gender or race and computer science (Whitley 1997), and that merely being reminded of such stereotypes can lessen performance and engagement (Good et al. 2003). Signifiers of these stereotypes are inherently present in traditional classrooms, but online lack any inherent need to be disclosed. It is worth considering whether hiding these signifiers is a missed opportunity in the long run, but it nonetheless presents a path around stereotype threats worth considering.

Other applications of this anonymity are even more delicate, demanding caution in conducting more rigorous studies, but they nonetheless reveal enormous potential for equity through the relative anonymity of the online delivery mechanism. Students have on multiple occasions confided in trusted instructors or teaching assistants the presence of mitigating issues that alter their in-person interactions, including physical disabilities or deformities, obesity, speech impediments, transgenderism, and behavioural disorders. The online environment removes these as a first impression among classmates and with instructors, creating an equity of experience among those populations least likely to find it in person.

5.5 Consistency

As a design principle, consistency appears across multiple sets of guidelines and heuristics. We apply the definitions from three different such sets. First, Norman states (Norman 2013),

> Consistency in design is virtuous. It means that lessons learned with one system transfer readily to others … If a new way of doing things is only slightly better than the old, it is better to be consistent.

Nielsen prescribes a similar heuristic, stating, "Users should not have to wonder whether different words, situations, or actions mean the same thing. Follow platform conventions" (Nielsen 1995). Constantine and Lockwood echo these sentiments as well with their Reuse Principle, stating (Constantine and Lockwood 1999),

> The design should reuse internal and external components and behaviors, maintaining consistency with purpose rather than merely arbitrary consistency, thus reducing the need for users to rethink and remember.

With regard to this case study, we consider especially consistency within the class: just as consistency is used to set expectations among users of the outcomes of different interactions, so also consistency is used to set expectations among students of certain responsibilities or deliverables. Efforts are underway as well to extend consistency across courses, especially as they relate to administrative elements of course delivery.

5.5.1 Assignment Cadence

Early on, we observed that in delivering an asynchronous class, a forcing function for students' regular engagement was lost. On campus, that engagement came from lectures: even if assessments were only due every month, students were still incentivized to remain engaged by the fleeting lectures which could not be recovered once lost. In this online design, all lecture material is persistently available: what, then, is there to motivate students to remain engaged long before assessments are due?

Our approach to this is to manually recreate that cadence of a weekly engagement through weekly deliverables. The class requires student submissions every week of the semester, each of which directly corresponds to the recommended lecture material for the week. Flexibility (and its effect on equity) are preserved in that lectures and assignment descriptions are all provided at the start of the semester, so students who need to work around other constraints may do so by working ahead; regular deadlines, however, force the majority of students to remain engaged with the course on a weekly basis. Just as through the principle of consistency in interface design a user can interact with a new interface and understand the outcomes of their actions, so also a student can enter a new week of the course and understand the expectations without re-reading the calendar.

5.5.2 Announcement Cadence

Just as in-person lectures serve as a forcing function for continued student engagement, we also observed that they serve as a hub for course communication. A natural expectation arises (even if only in the minds of instructors) that weekly lectures will set expectations for the week or recap the week. The loss of this dynamic risks a class becoming a single amorphous semester rather than a regimented curriculum, especially with students' tendencies to do work at non-traditional times [e.g. weekends (Joyner 2017)].

To combat this, the course leverages consistent weekly announcements, sent to students every Monday morning and Friday evening. Monday announcements remind students what they are expected to watch, read, and do for the week, while Friday announcements typically recap significant occurrences or reemphasize key points from the week's material. These announcements aim to further emphasize that classroom cadence, replicating the effect of a teacher walking in on Monday morning and beginning lecture. As an application of consistency, this replicates common interaction designs such as weekly reports or digests of activity, acting as consistent reminders that the course is ongoing.

The announcement cadence plays a more significant role as well with regard to the course's emphasis on distributed cognition, explained further in the next section. Either way, these weekly announcements are the single most well-praised element of the course's delivery, and have been incorporated into recommendations issued to all classes in the program.

5.5.3 Administrative Decisions

As a more literal application of the principle of consistency, the course makes several administrative decisions to create consistent expectations among students regarding more trivial elements of the course experience. The course's smallest unit of time is one week: there are no in-week deadlines (excepting a small incentive for early peer review discussed later). Sunday night at 11:59 PM UTC-12 (anywhere on earth) time marks the end of each week; all of the week's work is due at this time, and one minute later marks the start of the next week. Anywhere on Earth time is chosen to simplify planning for students: if it is before midnight their local time, the assignment is not due. We encourage students to submit by their own midnight for simplicity, although our experience is that students maximize the time available, and submissions role in late in the evening on Sunday nights.

Few course components are time-gated (exams, periodic course surveys), but those that are open at 12:00 AM UTC-12 on Mondays, closing at the typical deadline as well. Thus, students do not devote cognitive resources each day to considering what is required; only on Sundays are students required to ensure they have accomplished the week's deliverables. As a principle of consistency, this process similarly aims to diminish students' reliance on repeated manual checks and increase the time allotted to focus on the course material and assessments.

Interestingly, we have attempted to leverage the principle of consistency in other ways, such as scheduling the aforementioned announcements to go out at the exact start of the week. Feedback we have received from students, however, indicates this is actually somewhat counterproductive as it diminishes the personal feel of these announcements: students feel more connected to the class knowing the instructor was physically present to send the announcement, even if it is delayed. This suggests this principle is best applied to items around which students plan, such as deadlines and release dates, rather than every element of the course delivery. It may also be the case that students are patient with late announcements because expectations of consistency and fairness are set in these other ways.

5.6 Distributed Cognition

Where the previous four design principles were stated with some clarity in a well-known prescriptive set of guidelines, distributed cognition is a more general theory through which we may examine human-computer interfaces (Hollan et al. 2000). Key to this idea is the notion that human cognitive tasks like reasoning, remembering, and acting could be offloaded onto a computer interface to lighten the cognitive load on the user. As applied to education, this suggests using an interface to lessen the attention paid by students to course administration to support greater attention to course content.

5.6.1 Offloading Through Announcements

As referenced above, in addition to creating consistent expectations, a major function of regular announcements is to offload the attention students may otherwise spend thinking about course procedures, assignment deadlines, and so on onto the interface, allowing them instead to focus on the course material. This role of these announcements comes from an early observation from students: whereas traditional in-person courses operate on a "push" structure, online courses emphasize a "pull" structure. These terms, derived from principles of HCI as well, mean that students in a traditional class can usually rely on the instructor to push information to them, such as by standing in front of a lecture hall and giving announcements. Online classes usually operate by making all information available to the students, but that relies on students pulling the right information at the right time.

Weekly announcements approximate that in-person dynamic by pushing immediately pertinent information to students. Students thus do not need to trust that they have pulled all critical information at the right time; absent this trust, students devote significant cognitive resources to attending to the class's administration, which diminishes the resources that may be devoted to learning the actual course material. As noted above, this is a small feature, but it is one of the most well-praised features in the program; student reviews on a public student-run review site praise this repeatedly, and other pieces of negative feedback could be similarly addressed by offloading these roles onto the interface.

5.6.2 *Offloading Through Documentation*

A second application of distributed cognition to the course design leverages the student community more heavily. As referenced previously, the online environment makes heavy use of the course forum, but it takes on a unique role in the online course: it *is* the classroom, but it is a classroom where any student can contribute at any time (Joyner et al. 2016). Student answers to classmates' questions are not often emphasized in traditional lectures where students inherently pose questions to the professor, but the online board affords student-to-student discussion more fully.

This provides an answer to another implicit question in course design: what information should be incorporated into the course's fundamental documentation, and what should be pushed to students through announcements and discussions? This course errs heavily on the side of the documentation specifically because it leverages this student community: the community as a whole can come to a common understanding of the course's administration and policies because the entire documentation is available to everyone. Any single student likely will not read all the documentation, but enough students will read each part that if a student has a question that is covered in the documentation, some classmate will have the answer. Thus, knowledge of the course is distributed among the student body rather than solely relying on the communication of the instructor.

5.6.3 *Offloading Through Assessment Design*

Finally, the course deliberately designs assessments to encourage students to leverage distributed cognition. While this is natural in essays and projects where course access is persistent during work, the course tests are also designed to be open to any non-collaborative information seeking. These open-book, open-note, open-video, open-forum tests are created with the knowledge that students will have access to course resources, and thus should focus less on the knowledge they are able to draw to mind immediately and more on their ability to solve questions quickly with the available resources.

Students are informed of this paradigm in advance of the exams, and encouraged to organize their test-taking environment accordingly. Ready access to course material, their notes, the readings, and even the course's discussions are encouraged. These tests emphasize that it is the system comprised of the student, their resources, and their environment that is being assessed on the test rather than just their cognition. Distributed cognition is thus simultaneously a lesson in the course, a principle for students to apply to the course, and a theory for us to apply in evaluating the course.

5.7 Additional Principles

Additional principles are at play in the course as well, although we generally note that many of these principles apply equally well to traditional courses using modern-day learning management systems. Nonetheless, they are worth including as they further broaden the view of how interface design principles may be applied to learning design.

5.7.1 Structure

With regards to structure as a principle of design, we leverage the principle defined by Constantine and Lockwood (1999). In many ways, our applications of structure are not inherently restricted to online environments; however, we observe that specific details of the online environment more clearly afford visible structure. We observe, for example, that organizing lecture material into pre-produced videos allows the presentation of it in a way that brings out the underlying structure of the content rather than forcing it into a prescribed lecture schedule. This, then, allows students to construct their consumption of course material around the actual structure of the content.

This similarly connects to the structure of a course calendar offered to students: without requirements that a pre-set amount of time be spent in certain weeks in lecture, the structure of the course can be more deliberately designed not only for the content, but also for the assessments. Other classes in the program, for example, implicitly require students to "attend" ten hours of lecture in the early weeks of the class, then shift to a strict project-based mode in the later weeks. Such a structure would not be possible in a traditional system of prescribed lecture times.

5.7.2 Perceptibility

On perceptibility, Nielsen writes, "The system should always keep users informed about what is going on, through appropriate feedback within reasonable time" (Nielsen 1995). An education application of this heuristic has emerged as a somewhat natural consequence of the advent of learning management students: students retain persistent access to the gradebook for immediate perceptibility of their current status in the class. Although Nielsen focuses on this as a pushing relationship where relevant information is pushed to the user, this availability instead facilitates a pulling behavior allowing the student to pull information when pertinent to them.

We have seen this principle emphasized more heavily in other courses, especially those reliant more on automated evaluations. An online CS1 course offered by the same university provides automated evaluators for every course problem, all of which feed an immediately-available gradebook (Joyner 2018). This even more dramatically the perceptibility of what is going on with a student's grade, and while this is compatible with traditional classes, it takes on a new emphasis when the entire experience is in an online environment based on immediately-perceptible feedback.

5.7.3 Tolerance

Regarding tolerance, the Principles of Universal Design state that a good design "minimizes hazards and the adverse consequences of accidental or unintended actions" (Story et al. 1998). In education, the level of tolerance for content-specific answers is often dictated by the field rather than by the learning design. However, interface design and learning design can merge to create a tolerance for mistakes more related to administration and policies instead of content errors. In this course's learning management systems, it is possible to separate an assignment deadline (shown to the students) and an assignment close date (hidden from the students); this course uses these features to set a two-hour grace window after the official deadline where submissions are still accepted. This creates a tolerance for minor errors, such as incorrectly converting the UTC-12 time zone to one's local time zone or underestimating the time it will take to move through the submission screens to upload an assignment.

This course also builds tolerance for late work into its process for rapidly evaluating assignments. After an assignment's close date, a gradebook is exported with individual students assigned to individual grades. In the event that a student submits work even later than the grace period allowed by the learning management system, the course staff may quickly attach the submission to the row; if the grader has not yet completed their tasks, then accepting the late submission costs the grading team no time compared to if it had been submitted on time. While others address this with a strict grading policy, the size of the class means that a non-trivial number of assignments will have earnest reasons for late submission, and so the course builds tolerance into the grading workflow design.

5.7.4 Feedback

Regarding the common need for feedback, Norman writes (Norman 2013),

> Feedback must be immediate. … Feedback must also be informative. … Poor feedback can be worse than no feedback at all, because it is distracting, uninformative, and in many cases irritating and anxiety-*provoking*

Among all usability principles, the principle of feedback is likely the most easily transferrable between interface and learning design. Feedback holds the same meaning in both domains, providing actionable information on the outcome and correctness of an action.

As it relates to online course design, we see in this course two interesting applications where the course facilitates more rapid feedback. First, the scale of the course dictates heavy organization; the grading workflow described above follows almost an assembly line approach, where assignments are automatically distributed to graders, rubrics are formalized, and results are processed in batch. Research on the program shows that a significant amount of attention in the learning design process goes into exactly these grading workflows (Joyner 2018), and the result is a more rapid return rate than seen on campus due to the benefits of scale.

A second component comes from the course's method for implementing peer review. Students complete peer reviews as part of their participation grade, but as rapid feedback is more desirable, students are explicitly incentivized to complete peer reviews early. This is the only place in the course where a mid-week semi-deadline exists: students receive 50% more credit (1.5 points) for a peer review submitted within three days of its assignment's deadline, and 50% less credit (0.5 points) for a review submitted more than a week after the deadline. With each assignment reviewed by 3–4 classmates, this raises the likelihood that feedback will arrive rapidly; in the most recent semester, 58% of all peer reviews were submitted within 3 days, and 69% within one week.

5.8 Course Evaluation

Course evaluation has been the topic of considerable discussion in the learning sciences literature. Attempts have been made to create explicit evaluators of course or teaching quality (Biggs and Collis 2014; Ramsden 1991), but these often require standardized tests or high-effort qualitative analyses. In place of these, student reviews are often used as a low-cost approximation of course quality. While some early research found these types of surveys are decently correlated of learning outcomes (Cohen 1981), more recent research casts doubt on this correlation (Greenwald 1997; Uttl et al. 2017), suggesting student reviews are too biased especially by gender differences to be useful for comparisons (Andersen and Miller 1997; Centra and Gaubatz 2000).

In this analysis, we nonetheless use student reviews to add to the overall picture of the class in this case study. We acknowledge the weaknesses of student reviews as comparative tools, but note that (a) we are not using these student reviews to compare against another class, but rather merely to attest that the class is generally well-received by students, and (b) while most research on the validity of student reviews has been performed at the K-12 or undergraduate level, these reviews are submitted by graduate students who are also mid-career professionals, and thus we hypothesize are more valid assessors of course quality. Anecdotally, several professors in the program agree to the observation that online students appear to have far higher standards than their traditional counterparts.

These student surveys come from two sources: first, the institute issues a Course Instructor Opinion Survey open to every student in every class. Student identifies are strictly hidden in these surveys, and the results are known to inform institute-level evaluations of teaching. Second, the course itself issues an end-of-course survey asking questions more specific to its own unique details.

5.8.1 Institutional Surveys

At time of writing, the course from this case study has been offered four times: Fall 2016, Spring 2016, Summer 2016, and Fall 2017. At the end of each of these semesters, students were offered the opportunity to complete the institute's Course Instructor Opinion Survey for the course. The questions on this survey are dictated by the institute, and although no explicit incentive exists for students to participate, students are nonetheless highly encouraged to do so by the school and instructor.

All questions on this survey offer 5-point Likert-scale responses. Table 5.2 provides the interpolated medians to each of these prompts.

Based on these results, we make two notable observations. First, the ratings of course effectiveness and quantity learned have not changed semester to semester. This is notable because the course has undergone significant revisions semester to semester, suggesting that either these revisions do not affect the student experience (or the effect is too small for detection), or that students are unable to evaluate the effect of these changes absent a target for comparison. In particular, Fall 2017 added a significant reading component to the course requiring an additional 1–2 h per week of reading. With this change, 61.7% of the Fall 2017 class estimated they put 9 or more hours per week into the course, which is statistically significantly different from the percent reporting 9 or more hours in Spring 2017 (43.6%, $X^2 = 9.193, p = 0.0024$) or Fall 2016 (51.5%, $X^2 = 5.322, p = 0.0211$).[1] Despite this, student assessments of the amount of material learned did not change.

Secondly, these reviews suggest that the design decisions described herein are at least somewhat effective in supporting the student experience as students specifically comment positively on criteria that typically are considered lacking in online courses. Most notably, whereas online instructors are often considered detached or uninvolved (De Gagne and Walters 2009), students in this class specifically reflected positively on the instructor's enthusiasm (4.96/5.00), respect (4.96/5.00), availability (4.90/5.00), and ability to simulate interest (4.89/5.00). We hypothesize this is due in part to the singular ownership over course announcements, documentation, and scheduling attributed to the instructor, in line with existing research on the effectiveness of immediacy behaviors (Arbaugh 2001).

---

[1] Summer 2017 is excluded from this comparison as the semester is shorter and more work is deliberately expected per week.

Table 5.2 Interpolated medians of student responses to eight prompts on the institute-run end-of-course opinion surveys

Prompt	Fall 2016	Spring 2017	Summer 2017	Fall 2017
Response rate (%)	83	69	70	61
How much would you say you learned in this course?[a]	4.53	4.45	4.41	4.45
Considering everything, this was an effective course[b]	4.82	4.74	4.85	4.80
The instructor clearly communicated what it would take to succeed in this course[a]	4.89	4.89	4.93	4.90
Instructors respect and concern for students[c]	4.95	4.96	4.96	4.94
Instructors level of enthusiasm about teaching the course[d]	4.95	4.97	4.97	4.95
Instructors ability to simulate my interest in the subject matter[e]	4.90	4.86	4.89	4.89
Instructors availability for consultation[f]	4.88	4.89	4.93	4.87
Considering everything, the instructor was an effective teacher[a]	4.92	4.95	4.94	4.93

[a]From 5—Exceptional amount to 1—Almost nothing
[b]From 5—Strongly agree to 1—Strongly disagree
[c]From 5—Exceptional to 1—Very poor
[d]From 5—Extremely enthusiastic to 1—Detached
[e]From 5—Made me eager to 1—Ruined interest
[f]From 5—Highly accessible to 1—Hard to find

5.8.2 Course Surveys

While the institute-wide course surveys give some useful information, they are a bit constrained by the need to apply universally to all courses. To supplement these, the course offers its own end-of-semester survey asking questions more specifically targeted to the design and structure of the course itself. Table 5.3 provides these results.

As with the institute-level survey, the course-level survey provides some interesting insights. First, the numbers across most categories do not change semester to semester. This is notable not only because of changes made to the course as time goes on, but also because of semester-specific factors. Fall 2016, for example, was the first semester of the course, and students popularly consider the first semester a "trial run"; anecdotally, many students specifically avoid first-semester classes knowing the second run will be smoother, while other students deliberately take new classes because

Table 5.3 Interpolated medians of student responses to eleven prompts on the course-run end-of-semester opinion survey

Prompt	Fall 2016	Spring 2017	Summer 2017	Fall 2017
Response rate (%)	63	65	83	52
"The lectures were informative and easy to understand"[a]	6.71	6.60	6.56	6.66
"The exercises during the lectures kept me engaged"[a]	5.95	5.74	5.80	5.85
"The video lessons were valuable in helping me learn"[a]	6.78	6.56	6.59	6.67
"[The forum] improved my experience in this class"[a]	5.90	5.42	5.56	5.45
"The [peer review] system improved my experience in this class"[a]	5.29	5.51	5.46	4.92
Jump around in the lessons instead of watching in order[b]	1.82	1.84	1.91	2.13
Fall behind the recommended schedule in the syllabus[b]	2.17	2.17	2.12	2.26
Watch ahead of the recommended schedule[b]	2.55	2.05	2.11	2.15
Re-watch an entire lesson[b]	3.02	2.73	2.71	2.93
Re-watch only a portion of a lesson after having previously finished a lesson[b]	3.72	3.74	3.49	3.41
Watch videos through an app[b]	1.41	1.36	1.72	1.40
Download course videos for offline viewing[b]	1.38	1.31	1.37	1.34

[a]Agree or disagree, from 7—Strongly agree to 1—Strongly disagree
[b]How often, from 5—Always to 1—Never

they enjoy being early adopters. This may be visible in the data: students reported slightly more re-watching and watch-ahead behaviors during the first semester. It is unclear why peer review ratings are lower during Fall 2017.

Second and more significant to this analysis, however, is that we see a significant incidence of behaviors corresponding to the claims regarding equity from earlier in this analysis. Nearly all students report some re-watching behaviors with an interpolated median corresponding to 3 ("Occasionally") for rewatching lectures in their entirety and closer to 4 ("Frequently") for rewatching only specific parts. While data does not exist regarding why students engage in these behaviors, they are closely aligned with potential supports for sensory or attentional deficits. Similarly, while behaviors related to watching ahead, falling behind, or taking lectures "on the go" are rarer, a non-trivial portion of the class still reports leveraging these capabilities. These correspond to the applications of flexibility discussed previously, allowing students to integrate their course performance flexibly into their routine and schedule. Anecdotally, students report these behaviors most commonly in working around vacation or work schedules or integrating course participation into train commutes or travel plans.

5.9 Conclusion

In this case study, we have taken common principles from well-renowned literature on human-computer interact (Constantine and Lockwood 1999; Nielsen 1995; Norman 2013; Story et al. 1998) and applied it to the design of an entirely-online for-credit graduate-level course in human-computer interaction. We find that whether by analogy or by direct application, many of these principles are strongly related to both the goals and design of online education. Just as interface design aims to accommodate flexibility with regard to user preferences, so also a major objective of online education is to accommodate audiences for whom traditional education is too inflexible to fit into their lifestyle. Just as interface design strives to accommodate all audiences regardless of experience and personal factors, so also online education aims to give access to anyone who may succeed at the course material. Just interface design aims to shrink feedback cycles and emphasize attention to the underlying task, so also learning design in online education aims to offload non-content tasks onto the interface or leverage consistent expectations to minimize time spent thinking about course administration. Most notably, there are places where the lines between learning design and interface design blur: instructors take certain actions in the interface to implement the learning design, such as setting consistent deadlines to minimizes cognitive load or pushing announcements to students to offload progress-tracking onto the interface.

References

Andersen K, Miller ED (1997) Gender and student evaluations of teaching. PS: Polit Sci Polit 30(2):216–220

Arbaugh JB (2001) How instructor immediacy behaviors affect student satisfaction and learning in web-based courses. Bus Commun Q 64(4):42–54

Biggs JB, Collis KF (2014) Evaluating the quality of learning: the SOLO taxonomy (Structure of the observed learning outcome). Academic Press.

Bjork RA (2013) Desirable difficulties perspective on learning. Encycl. Mind 4:243–245

Boud D, Cohen R, Sampson J (eds) (2014) Peer learning in higher education: learning from and with each other. Routledge

Centra JA, Gaubatz NB (2000) Is there gender bias in student evaluations of teaching? J Higher Educ 71(1):17–33
Chandler J (2003) The efficacy of various kinds of error feedback for improvement in the accuracy and fluency of L2 student writing. J Second Lang Writ 12(3):267–296
Cho V, Cheng TE, Lai WJ (2009) The role of perceived user-interface design in continued usage intention of self-paced e-learning tools. Comput Educ 53(2):216–227
Cohen PA (1981) Student ratings of instruction and student achievement: a meta-analysis of multisection validity studies. Rev Educ Res 51(3):281–309
Constantine L, Lockwood L (1999) Software for use: a practical guide to the models and methods of usage-centered design. Pearson Education.
De Gagne J, Walters K (2009) Online teaching experience: a qualitative metasynthesis (QMS). J Online Learn Teach 5(4):577
Fishwick M (2004) Emotional design: why we love (or hate) everyday things. J Am Cult 27(2):234
Freeman M, Bamford A (2004) Student choice of anonymity for learner identity in online learning discussion forums. Int J ELearn 3(3):45
Goel A, Joyner DA (2016) An experiment in teaching cognitive systems online. In: Haynes D (ed) International journal for scholarship of technology-enhanced learning, vol 1, no 1
Good C, Aronson J, Inzlicht M (2003) Improving adolescents' standardized test performance: an intervention to reduce the effects of stereotype threat. J Appl Dev Psychol 24(6)
Goodman J, Melkers J, Pallais A (2016) Can online delivery increase access to education? (No. w22754). National Bureau of Economic Research
Greenwald AG (1997) Validity concerns and usefulness of student ratings of instruction. Am Psychol 52(11):1182
Hiltz SR, Wellman B (1997) Asynchronous learning networks as a virtual classroom. Commun ACM 40(9):44–49
Hollan J, Hutchins E, Kirsh D (2000) Distributed cognition: toward a new foundation for human-computer interaction research. ACM Trans Comput-Hum Interact (TOCHI) 7(2):174–196
Jones MG, Farquhar JD (1997) User interface design for web-based instruction. Khan 62:239–244
Joyner DA, Goel AK, Isbell C (April 2016) The unexpected pedagogical benefits of making higher education accessible. In: Proceedings of the third ACM conference on Learning@ Scale. ACM pp 117–120
Joyner DA (April 2017) Scaling expert feedback: two case studies. In: Proceedings of the fourth (2017) ACM conference on Learning @ Scale. ACM
Joyner DA (June 2018) Squeezing the limeade: policies and workflows for scalable online degrees. In: Proceedings of the fifth (2018) ACM conference on Learning @ Scale. ACM
Joyner DA (June 2018) Towards CS1 at scale: building and testing a MOOC-for-credit candidate. In: Proceedings of the fifth (2018) ACM conference on Learning @ Scale. ACM
Kulkarni C, Wei KP, Le H, Chia D, Papadopoulos K, Cheng J, Koller D, Klemmer SR (2015) Peer and self assessment in massive online classes. In: Design thinking research. Springer, Cham, pp 131–168
Kizilcec RF, Schneider E, Cohen GL, McFarland DA (2014) Encouraging forum participation in online courses with collectivist, individualist and neutral motivational framings. In: EMOOCS 2014, Proceedings of the European MOOC stakeholder summit, pp 80–87
Koppelman H, Vranken H (June 2008) Experiences with a synchronous virtual classroom in distance education. In: ACM SIGCSE bulletin, vol 40, no 3. ACM, pp 194–198
Kulkarni CE, Bernstein MS, Klemmer SR (March 2015) PeerStudio: rapid peer feedback emphasizes revision and improves performance. In:Proceedings of the second (2015) ACM conference on Learning @ Scale. ACM, pp 75–84
Li X, Chang KM, Yuan Y, Hauptmann A (February 2015) Massive open online proctor: protecting the credibility of MOOCs certificates. In: Proceedings of the 18th ACM conference on Computer-Supported Cooperative Work & Social Computing. ACM, pp 1129–1137
Martin F, Parker MA, Deale DF (2012) Examining interactivity in synchronous virtual classrooms. Int Rev Res Open Distrib Learn 13(3):228–261

McBrien JL, Cheng R, Jones P (2009) Virtual spaces: employing a synchronous online classroom to facilitate student engagement in online learning. Int Rev Res Open Distrib Learn 10(3)
McDaniel MA, Butler AC (2011) A contextual framework for understanding when difficulties are desirable. In: Successful remembering and successful forgetting: A festschrift in honor of Robert A. Bjork
Najjar LJ (1998) Principles of educational multimedia user interface design. Hum Factors 40(2):311–323
Nielsen J (1995) 10 usability heuristics for user interface design, vol 1, no 1. Nielsen Norman Group
Norman D (2013) The design of everyday things: revised and expanded edition. Basic Books (AZ)
Northcutt CG, Ho AD, Chuang IL (2016) Detecting and preventing "multiple-account" cheating in massive open online courses. Comput Educ 100:71–80
O'Malley PJ, Agger JR, Anderson MW (2015) Teaching a chemistry MOOC with a virtual laboratory: lessons learned from an introductory physical chemistry course. J Chem Educ 92(10):1661–1666
Ramsden P (1991) A performance indicator of teaching quality in higher education: the course experience questionnaire. Stud High Educ 16(2):129–150
Story MF, Mueller JL, Mace RL (1998) The universal design file: designing for people of all ages and abilities
Swan K, Shea P, Fredericksen E, Pickett A, Pelz W, Maher G (2000) Building knowledge building communities: consistency, contact and communication in the virtual classroom. J Educ Comput Res 23(4):359–383
Tu CH, McIsaac M (2002) The relationship of social presence and interaction in online classes. Am J Distance Educ 16(3):131–150
Uttl B, White C, Gonzalez D (2017) Meta-analysis of faculty's teaching effectiveness: student evaluation of teaching ratings and student learning are not related. Stud Educ Eval 54:22–42
Whitley BE Jr (1997) Gender differences in computer-related attitudes and behavior: a meta-analysis. Comput Hum Behav 13(1)

Part II
Applications and Case Studies

Chapter 6
User Requirements When Designing Learning e-Content: Interaction for All

Pilar Orero and Irene Tor-Carroggio

Abstract Learning is a fundamental Human Right and in the Information Society learning has become an audiovisual experience. Audiovisual interactive learning materials, virtual learning environments and platforms, and online applications are the standard format where learning happens. Having access to this e-learning environment and content is fundamental to fulfil the right to education, but also the UN Convention on the Rights of Persons with Disabilities, which mentions "nothing about us without us" leading to take into consideration persons with disabilities when designing all learning elements. Therefore, accessibility has to be integrated in every step of the design process to avoid costly and unsatisfactory ad hoc solutions. How to contact end users and request their information and participation is an unavoidable challenge. Questionnaires have been the traditional tool to enquire users about their needs and preferences. Still, how to draft pertinent questionnaires to gather meaningful information is not a straightforward activity, but one that varies with fashions and schools of thought. For example, the Medical and the Social Models share equal popularity to classify user disabilities. In this chapter we will depart from the fact that access to education is a Human Right, and from the experience of designing an accessible MOOC. The second part of the chapter will revise some of the most used models of disability and we will explore a more holistic approach based on user capabilities. This will allow researchers in Education to focus on the aspects they can provide a solution to, instead of dealing with physiological tags that offer a simplified view of reality.

This article is related to the research carried out in the European funded projects ImAC (GA: 761974) and EasyTV (GA: 761999). Both authors are TransMedia Catalonia members (2017SGR113, 2017).

P. Orero (✉) · I. Tor-Carroggio (✉)
Universitat Autònoma de Barcelona, Barcelona, Spain
e-mail: pilar.orero@uab.cat

I. Tor-Carroggio
e-mail: irene.tor@uab.cat

E. Kapros and M. Koutsombogera (eds.), *Designing for the User Experience in Learning Systems*, Human–Computer Interaction Series,
https://doi.org/10.1007/978-3-319-94794-5_6

6.1 Introduction

Education is considered one of the most basic human rights. This can be read in Article 26 of the Universal Declaration of Human Rights.[1]

"Everyone has the right to education. Education shall be free, at least in the elementary and fundamental stages. Elementary education shall be compulsory. Technical and professional education shall be made generally available and higher education shall be equally accessible to all on the basis of merit. Education shall be directed to the full development of the human personality and to the strengthening of respect for human rights and fundamental freedoms. It shall promote understanding, tolerance and friendship among all nations, racial or religious groups, and shall further the activities of the United Nations for the maintenance of peace. Parents have a prior right to choose the kind of education that shall be given to their children."

The right to education is also mentioned in Articles 13 and 14 of the International Covenant on Economic, Social and Cultural Rights.[2] The right to education has also been reaffirmed in the 1960 UNESCO Convention against Discrimination in Education,[3] the 1981 Convention on the Elimination of All Forms of Discrimination Against Women (CEDAW),[4] the 2006 Convention on the Rights of Persons with Disabilities (CRPD),[5] and the African Charter on Human and Peoples' Rights.[6]

As early as 1952 in Europe, Article 2 of the first Protocol to the European Convention on Human Rights[7] states that the right to education is recognized as a human right and is understood to establish an entitlement to education. This right encompasses also the obligation to eliminate discrimination at all levels of the educational system, to set minimum standards, and to improve quality.

Universal legislation regarding education is in place, still the Internet and the new Information Technology (IT) technologies have changed the field of education in general, and learning in particular. Learning possibilities and approaches have multiplied. The Internet has made possible new learning paradigms like Massive Online Open Courses (MOOC) (Seale 2014). The need to have an inclusive approach for learning is today more pertinent than ever to comply with all the above-mentioned legislation from the area of Human Rights (Sánchez-Gordón and Luján-Mora 2014, 2016; Iniesto and Rodrigo 2016; Orero 2017).

Technology allows for automatic translation of content, for interaction in virtual reality environments, and Artificial Intelligence (AI) will soon tailor our learning interests, recommendations, and will produce bespoke assessments. Still, the human factor is at the centre of all human learning activities and having the right of access

---

[1] See http://www.un.org/en/universal-declaration-human-rights/ [retrieved 14/03/2018].

[2] See https://treaties.un.org/Pages/showDetails.aspx?objid=080000028002b6ed [retrieved 14/03/2018].

[3] See https://goo.gl/9oipD5 [retrieved 14/03/2018].

[4] See http://www.un.org/womenwatch/daw/cedaw/cedaw.htm [retrieved 14/03/2018].

[5] See http://www.ohchr.org/EN/HRBodies/CRPD/Pages/CRPDIndex.aspx [retrieved 14/03/2018].

[6] See http://www.achpr.org/instruments/achpr/ [retrieved 14/03/2018].

[7] See https://rm.coe.int/168006377c [retrieved 14/03/2018].

to the e-ecosystem and its content is not yet a mainstreamed requirement when designing content.

Since many learning environments are online, each browser has its own tools allowing for alternative interaction. Much effort has been dedicated to design alternative interactive e-technology such as JAWS or Classroom Screen Reader,[8] or the many speech-to-text programmes, and even a Google Draw Braille.[9] Regarding web pages, the World Wide Web Consortium (W3C) launched the Web Accessibility Initiative (WAI) as an effort to improve the accessibility of the World Wide Web (WWW) for people with disabilities, and to fulfil the UN CRPD since people with disabilities and the elderly require non-standard devices and browsers. The W3C launched the Web Accessibility Initiative in 1997 and started working on the Web Content Accessibility Guidelines (WCAG). They are a set of guidelines that specify how to make content accessible, primarily for people with disabilities. The current version, WCAG 2.0, was published in December 2008 and became an ISO standard, ISO/IEC 40500:2012, in October 2012.[10]

While much effort has been made in the technical side of accessibility and e-learning, little dedication has been made to address the interaction and accessibility with the media learning content. Recently, the field of Media Accessibility was established as a "set of theories, practices, services, technologies and instruments providing access to audiovisual media content for people that cannot, or cannot properly, access that content in its original form (Szarkowska et al. 2013; Greco 2016). It is now established how technology is basic for Media Accessibility, since it determines the service, its production, distribution and reception, and it also has a direct impact on the quality. At the other side of the spectrum, we find the user who will be learning. The user, in a way, determines the technology to be used and also how to access the learning content.

6.2 Accessible MOOC

Designing an accessible MOOC is a challenge (Iniesto et al. 2014; Seale 2014). Accessibility requirements (Sánchez-Gordón and Luján-Mora 2016) should be met from: platform services, user interface, learning content and resources, and learning assessment activities. While much literature focuses on the platform interaction (Iniesto and Rodrigo 2016) and user interface requirements (Ngubane-Mokiwa 2016) little is dedicated to the content or assessments (Sánchez-Gordón and Luján-Mora 2014). This difference is probably due to the nature, field of knowledge, and format of the learning content. It is not the same to access mathematical formulae or statistics than to read a music score or follow any of these as a PowerPoint presentation or a movie. Multiplicity of topics and formats defy unified solutions or guidelines

---

[8]See http://bit.ly/2D1sKA1 [retrieved 18/01/2018].

[9]See https://support.google.com/docs/answer/6057417 [retrieved 18/01/2018].

[10]See https://www.iso.org/standard/58625.html [retrieved 18/01/2018].

following a mainstreamed Universal Design approach (Ngubane-Mokiwa 2016). Also, the multiple end user requirements should be taken into consideration, and to this aim the first accessible MOOC on media accessibility was designed in 2015 for the EU funded project HBB4ALL.[11] HBB4ALL MOOC had a double objective. The content of the course teaches the many issues related to accessibility services for media content: subtitling, audio description and Sign Language interpreting. The course interaction is in itself a demo on how to make MOOCs content accessible. This was a timely proposal since existing prestigious MOOCs, such as those from Harvard University and MIT, have been sued for their lack of accessibility[12] and Bohnsack and Puhl (2014) showed how none of the largest platforms (Udacity, Coursera, edX, OpenCourseWorld and Iversity) were accessible or allowed for accessible content beyond sound transcription.

HBB4ALL MOOC took into consideration the following accessibility user requirements:

- Visual media had to be accessible for persons with sight and low vision impairments.
- Spoken dialogue had to be subtitled in the same language, for people with hearing impairments.
- The module on Sign Language needed an interpretation into Sign Language, for deaf users.

For this we prepared subtitles, audio description and Sign Language as the basic services interaction access services. While subtitling is the most widespread service, Sign Language interpretation is perhaps the most obvious. The reason is because it takes a good share of the screen, and it presents two videos simultaneously challenging the challenging viewers with split attention (Fig. 6.1).

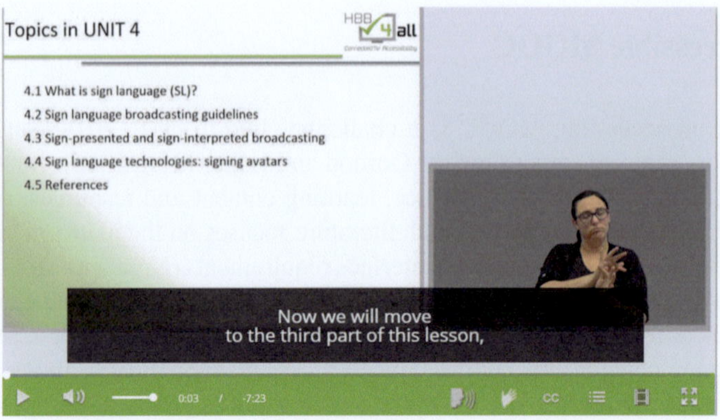

Fig. 6.1 Subtitles, PPT and Sign Language screen sharing student attention

[11] See http://accessguide.tv/course/ [retrieved 14/03/2018].

[12] See https://goo.gl/vqdjv6 [retrieved 14/03/2018].

For the HBB4ALL MOOC the platform used was developed as part of the project, and other user requirements, such as multilanguage, while available in the technological side, were not possible given the cost of translations. EMMA,[13] the EU funded multilanguage MOOC platform, allows for this, solving one of the biggest accessibility issues, since in Europe the wealth of languages challenges the sharing learning materials because of language specific content (Sánchez-Gordón and Luján-Mora 2015).

The personalisation of the MOOCs accessibility features was built with an online platform called AccessGUIDE. It allows the personalisation of accessible online video services on PCs and mobile platforms. This Software is a Service (SaaS) platform that can be used by application developers to include personalized accessibility features into their applications. It comes along with an online multilingual text-to-speech function that can be used for screen reader and spoken subtitle functionality. It supports the personalisation of the applications' user interface, the subtitles in video on demand applications as well as the text-to-speech service.

AccessGUIDE service supports accessibility features such as a screen reader functionality (Fig. 6.2), customizable multilingual subtitles with the possibility of choosing language, size and position (Fig. 6.3), spoken subtitles in different languages as well as the possibility to switch between signed and unsigned video content (Fig. 6.4).

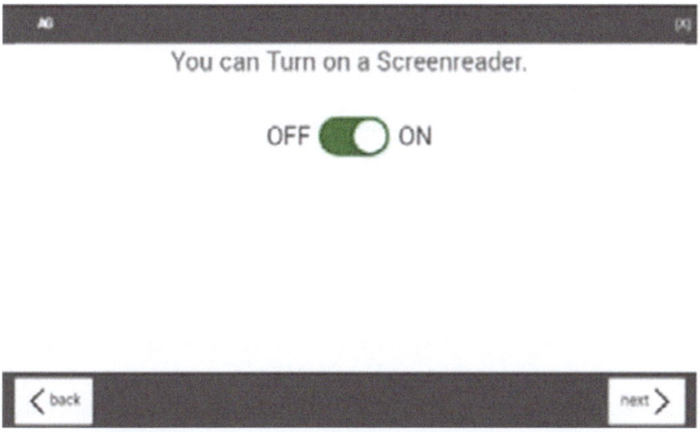

Fig. 6.2 Screen reader functionality

[13]See http://project.europeanmoocs.eu/about/ [retrieved 14/03/2018].

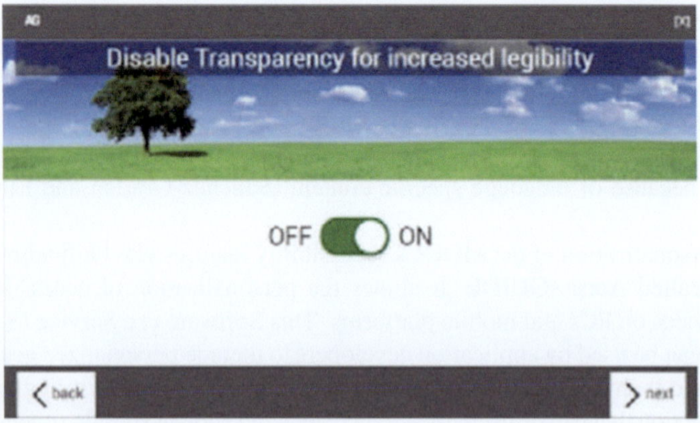

Fig. 6.3 Subtitle personalisation

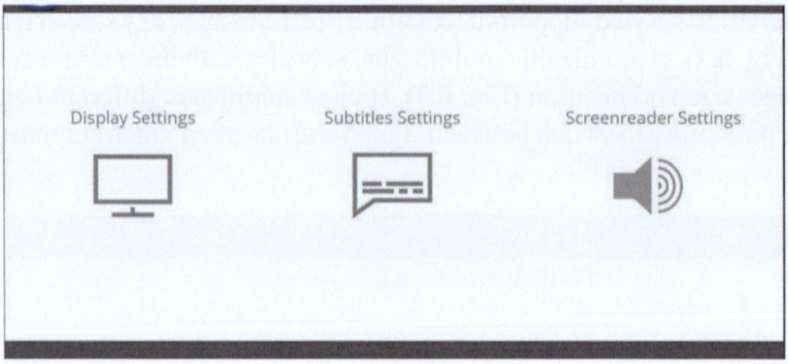

Fig. 6.4 Display functionalities

After this first attempt at generating accessible online media content, a new MOOC was designed within the European funded project ACT (Orero 2017). ACT aims at training the expert on accessibility for live cultural events: theatre productions, operas, conferences, etc. Given the fact that the MOOC trains on accessibility services for cultural contents, it had to be accessible and it was considered that a MOOC would be a good way to showcase the project.

The HBB4ALL MOOC was developed in a platform which aimed at offering accessibility services and interaction. The ACT MOOC was developed for Coursera, a standard platform which lacks most accessible functionalities, so creativity was required when dealing with services such as audio description. The solution was to apply "accessible cinema" (Romero-Fresco 2012) guidelines from the course design. For audio description this meant to include in the narrative or presentation the audio description. For example, when a teacher was introduced, the presentation included their physical appearance. When a movie was shown, the movie could not be audio described, but the approach then was to add an audio introduction (Fryer and Romero-Fresco 2014).

ACT took care to find out user requirements from the three groups identified as "end users",[14] who were:

- Managers of cultural venues;
- members of artistic teams; and
- diverse audiences including people with varying physical, linguistic, sensory, and cognitive abilities.

While in the HBB4ALL MOOC persons with disabilities (PwD) were the focus of interaction, for ACT MOOC they were only one of the three groups used to gather requirements. For this ACT MOOC there were two challenges:

- The use of Coursera as a closed and standardise platform didn't allow for any accessibility add-on services.
- PwD were no longer the target student.

Looking at the bibliography on accessibility and MOOCs to understand solutions it became clear the approach used to gather requirements. Sánchez-Gordón and Luján-Mora (2016) literature review shows that to date end user requirements are gathered following the UN International Classification of Functioning, Disability and Health WHODAS 2.0[15]:

- Blindness and low vision
- Deafness and reduced hearing needs
- Speech needs
- Motor needs
- Cognitive needs
- Psychological needs
- Elderly needs
- Non-native speakers' needs
- Cross-cultural needs
- Technology needs.

Out of the ten categories only the last three are not health-related. This biased profiling approach has a direct implication in three areas:

- It displaces learning from a universal human right to an "Assisted Living" territory, where each medical condition requires a uniquely designed solution.
- Assisted living raises the issue of "reasonable accommodation" as a possibility to avoid thinking about accessibility solutions as a default usability feature.
- Defines profiling from a pathological perspective, reinforcing the bipolar inclusive/exclusive model, away from mainstreaming possibilities.

Designing the two MOOCs, and looking at ways to optimise accessibility services for PwD made us identify the basic flaw: profiling end users from a Medical Model. MOOCs are related to learning, and access to content and interaction is more related

[14]See http://pagines.uab.cat/act/content/io1-accessibility-profiling [retrieved 14/03/2018].

[15]See http://www.who.int/classifications/icf/en/ [retrieved 14/03/2018].

to capabilities than to disabilities. The MOOCs we generated will not solve the functioning or health items gathered by Sánchez-Gordón and Luján-Mora (2016) since interaction is related to communication. It is for this reason that for the ACT MOOC, and the research we have currently embarked in other H2020 funded projects (1), we decided to challenge the medical approach to understand end user needs. The objective is to mainstream media accessibility in all human communication activities, such as learning, where media is nowadays the most popular format. In order to propose a new profiling model, a critical revision of existing models is performed in the next section.

6.3 Background: The Most Common Models of Disability

Disability has always been difficult to define, no matter what approach is chosen. One of the reasons may be that "disabled people belonging to the same 'impairment category' as those who have visual, hearing or mobility impairments vary enormously" (Marks 1997: 85). Nevertheless, that is no excuse to not being able to identify it, since it still needs to be dealt with. To be able to stand up to scrutiny, a definition of disability should be applicable to all people, without segregation into groups such as "the visually impaired" or "the hearing impaired", and be able to describe the experience of disability across many areas of functioning (Leonardi et al. 2006). It is not a matter of benevolence, but, as we have previously stated, of Human Rights. Although disability has traditionally been closely linked to medical models, there are also other approaches that try to tear the medical tags in order to place the disabled person in context. Actually, it is a matter of fact that more recent models of disability acknowledge the central role of social factors in understanding the causes and consequences of disability, supporting a more integrative biopsychosocial model of disability (Peterson and Elliott 2007). This variety of models is what makes the definition of disability so hard to come up with; however, at the same time, this wide range of ideas evidences the effort that has been put towards attaining one goal: understanding disability from different angles to achieve full inclusion.

In this section presented some of the most traditional and used models to classify disability are going to be put forward, as well as some new approaches, so as to analyse their strong points and weaknesses, always bearing in mind that our final objective is to find an approach that allows non-medical researchers, in this case researchers who want to develop accessible learning tools for the disabled, to design research materials, such as questionnaires, which can truly be helpful to obtain the needed information that can be both useful and relevant.

6.3.1 The Moral Model

Even though it may sound dated, it is worth mentioning due to it being the oldest paradigm for understanding disability in the Western World. Based on religious beliefs, it considers disability a test of faith, the notion that "God gives us only what we can bear". The Moral Model links disability with sin and shame. In this sense, as disability impairs one sense, it heightens another (Olkin 2001). Charity and condescendence are the social reply to disability, and while the concept is dated, is very much alive today. It is common to find someone speaking slowly to someone in a wheelchair or helping a blind person to cross the street. These today are considered morally good actions.

6.3.2 The Medical Model

The Medical Model takes the moral aspect out and substitutes it for a more patronising perspective. It is not an explicitly described model, but rather label attached to a large body of research with a focus mainly on biomedical explanations (Bøttcher and Dammeyer 2016). According to this model, disability is a pathological and permanent issue that exclusively belongs to the disabled person, and that needs to be fixed, even if it does not cause pain or illness. For example, if a signing deaf person wants to attend a university lecture but is unable to do so because there is no Sign Language interpreter, the Medical Model would suggest that this is because of the person's hearing loss problems, rather than the lack of Sign Language interpreters. Another example would be a researcher who refuses to produce a questionnaire in a larger font for a visually impaired person. By doing so, the researcher is depriving that particular informant of participating.

This kind of approach has proved to be beneficial to improve medical diagnosis and treatment and, thus, to have better results in that particular field, but it also has a series of weaknesses. Doctors are the experts, whereas patients are passive and not collaborators. The goal is to "fix" what is "wrong" with the person aiming at "normality". The problem is individual isolated from society; the fact that it creates low expectations and results in people losing independence and choice; and, finally, its lack of human touch. It can be seen that this model fails to empower people with disabilities and to make inclusion a reality. This model emphasizes the injury that leads to disability rather than the individual, and, therefore, people can be regarded as disabled only because of the characteristics of some organs, which are seen as a whole, which, in turn, causes the subject to be lost (Edler 2009).

6.3.3 The Social Model

The Social Model, was developed in opposition to the medical approach, first in the United Kingdom in the 1960s and 1970s (Bøttcher and Dammeyer 2016). It was mainly developed by Michael Oliver, who "sees disability, by contrast with impairment, as something imposed on disabled people by oppressive and discriminating social and institutional structures" (Terzi 2005: 201). It believes the medical explanation is insufficient to understand the relationship between people and their environment, and that not enough importance is attached to human diversity (Edler 2009). The Social Model shifts the focus from the defective person to society . Disability now is not the physical impairment, but the failure of society to consider individual differences (Bøttcher and Dammeyer 2016). According to this model, impairments are not what makes people disabled, but the world around them. This is to say negative connotations, social barriers and lack of accessibility are the actual problem, not disability itself. Disability is an experience, not an injury (Edler 2009). Using one of the examples presented in the previous model, the problem of the deaf person being unable to attend a lecture would be the lack of Sign Language interpreters at that university, not the person's hearing impairment. Thus, accessibility is seen as a matter of civil rights, as the way to balance the treatment that society offers to its citizens. This model concludes that accessibility makes the world less disabled and leaves people just with their impairments.

Nonetheless, the popularity of the Social Model has been increasingly criticised in the past number of years, mainly for ignoring that disabilities are grounded in biological impairments, and for overlooking individual psychological perspectives of people with disabilities (Bøttcher and Dammeyer 2016). According to Shakespeare, "the simplicity which is the hallmark of the social model is also its fatal flaw" (Shakespeare 2010: 271) since it misses a disability as a core feature of many disabled people's lives and the concept of the barrier-free utopia. Terzi (2005) considers there is an aspect of over-socialization of sources and causes of disability and the model overlooks the complex dimensions of impairment.

6.3.4 The Human Rights Model

As previously stated, the Social Model of disability was developed as a critique to the Medical Model of disability; however, within disability studies, the Social Model of disability has been almost as condemned as the Medical Model (Degener 2016). The UN CRPD was initially drafted as a human rights convention that aimed to substitute the Medical Model of disability for the Social Model of disability. Yet, according to Degener (2016)-who in 2001 was a legal expert to the UN High Commissioner for Human Rights as co-author of the background study to the UN CRPD-the drafters went beyond the Social Model and came up with a treaty based on the Human Rights Model of disability (in fact, what these two models have in common is that both are built on the premise that disability is a social construct). Thus, the Human Rights Model offers an alternative to both the Social and Medical Models of disability and is a tool to implement the CRPD.

Degener (2016) suggests six propositions to explain in which ways the Human Rights Model differs from the Social and also why it goes one step further:

- The human rights model can vindicate that human rights do not require a certain health or body status, whereas the social model can merely explain that disability is a social construct.
- The human rights model encompasses both sets of human rights, civil and political as well as economic, social and cultural rights and thus not only demands anti-discrimination rights for disabled persons.
- The human rights model embraces impairment as a condition which might reduce the quality of life but which belongs to humanity and thus must be valued as part of human variation.
- The human rights model values different layers of identity and acknowledges intersectional discrimination.
- Unlike the social model, the human rights model clarifies that impairment prevention policy can be human rights sensitive.
- It is thought that the human rights model not only explains why 2/3 of the world's disabled population live in developing countries, but that it also contains a roadmap for change. Degener (2016: 19).

Regarding its weaknesses, Berghs et al. (2016) underline that many analyses have identified non-enforcement as a problem, and there is evidence of a lack of defined sanctions. Moreover, people with disabilities hold the belief that the link between the CRPD and other legislative institutions is still unclear. A frequent issue linked to the implementation and enforcement of the CRPD is how to understand what 'reasonable accommodation' means. This has particular implications for research. "The way environments should be 'modified' to accommodate and ensure disabled people can exercise their rights is open to interpretation. […] Inclusion tends to be defined in relation to access and, ignoring diversity among people with disabilities, assumes a universal research design will solve problems for all" (Berghs et al. 2016: 35).

6.3.5 The International Classification of Functioning Model

The International Classification of Functioning, Disability and Health (ICF) was approved by the World Health Organisation in 2001 and has been yearly revised since then, the last version being approved in 2017. Based on, theoretically, the integration between the Social and Medical Model of disability and initially drafted as the International Classification of Impairments, Disabilities, and Handicaps (ICIDH), the ICF was intended to complement its sister classification system, the International Classification of Diseases (ICD). The ICD classifies mortality and morbidity, whereas the ICF classifies functioning, disability, and health, and they are designed to be used together (Peterson and Elliott 2007). The ICF Model sees disability as the result of a combination of individual, institutional and societal factors that define the environment surrounding a person with an impairment (Dubois and Trani 2009). It is operationalised through the World Health Organization Disability Assessment Schedule II (WHODAS II) and it covers all types of disabilities, for various countries, languages and contexts, which makes it suitable for cross-cultural use.

The aims of the ICF[16] (WHO 2001: 5) are to:

- Provide a scientific basis for understanding and studying health and health-related states, outcomes, determinants, and changes in health status and functioning;
- establish a common language for describing health and health-related states in order to improve communication between different users, such as health care workers, researchers, policy-makers and the public, including people with disabilities;
- permit comparison of data across countries, health care disciplines, services and time; and
- provide a systematic coding scheme for health information systems.

ICF's novelty is combining health functionality with contextual factors (gender, race, age, fitness, religion, lifestyle, habits, upbringing, behaviour pattern and character, etc.), which supposedly gives it a biopsychosocial and interactional approach. It is believed that all these descriptors can impact health and functioning, and users are encouraged to consider these issues qualitatively while classifying other areas of health and functioning. Great interest has been expressed by a variety of stakeholders to further develop this component of the ICF (e.g., Hurst 2003).

The ICF has gained considerable influence globally. It is used for a variety of objectives, in descriptive as well as analytical studies and for policy. Yet, its rigid classification fails to reproduce a more accurate picture of the reality.

6.4 The Human Development Model of Disability, Health and Wellbeing (HDM)

Amartya Sen, 1998's winner of the Nobel Prize of Economics, along with Martha Nussbaum, are responsible for developing the capability approach, which has been used as a framework to analyse different concepts in welfare economics (Mitra 2006). This has been extrapolated to many different fields of knowledge to address a wide range us issues, such as: poverty, justice and even in disability studies. Under the capability approach, Sen and Nussbaum focus on the type of life that people are able to live, i.e., on their practical opportunities, called, according to these two authors, *capabilities*, and on their achievements, called *functionings* (Mitra 2006). Sen used the example of two women starving to contrast the two terms: both women have the same functioning (not being well nourished) but very different capabilities. One

[16]See http://www.who.int/classifications/icf/en/ [retrieved 05/03/2018].

has the capability, this is, the opportunity to be well nourished but decides to starve for her religious beliefs, and the other can't afford to buy food. This approach has also given rise to a new model of disability: The Human Development Model of Disability, which aims at providing a conceptual framework to describe and explain health conditions, impairments, disability, their causes as well as their consequences (Mitra 2018).

Disability can be understood as a deprivation in terms of capabilities or functionings that results from the interaction of an individual's (a) personal characteristics (age, impairment, etc.) and (b) available goods (assets, income) and (c) environment (social, economic, political, cultural) (Mitra 2006). Disability means lacking certain capabilities/functioning due to the interaction of the above-mentioned factors. Thus, disability depends on whether the impairment places restrictions on the individual functioning or capabilities.

It is worth to retrieve the example Mitra (2006) mentions in her article to explain how she departs from the Capabilities Approach to develop a new model of disability: a 19-year-old boy who suffers a brain injury is considered disabled if his practical opportunity to attend college is restricted (potential disability), in contrast to an individual with a similar basket of goods, in the same environment, and with similar personal characteristics except for the impairment. In case the 19-year-old cannot finally attend college, we would be facing actual disability but in case he finally goes to university, then he would not be considered disabled.

The Human Development Model uses capabilities and/or functionings as metric for wellbeing (Mitra 2018). It does not consider impairments/health conditions as individual characteristics; instead, they are themselves determined by resources, structural factors, and personal characteristics, and thus the model is informed by the socioeconomic determinants of health literature.

Mitra (2018) states that for the Human Development Model (HDM) the focus is on how health deprivations may relate to other dimensions of wellbeing. The aim of research or policy initiatives guided by this model is thus to enhance human development, this is, to expand the functionings/capabilities of individuals with health deprivations or to expand functionings/capabilities by preventing health deprivations.

Unlike the Social and Medical models, but like other interactional models such as the ICF, the human development model provides a comprehensive account of the variety of factors that might lead to deprivations. According to the HDM, and unlike the Medical Model, the impairment is not always the cause for disability and, unlike the Social Model, the environment is not always the disabling factor. Also, the ICF could benefit from becoming open-ended, with the recognition that not all dimensions of life may be specified and classified, and thus the classification does not, and cannot be expected to provide an exhaustive account of the lived experience of health deprivations.

It is with this HDM as a framework where user interaction requirements for accessing media learning environments should be based. In order to apply this new model to profile requirements.

6.5 Drafting User Experience Questionnaires

Traditionally, user interaction with persons with disabilities requested for the user to tick if they were: blind or low sighted or deaf and hard of hearing. Some even went as far as asking the % of disability in their condition. While offering important information regarding their condition, other more important traits were overseen, for example, if a person is a fast reader. After many tests across Europe (Romero-Fresco 2015), it was found that reading subtitles was not related to any condition, but to reading ability, usually related to education. Consequently, we feel it is high time to take into consideration a new approach when designing the steps of a process aiming at offering any e-learning product taking user needs and requirements into account.

As we have already seen, under Sen's approach, disability can be understood as a deprivation in terms of capabilities or functionings that results from the interaction of an individual's (a) personal characteristics (age, impairment, etc.) and (b) available goods (assets, income) and (c) environment (social, economic, political, cultural) (Mitra 2006). This is to say that disability means lacking certain capabilities/functionings due to the combination of the above-mentioned factors. Consequently, when working with users to design any content, platform or technology for e-learning two issues need to be considered: (a) their capabilities and functionings (where they are and where they want to be) and (b) their personal characteristics, commodities and environment.

To design the methodology of any project aiming at producing e-learning materials for all citizens we suggest the following steps.

1. First of all gather a small group of people representing end user capabilities to collect information regarding expectations and needs. This stage is basic also to understand the validation process. The users in this first interaction can be called "super users" since, besides their condition of regular users, they also have some knowledge on the items to be tested. It would make no sense to consult users with no knowledge or experience with neither functional diversity nor technological background since at this stage what we require is not their acceptance of the final service, but system requirements.

These "super users" can be interviewed in focus groups or requested information through a questionnaire, or both, for example. Some questions that could be asked are:

- What are the key capabilities/functionings that you value when it comes to…?
- What level of achievement would be sufficient?

2. Testing e-learning technology/platform/content with users.

After developing the requested functionalities, a further interaction with super-users is needed to check if needs and expectations were met.

3. Once the integration has taken place, interaction with end users take place. To this aim two questionnaires can be drafted-one to be answered before the test and the other one just after.

- In the first questionnaire end users map their current situation regarding the capabilities/functionings mentioned by super-users. To evaluate capabilities/functionings, question should be like: "Do you have difficulty in…?" and then offer a scale.
- After end users test the new e-learning content/platform/technology, a post-questionnaire is distributed, which has to reproduce the same questions regarding capabilities/functionings to understand their assessment. Also, a demographic section needs to be included to ask about personal characteristics, commodities and environment, which are the factors that can lead to disability.
- Capability based questionnaires will not offer quantitative profiling, as ICT does. Rather than considering students by their officially established % of disability, their impairment will be evaluated towards a dynamic evaluation and functional profile.

6.6 Conclusions

The chapter has revised the legal background required to guarantee access for all to educational e-content and applications, from a Human Right perspective, securing the accessibility of media formats used for education. While the legal framework is in place, and to some extent technologies and standards are available, the main e-learning platforms are not accessible. This Accessibility decreases further when dealing with the user interaction to learning content, usually in audiovisual formats.

In this chapter the experience of designing two MOOCs to teach media accessibility are described. The first is a MOOC designed to be accessible, showcasing the many technological available options to secure access. The second MOOC uses a ready platform, Coursera, that challenged accessibility, but some solutions were found. The design of the two MOOCs shared the user centric methodology where persons with disabilities defined interaction requirements. Data from this interaction is usually gathered through questionnaires, which need to address the functionality of the interaction (impairment), rather than the user physiological condition (disability). For example, the literature showed that screen reading (subtitles) is associated to persons with hearing impairments. The chapter proposes a new approach to profiling students to design and validate e-learning platform requirements. The use of a capability approach-based model to reflect the needs of all citizens in society, following a Universal Design approach to mainstream accessibility. Adapting Sen's capability model to education and student profiling should offer an open-ended capability approach rather than a prescriptive medical taxonomy. It is expected that the proposal presented in this chapter should open the door to mainstreamed accessibility. This new impairment and capability—rather than disability—perspective has many implications for all issues related to e-learning and the future of student interaction with multimedia educational content. It is hoped this chapter raises awareness on the need to implement accessibility in the production phase of any learning material to secure universal access to all.

References

Berghs MJ, Atkins KM, Graham H (2016) Scoping models and theories of disability. Implications for public health research of models and theories of disabilities: a scoping study and evidence synthesis. Public Health Res 4(8):23–40

Bohnsack M, Puhl S (2014). Accessibility of MOOCs. In: Proceedings of the 14th international conference of computers helping people with special needs (ICCHP 2014), pp 141–144. https://doi.org/10.1007/978-3-319-08596-8_21

Bøttcher L, Dammeyer J (2016) Beyond a biomedical and social model of disability: a cultural-historical approach. In: Development and learning of young children with disabilities. International Perspectives on Early Childhood Education and Development, vol 13. Springer, Cham, 3–23

Degener T (2016) Disability in a human rights context. Laws 5(3):35

Dubois J, Trani J (2009) Extending the capability paradigm to address the complexity of disability. ALTER, Eur J Disabil Res 3:192–218

Edler R (2009) La clasificación de la funcionalidad y su influencia en el imaginario social sobre las discapacidades. In: Brogna P (ed) Visiones y revisiones de la discapacidad. Fondo de Cultura Económica, México D.F., pp 137–157

Fryer L, Romero-Fresco P (2014) Audio introduction. In: Maszerowska A, Matamala A, Orero P (eds) Audio description: new perspectives illustrated. John Benjamins, Amsterdam, pp 11–28

Greco GM (2016) On accessibility as a human right, with an application to media accessibility. In: Matamala A, Orero P (eds) Researching audio description: new approaches. Palgrave, London, pp 11–33

Hurst R (2003) The international disability rights movement and the ICF. Disabil Rehabil 25:572–576

Iniesto F, Rodrigo C, Teixeira AM. (2014). Accessibility analysis in MOOC platforms. A case study: UNED COMA and UAB iMOOC. In: International conference on quality and accessibility of virtual learning (CAFVIR 2014), pp 545–550

Iniesto F, Rodrigo C (2016) Strategies for improving the level of accessibility in the design of MOOC-based learning services. In: IEEE international symposium on computers in education (SIIE 2016), pp 1–6. https://doi.org/10.1109/siie.2016.7751841

Leonardi M, Bickenbach J, Ustun TB, Kostanjsek N, Chatterji S, MHADIE Consortium (2006) The definition of disability: what is in a name? Lancet 368(9543):1219–1221

Marks D (1997) Models of disability. Disabil Rehabil 19(3):85–91

Mitra S (2006) The capability approach and disability. J Disabil Policy Stud 16(4):236–247

Mitra S (2018) The human development model of disability, health and wellbeing. In: Disability, health and human development. Palgrave Studies in Disability and International Development. Palgrave Pivot, New York

Ngubane-Mokiwa SA (2016) Accessibility strategies for making MOOCs for people with visual impairments: a universal design for learning (UDL) perspective. In: 8th pan-commonwealth forum on open learning (PCF8)

Olkin R (2001) What psychotherapists should know about disability. The Guilford Press, London, New York

Orero P (2017) The professional profile of the expert in media accessibility for the scenic arts. Rivista internazionale di tecnica della traduzione 19:143–161

Pascual J, Castillo C, García-Díaz V, González R (2014) Method for analysing the user experience in MOOC platforms. In Proceeding of IEEE international symposium on computers in education (SIIE 2014), pp 157–162. https://doi.org/10.1109/siie.2014.7017722
Peterson D, Elliott T (2007) Advances in conceptualizing and studying disability. In: Brown S, Lent R (eds) Hand book of counseling psychology. John Wiley, Hoboken, NJ, pp 212–230
Romero-Fresco P (2012) Accessible filmmaking: joining the dots between audiovisual translation, accessibility and film making. JosTrans 20:201–223
Romero-Fresco P (2015) The reception of subtitles for the deaf and hard of hearing in Europe. Peter Lang, Bern
Seale JK (2014) E-learning and disability in higher education: accessibility research and practice. Routledge, London
Sanchez-Gordon S, Luján-Mora S (2014) Web accessibility requirements for massive open online courses. can MOOCs be really universal and open to anyone? In: Conference on quality and accessibility of virtual learning (CAFVIR 2014), pp 530–535
Sanchez-Gordon S, Luján-Mora S (2015) Accessible blended learning for non-native speakers using MOOCs. In: Proceedings of IEEE international conference on interactive collaborative and blended learning (ICBL), pp 19–24. https://doi.org/10.1109/icbl.2015.7387645
Sánchez-Gordón S, Luján-Mora S (2016) Research gaps in ccessibility and MOOCs: a systematic literature review 2008–2016. http://hdl.handle.net/10045/61628
Shakespeare T (2010) The social model of disability. In: Lennar J (ed) The disability studies reader. Routledge, New York, pp 266–273
Szarkowska A, Krejtz I, Krejtz K, Duchowski A (2013) Harnessing the potential of eye-tracking for media accessibility. In: Grucza S, Płużyczka M, Zając J (eds) Translation studies and eye-tracking analysis. Peter Lang, Frankfurt am Main, pp 153–183
Terzi L (2005) A capability perspective on impairment, disability and special needs: towards social justice in education. Theory Res Edu 3(2):197–223

Chapter 7
iMuSciCA: Interactive Music Science Collaborative Activities for STEAM Learning

Vassilis Katsouros, Evita Fotinea, Renaat Frans, Erica Andreotti, Petros Stergiopoulos, Manolis Chaniotakis, Thomas Fischer, Robert Piechaud, Zoltan Karpati, Pierre Laborde, Daniel Martín-Albo, Fotini Simistira and Marcus Liwicki

Abstract iMuSciCA supports mastery of core academic content on STEM subjects for secondary school students alongside with the development of their creativity and deeper learning skills, through engagement in music activities. To reach this goal, iMuSciCA introduces new methodologies and innovative technologies supporting active, discovery-based, collaborative, personalised, and more engaging learning. In particular, iMuSciCA delivers a suite of activity environments and tools on top of

www.imuscica.eu.

V. Katsouros (✉) · E. Fotinea
Athena Research and Innovation Center, Athens, Greece
e-mail: vsk@ilsp.gr

R. Frans · E. Andreotti
University College Leuven-Limburg, Limburg, Belgium

P. Stergiopoulos · M. Chaniotakis · T. Fischer
Ellinogermaniki Agogi, Pallini, Greece

R. Piechaud
Institut de Recherche et de Coordination Acoustique Musique-IRCAM, Paris, France

Z. Karpati
Leopoly, Budapest, Hungary

P. Laborde
Cabrilog, Grenoble, France

D. Martín-Albo
Wiris, Barcelona, Spain

F. Simistira · M. Liwicki
University of Fribourg, Fribourg, Switzerland

E. Kapros and M. Koutsombogera (eds.), *Designing for the User Experience in Learning Systems*, Human–Computer Interaction Series,
https://doi.org/10.1007/978-3-319-94794-5_7

core enabling technologies integrated on a web-based platform. These include: a 3D environment for designing virtual musical instruments; advanced music generation and processing technologies to apply and interpret related physics and mathematics principles; gesture and pen-enabled multimodal interaction for music co-creation and performance; and 3D printing for realizing the virtual instruments. The educational deployment of the iMuSciCA workbench is built around a suite of interdisciplinary project/inquiry-based educational scenarios for STEAM, integrating innovative methods in teaching and learning. iMuSciCA is pilot-tested and evaluated in real learning contexts in secondary schools from three European countries. The chapter presents the innovative STEAM pedagogical framework, the implementation of the advanced activity environments and core enabling technologies, the design aspects of the educational scenarios and exemplar lesson plans, and the overall evaluation framework that is adopted in successive pilot testing in secondary schools of three European countries.

7.1 Introduction

Improving Science, Technology, Engineering, and Mathematics (STEM) education has been a priority on the political agenda of many European countries since the end of the 1990s. In Europe, over the last years a great number of STEM programs and projects have been set up and a wide range of measures, starting with the earliest school years have been introduced.[1] The key objectives have been to encourage more students to study subjects of STEM as well as to improve the initial education and continuing professional development of teachers. High quality STEM education contributes to sustained economic growth, as well as sustainable development by fuelling R&D, innovation, productivity, and competitiveness. Also, in recent years, in the US and in European countries there has been increasing focus on integrated STEM, while Arts subjects are mostly left apart. Despite these efforts, recent evidence seems to illustrate that in both mathematics and science, underachievement of 15-year-olds remains above the ET 2020 benchmark of 15%. Moreover, most European countries continue to have a low number of students interested in studying or pursuing a career in STEM (Kearney 2016). Specifically, according to the 2012 PISA assessment results (OECD 2014), 23% of the 15-year-old students who participated in the PISA assessment across OECD countries are low achievers, as they performed below the baseline level (level 2) in mathematics, i.e. they are able to "answer questions involving familiar contexts where all relevant information is present, and the questions are clearly defined. They are able to identify information and to carry out routine procedures according to direct instructions in explicit situations. They can perform actions that are obvious and follow immediately from the given stimuli" (OECD 2013). Only 12.6% are top performers in mathematics (Level 5 or

[1] See indicatively the list of STEM-related projects at the European Schoolnet: http://www.eun.org/projects/stem.

6). The situation is equally disappointing in the field of science. Roughly 18% of the students in OECD countries performed below the baseline level and are thus defined as low achievers who "have such a limited scientific knowledge that it can only be applied to a few, familiar situations. They can present scientific explanations that are obvious and follow explicitly from given evidence" (OECD 2013). Less than 1 out of 10 students (8.4%) were assessed as top performers in science literacy.

STEAM (Science, Technology, Engineering, and Mathematics combined with Arts) is a movement in the field of education which initiated from the United States of America and was driven forward in Europe. The STEAM initiative's aim is to place Arts at the heart of education systems to cultivate the creative skills of young people, alongside with the knowledge and skills they acquire in STEM fields. The interconnectivity of Arts and Sciences is a request and a challenge not only in education, where the STEM fields are actually the starting point and Arts are employed to increase the students' engagement, motivation and impact of learning, but also in Arts as a profession. Among the several Arts subjects, music has received great attention with examples in educational settings demonstrating how it can be exploited to cultivate important skills of young people and how it can be part of STEAM learning initiatives. Music is considered as essential to cognitive development from the early years of life. Studies on the links between music education and cognitive abilities report that participation in music lessons is associated with higher IQ and higher academic abilities of students (OECD 2011).

Recently, the EU initiated, in the framework of the Horizon 2020 Programme, a specific challenge on technologies for deeper learning of STEAM education. In this framework, the eCraft2Learn[2] aims to engage students with science and arts though digital fabrication, or by creating artistic artifacts with the use of technological tools. An example use case of eCraft2Learn is the creation of a 3D printed lighthouse in which the light is regulated by an Arduino controller which considers the external light conditions. STORIES[3] promotes the storytelling concept as a key element for interacting arts with STEM. It provides a user interface targeted to young students to create multi-path stories expressing thus their creativity and imagination, along with the use of latest Augmented and Virtual Reality (AR/VR) technologies combined with 3D printing to materialize elements of these stories. The weDraw[4] project explores on how various human sensory modalities are involved to the learning of specific concepts by primary school students. The STEAM direction of weDraw is to allow students to investigate the relationships of important components of music such as melody and rhythm with numbers and fractions, as well as the study of geometry in drawing and painting.

On the other hand, iMuSciCA proposes a platform supporting ICT-enhanced environments with new enabling technologies for deeper learning of STEAM subject matters to encourage learners in co-creative music activities. The general goal is to pursue the research and development of state-of-the-art concepts and proto-

[2]https://project.ecraft2learn.eu/.

[3]http://www.storiesoftomorrow.eu/.

[4]https://www.wedraw.eu/project.

types towards a novel framework of a workbench that involves advanced toolkits for music co-creation activities deployed in lesson plans for STEAM learning/teaching. The iMuSciCA workbench addresses secondary school students with the aim to support mastery of core academic content on STEM subjects (Physics, Geometry, Mathematics, and Technology) alongside with the development of creativity and deeper learning skills through student engagement in music activities.

The rest of the chapter is organized as follows. Section 7.2 presents an envisioned use case scenario for STEAM teaching/learning and gives an overview of the proposed pedagogical approach. In Sect. 7.3 we present the various activity environments and tools with reference to corresponding core-enabling technologies that constitute the iMuSciCA web-based workbench. Section 7.4 deals with the principles of designing lesson plans that are implemented with the iMuSciCA workbench, while Sect. 7.5 presents the overall evaluation framework of the pedagogy, the lesson plans and the usability of the iMuSciCA workbench. Section 7.6 concludes this chapter with discussion and future plans.

7.2 Pedagogical Approach

The envisioned use case scenario of iMuSciCA is illustrated in Fig. 7.1, where students (John and Beatrice in this example) are enjoying interactive music science education in various collaborative activities involving physics, mathematics, geometry, informatics, engineering, technology, music, design, and history of arts using lesson plans that have been prepared by their teachers (e.g. Garry and Alexandra) of different disciplines (e.g. Music and Maths or Physics) who collaborate as a team for STEAM education.

7.2.1 Problem Statement

At the heart of the iMuSciCA pedagogy is the idea that concepts of different fields, mostly left unconnected in schools, are meant to be seen in relation to each other. However, although connecting science, technology, engineering, mathematics and art is at the agenda of STEM and STEAM reforms in education, the realization of this connection is far from evident (Quigley et al. 2017; Bartos and Lederman 2014; Czerniak and Johnson 2007; Lederman and Niess 1997; Frans et al. 2013; Tamassia and Frans 2014). So iMuSciCA is fostering renewal on this point. It is a huge challenge but one worth trying. From our first piloting experiences it soon became clear that teachers showed great interest in connecting STEAM-fields though they felt very unsure as to how to realize this (Tsuprost et al. 2009).

Most students nowadays in school see hardly any relation between concepts or skills that are being taught to them in different fields or subject matters (Honey et al. 2014; Bevan et al. 2015). Our small study showed that in the iMuSciCA countries

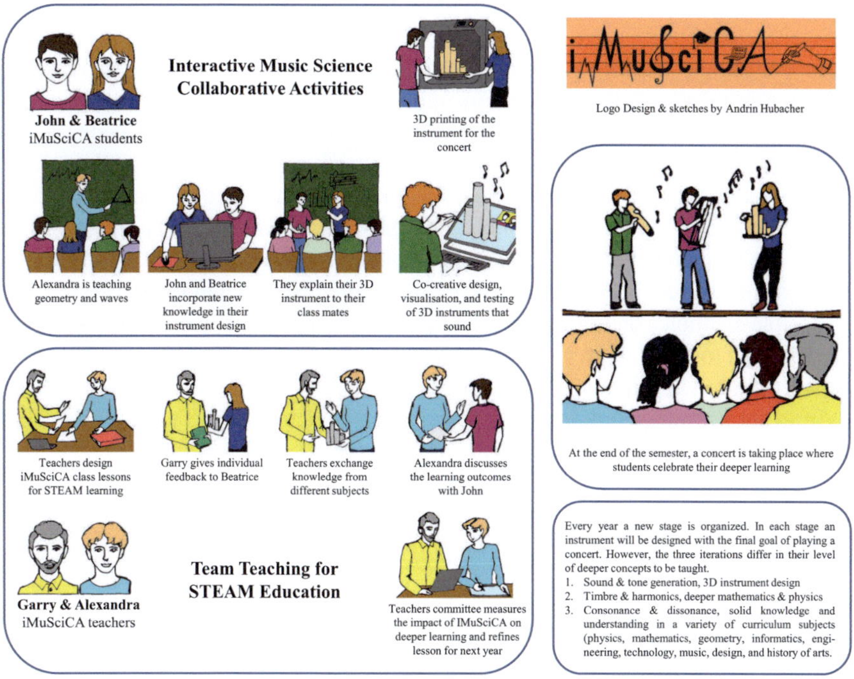

Fig. 7.1 Collaborative designed STEAM learning lesson plans used by students in music science collaborative activities

a pedagogy connecting Music with Science and Engineering can hardly be found in the standard curriculum.

For example, students in schools learn about waves and superposition in physics and mathematics, but they don't connect this to what they are experience in music: melody, timbre or harmony. The same goes for engineering: while designing an instrument (supposing they get a task like this in standard curriculum) students hardly realize that concepts of maths and physics are at stake there.

A prerequisite for STEAM education is one that has to be fulfilled by the school itself: there is no good way to STEAM teaching if there is no team of teachers, preferably of different STEAM disciplines, that can take this challenge 'as a team'. Indeed, teachers are mostly educated in one or two subjects at the most and understanding the language of another subject remains difficult. Different disciplines use different approaches, different tools, different ways. 'STEAM teaching' is a lot about 'TEAM teaching'.

To support teachers in overcoming the many challenges when implying an interdisciplinary STEAM pedagogy, iMuSciCA will help them by providing:

- A **workbench** with ready to use tools in order to connect the fields of Music, Science, and Engineering. Teachers can find tools for making or composing music, for analysing sounds and tones, for designing an instrument, etc.
- **Educational scenarios and lesson plans** that show teachers ways of how this workbench can be used in the class to bring iMuSciCA's STEAM pedagogy to life. The lesson scenarios are built on the basis of an inquiry-based methodology. At the same time, they give extra background to teachers and in some cases even working sheets for students which show how an interdisciplinary question and task can be handled and how students can lead inquiries by using the iMuSciCA workbench. These scenarios are meant to inspire teachers and demonstrate some possible examples on how to connect the fields by using the workbench. Teachers are invited to adapt them and use the workbench in a way that is most suitable for their situation in school.
- An **evaluation methodology** that teachers can use to observe whether this connected learning approach has the potential for deeper learning or not.

So, iMuSciCA's STEAM pedagogy tries to give tools to teachers to connect what has hitherto been left unconnected in schools. This combined way of learning has the potential for deeper and more meaningful learning.

7.2.2 Description of the Framework

iMuSciCA helps teachers to bring a contemporary STEAM teaching methodology in the class. iMuSciCA's STEAM pedagogy is designed according to the following principles:

a. **Interdisciplinarity**

The main design principle of the pedagogy behind iMuSciCA's workbench and lesson scenarios is to provide a STEAM-rich environment where interdisciplinary activities are at hand. Students can use a STEAM-rich palette of tools, concepts, and phenomena belonging to different subject matter fields. iMuSciCA's pedagogy lets them see and connect concepts and skills of music with those of science and engineering.

iMuSciCA scenarios do provide clear view for teachers: this is crucial since interdisciplinary subjects and inquiry paths might be a bit outside the 'known territory' of teachers, who might become unsure, even if they are experienced and working in a good team. Therefore, the iMuSciCA scenarios are full of background, example solutions and so on. The principle is not to tell teachers what they should do, but to inspire them and give them confidence in interdisciplinary STEAM education.

b. **Inquiry learning across STEAM fields**

iMuSciCA uses the following Inquiry Based Science Education (IBSE) phases: Engage, Imagine, Create, Analyse, Communicate, and Reflect. Classically, these or similar IBSE phases are applied in education though mostly they are seen as belonging to separate subject matter fields (see, for instance, Pedaste et al. 2015). But iMuSciCA now brings in an inquiry learning, where different STEAM disciplines are connected. This implies respect for the identity of each STEAM discipline, its concepts and practices, while, at the same time, broadening the IBSE phases to give room for questions and practices from other fields. This interdisciplinarity is usually not incorporated in science inquiry.

Work with the iMuSciCA workbench lets students experience that all these ways of inquiry learning are needed to come to a result. The engineer uses the scientific insights to predict how a musical instrument will behave in terms of fundamental, upper tones etc. The scientist tries to understand why these particular factors exist or which new ones lie ahead. The musician creates or performs a musical piece. In the end, the listener participates in the result of this process. All these are complementary and iMuSciCA tries to take the learner through the whole process.

c. **Different inquiry paths**

iMuSciCA reflects the open way in which real investigation occurs: as history of science shows, inquiry often follows rather unexpected paths (Matthews 1994).

The different inquiry phases in iMuSciCA are used as a model. This implies that the phases do not necessarily follow a standard sequence: variation and loopholes (sometimes certain phases reoccur a few times before going further). Besides alternating the sequence of the inquiry phases, iMuSciCA's pedagogy also varies the point of entrance and the level of guidance given (Tiberghien 2000).

Many times, though not always, iMuSciCA will let users start from the experience of music (music is then used as a context). On other occasions, scientific or engineering questions serve as a starting point like, for instance, in scenarios of the 'design your string instrument' or 'synthesize your preferred timbre' types.

Whatever the point of entrance, iMuSciCA's pedagogy tries to avoid one of the reported pitfalls concerning open forms of inquiry: if the necessary scaffolding to students is not sufficiently given, inquiry turns out to be negative, especially for the ones with less privileged backgrounds (Kirschner et al. 2006). Therefore, iMuSciCA shows pathways that will brush up the users' prior knowledge so that they succeed in their preferred inquiry. See below in Sect. 2.4 how, for different points of entry, students are referred to the appropriate basic scenarios where prior knowledge can be updated.

d. **Collaborative and co-creative learning across fields**

Science, Music, and Technology are all human collaborative activities: it is this diverse and interdisciplinary field of STEAM that iMuSciCA wants to show.

Therefore, iMuSciCA's workbench and lesson activities are designed to address the following characteristics that are known to support collaborative learning (Kirschner 2001):

1. **Active learning**: iMuSciCA's scenarios engage students from different perspectives: music, science, and engineering. Scenarios actively engage students in interdisciplinary investigations and, by doing so, they support a lot of collaborative skills and creativity (Honey and Kanter 2013; Martinez and Stager 2013).

2. **Teachers**: The role of the teachers is to provide guidance when needed, especially by attending to the less privileged. Teachers can recommend different pathways through different iMuSciCA scenarios depending on the student's background.
3. **Teaching and learning as shared experiences**: Teachers and learners create time for making joint conclusions to foster discussions around the learned concepts within student groups, within the group of iMuSciCA teachers, as well as joint discussions between these two groups. In iMuSciCA, we talk about teachers in plural, since iMuSciCA involves teachers from different backgrounds.
4. **Student participation in small-group activities**: iMuSciCA scenarios are built around inquiry activities that are preferably performed by a small group of students who later interact with the rest of the class to share their findings.
5. **Students taking responsibility for learning**: Small group activities of interdisciplinary nature allow students to take responsibility for their activities depending on their interest. For instance, some students can take the lead in a music activity while others can be in charge of coordinating a scientific experiment or designing an instrument.
6. **Students being stimulated to reflect** on their own assumptions and thoughts during iMuSciCA's 'communicate and reflect' phases.

e. **21st century skills across different STEAM-fields**

iMuSciCA translated the 21st century skills (Wagner 2008) into design principles that are somewhat more pedagogically operational. These are called the '9 lessons' for a 21st century pedagogy and are based on Saavedra and Opfer (2012). This is how they work for iMuSciCA as design principles:

1. **Make it relevant**. iMuSciCA activities connect contexts that engage students from different perspectives. The context of music 'resonates' evidently with students. Depending on the interests of learners, iMuSciCA allows teachers to switch contexts in order to make them relevant to learners (Perkins 2010).
2. **Teach through the disciplines**. In the classical model of education, teachers are restricted to a certain subject matter. This remains the dominant approach in compulsory education in much of the world (OECD 2009). Typically, students taught in this way do not have much practice in applying their knowledge to new contexts to solve new problems. The iMuSciCA pedagogy overcomes exactly these pitfalls from the design on by connecting disciplines and making knowledge transferable across fields and contexts.
3. **Develop thinking skills**. Connecting knowledge from different fields contributes highly to deeper and more applicable understanding (Schwartz and Fischer 2006). Students in iMuSciCA might practice, for instance, lower order skills by plugging numbers into an equation or a table when trying to understand the relationship between frequency and natural tones. But soon they apply this knowledge to another field: for example, they use this knowledge while designing an instrument or connect it to what they hear.
4. **Encourage learning transfer**. Transfer is hard, and students need support and practice to ensure that it happens (Fogarty et al. 1992). By connecting different

disciplines in the appealing context of music, iMuSciCA powerfully supports transfer: questions and tasks are given to make connections between scientific laws and situations in music, engineering, or life in general (Salomon and Perkins 1989).

5. **Teach students how to learn**. iMuSciCA's scenarios support students' metacognition by addressing reflection in different inquiry phases: talking through their own thinking, reflecting on their model or presenting it to peers. In this way, iMuSciCA supports the development of positive mental models by students: students are supported in their belief that intelligence and capacity increase with effort. The iMuSciCA workbench provides tools that enable them to inquire freely the phenomena. Thus, mistakes and failures become opportunities for growth (Dweck 2000).
6. **Address misunderstandings directly**. Learners evidently have a lot of misunderstandings about how the world really works, and they hold onto misconceptions until they can build alternative explanations based on experience (Perkins and Grotzer 2008). iMuSciCA's pedagogy confirms students' 'theory' every time with practice and evidence not only from music but also from other fields, such as science and engineering.
7. **Treat teamwork as an outcome**. iMuSciCA combines collaborative learning with inquiry. iMuSciCA's pedagogy works like a 'studio of learning' in which small groups of students work on a given issue and reflect upon this with their peers and teachers.
8. **Exploit technology to support learning**. The iMuSciCA workbench creates a technology environment based on experience, where virtual instruments can be tested or designed, and experiments can be performed. This way, students practice transferring skills and applying knowledge to different contexts. iMuSciCA's workbench makes practicing with instruments and devices easier and supports collaboration and dialogue with peers.
9. **Foster creativity**. Creativity is not a fixed characteristic that people either have or not. Rather, it is incremental, allowing students to learn to be more creative. Creative development requires structure and intentionality from teachers and students and can be learned especially 'through the disciplines' (Robinson 2001; Kim and Park 2012a; Kim and Park 2012b). It is reported that connecting disciplines makes lessons relevant to learners and works positively on students' motivation and creativity (Csikszentmihalyi 2008; Sternberg 2006). iMuSciCA directly addresses this creative process across different fields.

7.2.3 The iMuSciCA Curriculum and Structure of Scenarios

As explained in Sect. 2.2, the iMuSciCA curriculum foresees the possibility to use the workbench following a guided path or a more open one. To support the work of teachers, scenarios based on a certain theme have been developed in co-operation with groups of teachers in Belgium, France, and Greece. Belgium and France mainly focused on the 7th to the 9th grades, while Greece focused on the 9th and 10th grades. In all cases, the aim of the scenarios was to offer inspiration, support and background information to teachers, and let them free to choose their preferred path. By co-creating the scenarios together with the teachers in each country, it was possible to adapt them to the national curricula and also address specific situations.

As an example, we present in Fig. 7.2 the structure of the scenarios dedicated to grades 7th–9th developed in Belgium:

- In the centre, we find two ‘basic scenarios’ which contain basic concepts of music, physics and mathematics, e.g. what the sources of sound and tone are, what a tone is, what natural tones are, etc. These two scenarios are built in a guided form including direct links to the appropriate tools on the iMuSciCA workbench. This is very useful in the 7th and 8th grades, as groups of pupils can work independently (supervised by a teacher) by following a pre-set guided inquiry path.
- Around this, we find the ‘open’ scenarios, considered as the ‘entrance’ point into the iMuSciCA pedagogy: these are creative scenarios containing a description of activities to be implemented by students directly on the iMuSciCA workbench. Therefore, the inquiry path gives more degrees of freedom to students.

The idea behind this structure is that teachers can start working in class form an ‘open’ scenario (entrance point into the iMuSciCA pedagogy) which stimulates the students’ curiosity and interest. They can then go to basic scenarios whenever this is needed to deepen the knowledge and understanding of the underlying basic concepts. Of course, teachers can also choose to adapt these scenarios or to develop new ones. Furthermore, each scenario starts from one of the STEAM ‘points of view’, i.e. Science/Mathematics, Engineering/Technology, Music, and then builds a bridge towards the other STEAM fields.

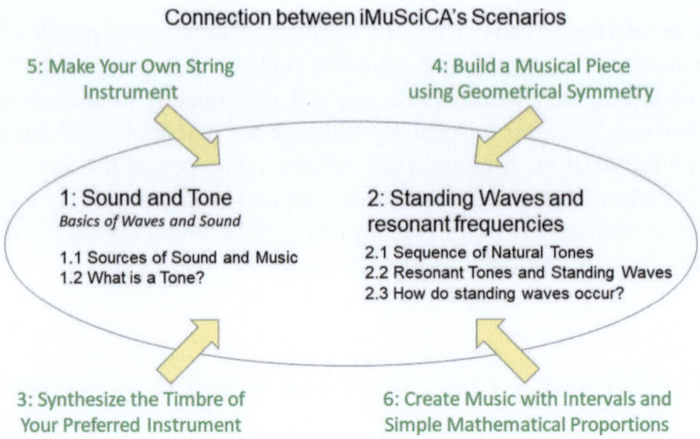

Fig. 7.2 Structure of exemplary educational scenarios for 7th–9th grades

7.2.4 *An Example of an 'Open' Scenario*

The scenario entitled 'Synthesize the timbre of your preferred instrument' is built around the 'Tones Synthesizer' activity environment of the workbench (see Fig. 7.7). In this scenario, the student's task is to recreate the timbre produced by his or her favourite instrument. Students must first play the same tone on different instruments to experience that the sound produced is somehow different. This is done first by listening and then by measuring the frequency spectrum and noticing that, when playing a tone on a musical instrument, more than one frequencies are produced. Students investigate then what happens by summing up different frequencies by using the 'Tones Synthesizer' and they conclude that it is the relative intensity of these frequencies which makes up a different timbre. At this point, they can proceed to the reproduction of the timbre of their chosen instrument. In principle, this scenario can be considered as independent. Although it is an example of a scenario starting from an *engineering* point of view, teachers could decide to make a deviation to deepen the understanding of the used concepts, such as tones and natural tones. In this case, they could implement alternative scenarios, which address these concepts from the points of view of *physics, mathematics, and music*.

7.3 The iMuSciCA Workbench

This section briefly describes the main components of the learning environment, and then focuses on the iMuSciCA workbench, which is the main user interface where innovative STEAM activities take place.

The learning environment consists of functional components allowing to create, manage, store, and use learning contents, as well as evaluate the learning outcomes. These include:

- The main entry point is the iMuSciCA Learning Management System (LMS) which is accessible at http://lms.imuscica.eu/. This builds on a standard Moodle environment (Dougiamas and Taylor 2003).
- The innovative iMuSciCA Learning Contents are provided to students in a unified workbench (https://workbench.imuscica.eu/).

On the LMS, the individual learning contents are available. These are typically generated or adapted by teachers using a Learning Content Authoring Tool (LCAT), which is based on the well-known Cabri authoring software (Cabri 2018), or directly added in Moodle using its own tools. Learning contents can be tagged using appropriate metadata, to allow for fast and efficient retrieval. When users follow a learning content, they produce some data (question answers, marks, current progress within an activity, etc.). These data are called 'learning records' and are stored in a repository, the Learning Record Store (LRS) (Tillett 2012).

The workbench is the place where students can perform STEAM-related activities according to the iMuSciCA pedagogical framework (see Sect. 7.2). It provides a set

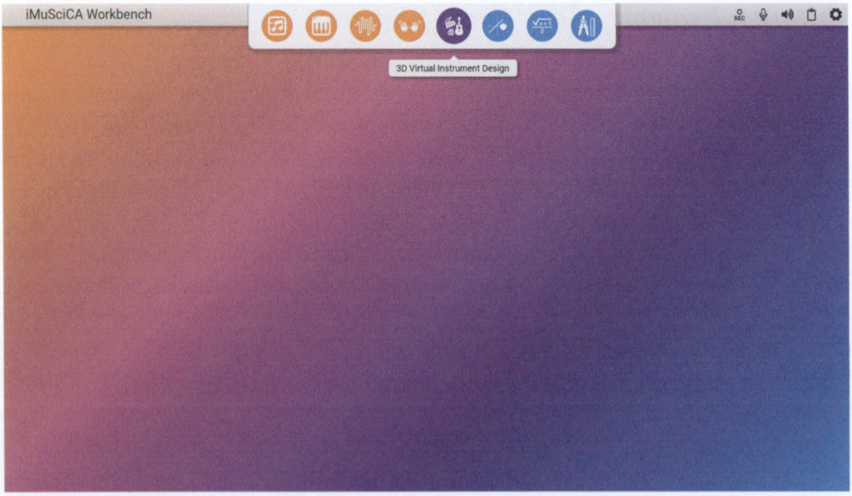

Fig. 7.3 Landing page of the iMuSciCA workbench

of Activity Environments and Tools (AE&T), categorised according to the different STEAM domains in music, science and mathematics, engineering and technology.

The activity environments and tools can be launched by clicking on the corresponding icon, located at the top of the window (see Fig. 7.3). Activity environments belonging to the same domain share the same colour. Furthermore, visualization and music tools, e.g., the very recent Snail from (Hélie and Picasso 2017) are available when users interact with an activity environment producing sound (see Fig. 7.7).

Virtual music instruments can be designed in an innovative 3D Music Instrument Design environment. In this environment, the user can load four pre-designed instruments: a multichord, a guitar, a membrane (circular or square), and a xylophone (Fig. 7.4). The ground-breaking novelty of iMuSciCA is that students can adjust various parameters (e.g. the length and chord tension) and then hear the produced sound from the instrument, the latter being excited using synthetic sound of physical instruments, building on the latest research outcomes of IRCAM.

In activities related to the interactive musical instrument environment (see Fig. 7.5), the student can either play pre-set instruments or load customized virtual instruments, previously designed in the 3D Musical Instrument Design. Students can use their hands (Leap Motion based interaction) and arms/body (Kinect-based interaction) to interact with the virtual musical instrument and their actions are translated into events that trigger the sound generating engine. The performance can be stored and re-played to be used in other activity environments and tools (visualization, sample sequencer, analysis).

The Performance Sample Sequencer (see Fig. 7.6) allows students to work on a performance sound recording, obtained from the interactive musical instrument performance activity environment. Students can explore combinations of segments

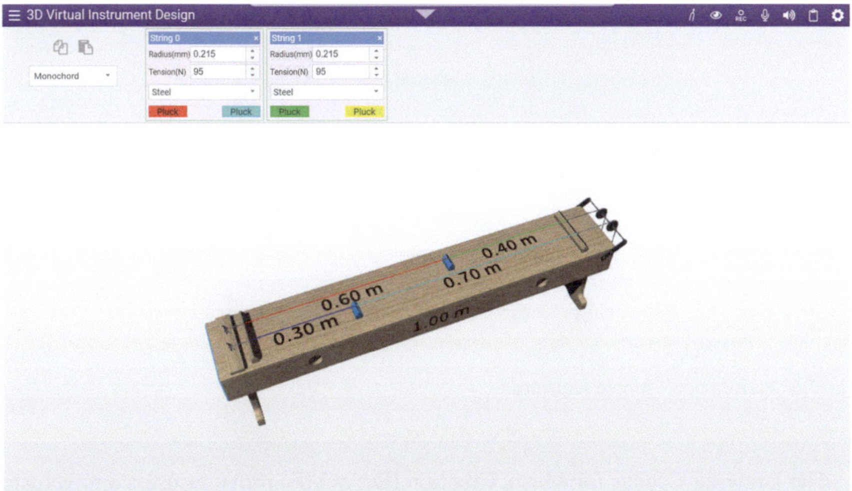

Fig. 7.4 The 3D musical instrument design environment

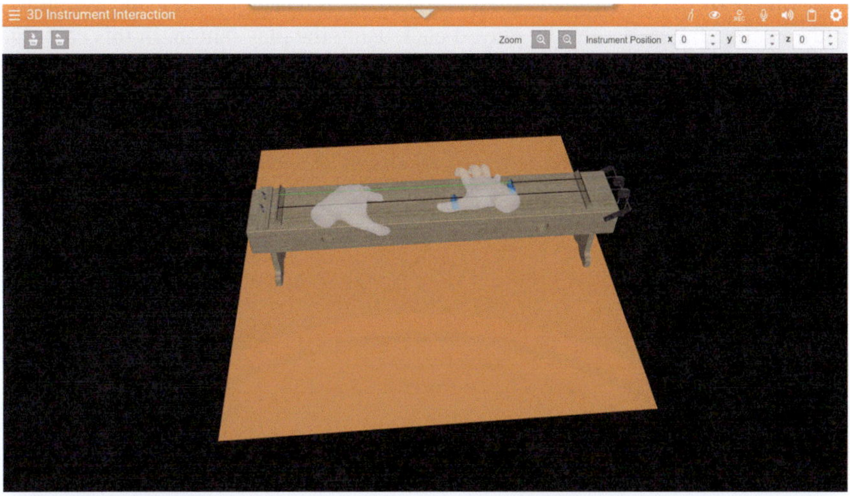

Fig. 7.5 Gesture-based interaction for virtual music instrument performance

of their recordings to generate new music. To this end, stored recorded performances can be imported in audio form into the sampler's interface. The student can then select segments from this performance recording as regions on the waveform and activate those samples on the sampler's matrix. Users can store the current settings of their composition and share it with other students, generating the conditions for co-creation.

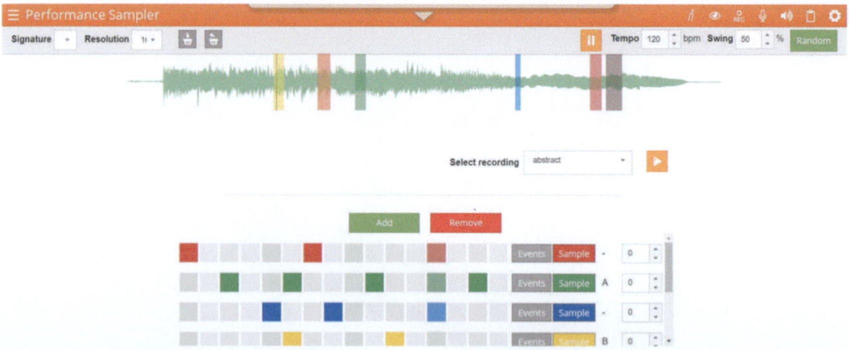

Fig. 7.6 Performance sample sequencer

The Drawing Canvas for Music Creation (DrAwME) provides users a novel and unique way that interconnects drawings with sounds. The y-coordinates of the canvas specify the frequency of the sound, while the colour of the drawing pen corresponds to the timbre of the sound (see Fig. 7.7). The sound is generated while the user draws on the canvas, but it can also be played back using the play button. In this case, the sound generation of the drawing is achieved by interpreting the x-coordinates as time which unfolds from left to write and playing the various frequencies (y-coordinates) of the drawing. The user may also select among a number of sound visualization tools. At the same time, the student may choose to see how a sound generated in the DrAwME can be visualized. Figure 7.7 presents the visualization of the Snail, which

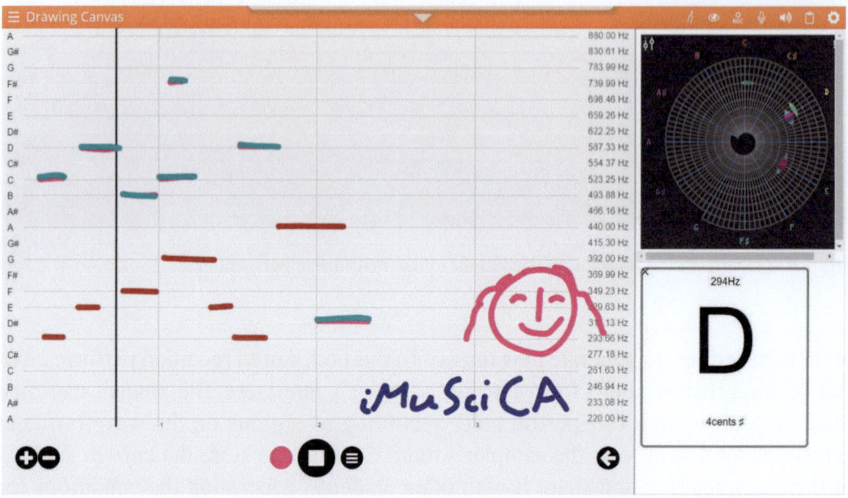

Fig. 7.7 Interactive drawing canvas for music creation with music visualization tools

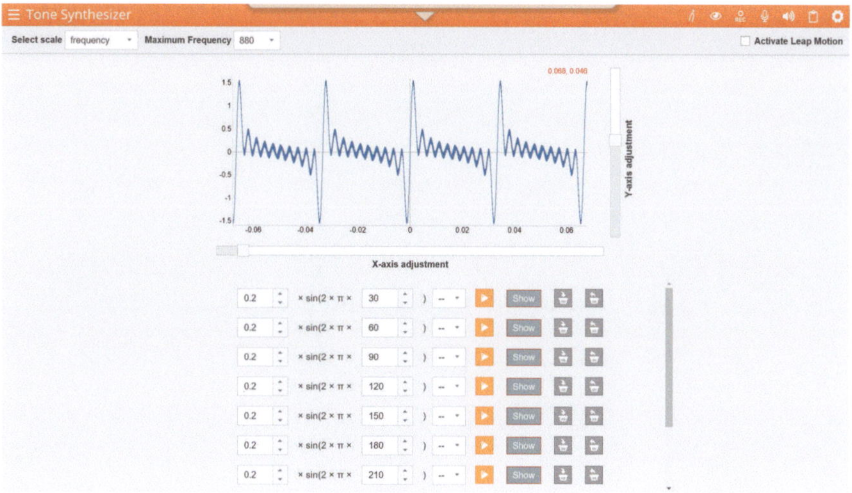

Fig. 7.8 Exploring timbres with the tones synthesizer

displays music tones around the spectrum of a sound as a "blob" with size and color that depend on the energy and phase shift in the Fourier decomposition and the tuner.

An alternative approach to study sound waves is provided by the Tones Synthesizer activity environment, which allows students to explore timbres as an addition of multiple sinusoidal elements. Students can listen to the sound produced by up to eight combined (summed) sinusoids, change their parameters (amplitude and frequency) and visualize the produced waveform, either as a whole or each element separately (see Fig. 7.8).

Finally, three scientific and mathematical activity environments and tools are available to students. In the sonification of mathematical expressions activity environment (Fig. 7.9), students can design mathematical equations and geometric curves and let them sound.

In the mathematical equation editor (Fig. 7.10), students can write math equations by handwritten recognition or using menus and keyboard.

In the geometry and algebra activity environment (Fig. 7.11), an all-purpose exploratory environment, students can use a wide range of tools suitable for mathematical and geometric design and analysis.

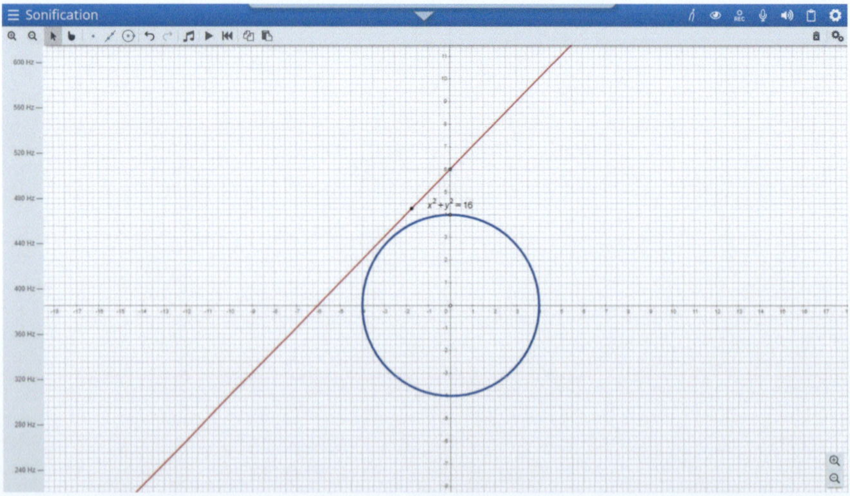

Fig. 7.9 Sonification of mathematical equations and geometric curves activity environment

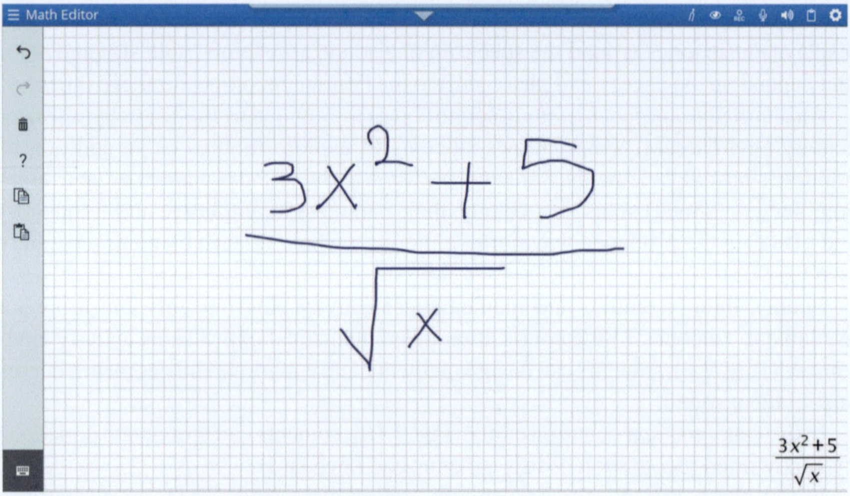

Fig. 7.10 Math equation editor using handwriting recognition

7.4 Lesson Plans Design

The educational scenarios of iMuSciCA implement the project's pedagogical design and, at the same time, harness the potential of iMuSciCA's workbench activity environments and tools through innovative learning activities. The educational scenarios are co-created by iMuSciCA experts and teachers and allow students to move from

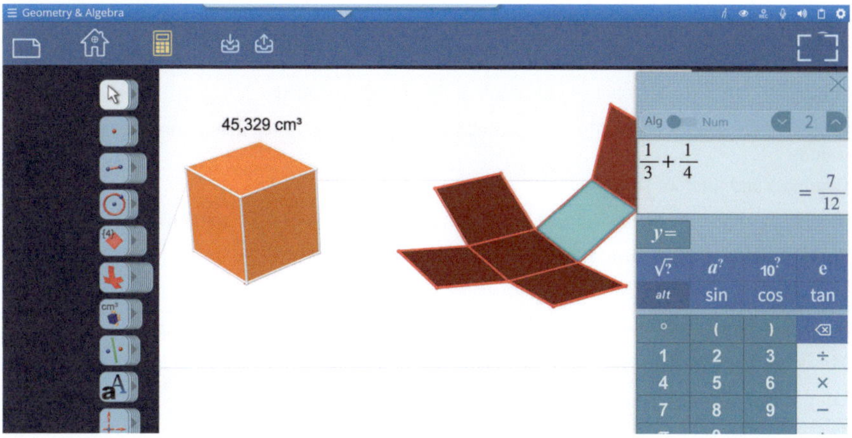

Fig. 7.11 Geometry and algebra activity environment

guided to free inquiry, as they implement the proposed activities, and further expand undertaking their own inquiries through the iMuSciCA workbench.

7.4.1 Connection with Subject Content Knowledge

Following the pedagogical framework of iMuSciCA, educational scenarios are closely aligned with the national STEM curricula in Belgium, France and Greece. At the same time, they address subject-specific misconceptions and difficulties that students face in secondary education (Table 7.1).

As the pedagogical approaches of iMuSciCA deal with principles of sound phenomena and their relationship with geometric and physical properties of sound bodies, they cover a wide range of subjects. Music teaching acts primarily as a catalyst demonstrating in very practical ways, i.e. through the creation of sound, that concepts such as the explanation of sound as a natural phenomenon through mathematical proportions and the harmonic arrangement in time as imposed by music creation are two faces of the same coin.

According to the existing body of knowledge, students often seem to have difficulties in terms of visualisation and analysis of both geometric and algebraic structures. iMuSciCA provides an innovative and highly interactive learning environment, in which students can experiment with geometric shapes in dynamic ways to create musical instruments aiming at addressing the above-mentioned difficulties. Furthermore, 3D-Geometry and its basic rules can be introduced in a playful manner through educational scenarios using the iMuSciCA workbench, which provides students with opportunities to interact with such objects, thus, enhancing their spatial reasoning.

Table 7.1 Students' misconceptions and difficulties in physics

Sounds can be produced without using any material objects
Hitting an object harder, changes the pitch of the sound produced
Human voice sounds are produced by a large number of vocal cords that all produce different sounds
Loudness and pitch of sounds are the same thing
In wind instruments, the instrument itself vibrates (not the internal air column)
Music is strictly an art form; it has nothing to do with science
Sound waves are transverse waves (like water and light waves)
Sound can be trapped in a container if the air is trapped; it needs holes to escape
Music has low volume (small amplitude) and noise has high volume (large amplitude)
Longer objects vibrate faster or produce higher notes
The sound box on a musical instrument is for making sound clearer
Vibrations and waves are the same thing
The pitch of a tuning fork will change as it "slows down", i.e. "runs out" of energy
Students often confuse wave period with frequency

Algebraic manipulations, either simple (e.g. manipulation of proportions) or advanced (e.g. manipulations of logarithmic and trigonometric functions) can be addressed by students if they research the functional dependencies of various parameters of the musical instruments they are designing.

Moreover, Engineering is a subject, which is not introduced systematically in standard K-12 Curricula. As opposed to Vocational Education and Training (VET), Engineering is mainly approached on a voluntary basis, e.g. through Project Based Learning (PBL), in extra-curricular/afterschool Student Clubs or as an elective subject. As a result, students' misconceptions about the engineering principles generally prevail and are not addressed in a systematic manner by many educational institutions.

The pedagogical design of iMuSciCA incorporates the engineering cycle of defining a problem by asking questions, imagining potential solutions, planning the design of a prototype, building it, testing it, assessing and optimizing the results, and providing the final product. Furthermore, the iMuSciCA workbench provides students with the opportunity to experiment with the design of a final product and comprehend the interrelations between Engineering, Science and Mathematics, as well as addressing the links between Music and STEM mentioned in the following table (Table 7.2).

7.4.2 Integration of the iMuSciCA Pedagogical Framework

The iMuSciCA educational scenarios follow the approach of IBSE across the STEAM fields. Students first engage with the subject, they wonder, they ask questions

Table 7.2 Links between music and science

Simple mathematical proportions and musical intervals
Natural tones and mathematical proportions
Natural tones and standing waves
Melody as a sequence of intervals
Harmony and the simultaneous sounding of musical intervals
The mathematical pattern in the upper tones and the musical consonance and dissonance
The concept of scale and the relationship of sounds
The concepts of musical time, rhythm and mathematical patterns
Elementary principles of musical composition and the relation with harmonics

Fig. 7.12 Inquiry based learning cycle. *Source* The OPEDUCA project (http://www.opeduca.eu/Inquiry_Based_Learning.html)

and they link the subject to their prior knowledge. Second, they imagine and formulate hypotheses and identify relevant parameters to investigate possible solutions. Third, they create prototypes, investigate the hypotheses they have been formulating beforehand and analyse the results of their investigations. Fourth, they connect the subject with different STEAM fields, they draw conclusions and evaluate the results. Fifth, they communicate the results of their activities to others, e.g. teachers, students, and peers. Finally, they reflect on the feedback they obtain and incorporate it in their further explorations (Fig. 7.12).

Thus, each educational scenario follows a vertical approach according to the successive steps that this model proposes but does not preclude teachers from delving deeper into the details of each field through dedicated lesson plans that can be adapted

Table 7.3 iMuSciCA's synopsis of educational scenarios

Title:					
Description:					
E: Engineering/Technology, S: Science/Mathematics, M: Music					
Phases	Field	Time	Description	Activity	Remarks

to different teaching needs. Furthermore, this structure allows students to perform their own inquiries by utilizing the acquired knowledge and feedback (Table 7.3).

The possibility of teachers themselves enriching and further developing pedagogical interventions in class led to the design of a synopsis table, in which all the above-mentioned possibilities of didactic actions using iMuSciCA's workbench can be briefly described and combined.

The Synopsis allows teachers to create the overall 'floor plan' of teaching practices in terms of duration, field and specific teacher-student actions in the iMuSciCA workbench.

7.4.3 Architecture of Educational Scenarios in iMuSciCA

Variations among National Curricula, structural differences among public schools, music schools and private schools as well as everyday practices in classrooms provide a landscape, which requires the iMuSciCA educational scenarios to be flexible and adaptable. Therefore, the design adapts to three possible settings: (i) long term Project Based Learning that can be carried out e.g. in School Clubs; (ii) medium term regular classroom interventions; or (iii) short term classroom interventions on a par with the curriculum.

In this framework, a modular architecture (Fig. 7.13) has been developed for the educational scenarios of iMuSciCA. Educational scenarios, which incorporate all IBSE phases and cover all STEAM fields usually have a duration of at least four hours and consist of smaller modules or Lesson Plans. Each Lesson Plan may incorporate one or more inquiry stages and has a typical duration of one or two teaching hours.

Educational Scenarios can be further combined, in order to produce a wider ranging and more comprehensive learning project, which consists of at least one scenario and can last from 20 h to the whole school year.

This structure allows flexibility not only with respect to the implementation setting, curriculum and time availability but also regarding the design of the Educational Scenarios. As Scenarios consist of Lesson Plans involving one or more Inquiry Phases and STEAM fields, those Lesson Plans can be easily combined, varied and re-arranged to contribute to different Educational Scenarios (Table 7.4).

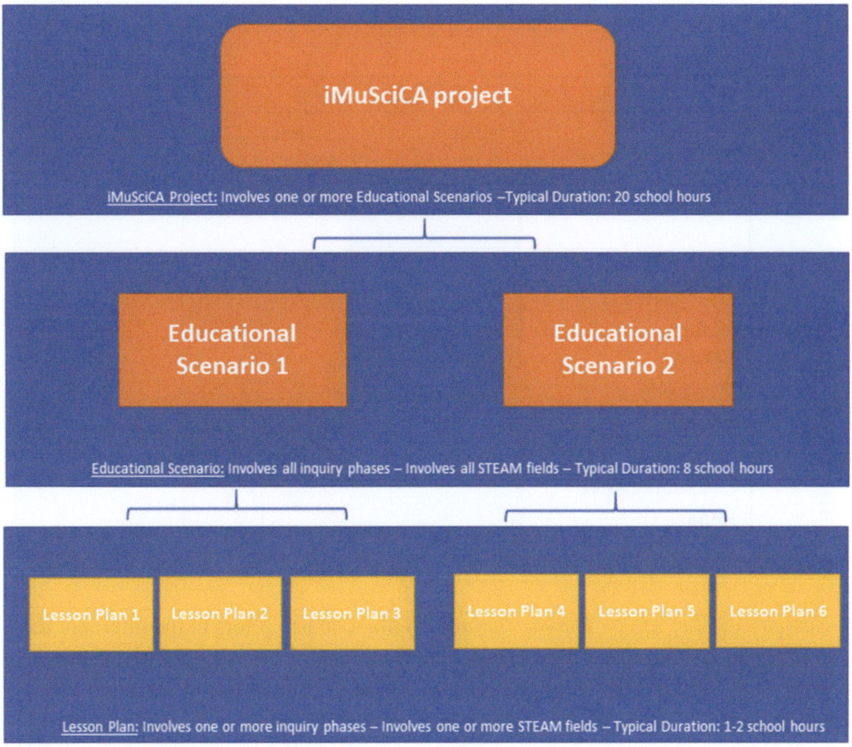

Fig. 7.13 Modular architecture of iMuSciCA's educational scenarios

7.4.4 Exemplary iMuSciCA Educational Scenarios

This section provides selected examples of Educational Scenarios for Lower and Upper Secondary Education developed by the pedagogical team of iMuSciCA in close co-operation with affiliated teachers coming from Belgium and Greece.

Scenario 1: Sound and tone: This scenario addresses students in lower secondary education. Students investigate vibrations as sources of sound. By means of the iMuSciCA visualisation tools they measure sounds and recognise that some are periodic, and others are not. They learn to connect this insight with what they hear: some sounds have more tones, some others less or no tone at all.

Scenario 2: Standing waves and resonant frequencies: This scenario also addresses lower secondary school students. Students investigate the natural sequence of tones that occur on string instruments and aerophones. They use the iMuSciCA sound visualization tools to measure the frequencies and discover their mathematical relation. Moreover, they try to understand how these precise sequences of tones can occur on an instrument where they do not change anything.

Table 7.4 Distribution of lesson plans of a generic educational scenario across STEAM fields and IBSE phases

		STEAM Field		
Inquiry Phase		Music	Science/ Mathematics	Engineering/ Technology
	Engage	*Lesson Plan 1*		
	Imagine		*Lesson Plan 1*	
	Create Investigate/Design	*Lesson Plan 4*	*Lesson Plan 2*	*Lesson Plan 2*
	Analyze		*Lesson Plan 3*	
	Communicate & Reflect	*Lesson Plan 4*	*Lesson Plan 3*	

Scenario 3: Let's hear Thales' theorem: This scenario refers to the intercept theorem of Thales of Miletus. Students of Upper Secondary Education use the iMuSciCA tools to divide a string length in parts keeping tension (and radius in the case of string) constant and then listen to the different generated sound. They select a number of string-lengths to form their own 'scale' in a polychord (bichord, trichord, etc.). With the help of their music teacher, they use this scale to compose motifs (i.e. sets of notes) making brief rhythmical patterns. By altering the tension, students can experiment to achieve the same frequencies used in the previous step. They compare their scientific results in table format and perform the same composition with the new models.

Scenario 4: Investigating the Monochord: This educational scenario introduces upper high school students to the science behind the sound produced by the simplest stringed instrument, the monochord. Students investigate and verify Mersenne's laws regarding the dependencies of the frequency of the sound produced by a virtual monochord on several parameters, such as string tension, radius and length. To do that, they will produce a virtual monochord using the iMuSciCA '3D Music Instrument Design Environment', experiment hands-on and minds-on with the relevant parameters and investigate the dependencies using simulated data produced by the performance of the virtual instrument.

Concerning more 'open' scenarios and lesson plans, a description of the activities has been developed following the Synopsis of iMuSciCA's Educational Scenarios presented in this section. These scenarios deal with concepts such as the timbre of musical instruments, the influence of length, tension and thickness of the string on the tone, recognition of patterns, transformations and combination of transformations in music and geometry. Below follow some examples addressing lower secondary school students:

The 'Synthesize the timbre of your preferred instrument' open scenario is built around the 'Tones Synthesizer' activity environment. In this scenario, the student has the task to create a sound, with a timbre similar to her/his favourite instrument.

The 'Build a musical piece using geometrical symmetry' open scenario uses various iMuSciCA tools such as the 'Performance Sample Sequencer', the 'Drawing Canvas for Music Creation', and the 'Geometry and Algebra tools' to teach students how to recognize patterns, transformations and combination of transformations in music and geometry.

7.5 Evaluation Framework

The in-depth evaluation of the pedagogical framework, the co-created educational scenarios and the associated iMuSciCA workbench activity environments and tools consist of two distinct assessment phases in Lower and Upper Secondary Education in three piloting countries (Belgium, France and Greece). In Belgium the pilot testing includes students in the 7th and 8th grades, in France it is applied in the 8th and 9th grades and in Greece it mainly addresses the 9th and 10th grades.

The first assessment phase is focused on the usability evaluation of the first versions of the learning environments as well as on the educational value and pedagogical relevance of the first versions of the educational scenarios.

A second assessment phase centres on the use and evaluation of the technological and pedagogical frameworks in real classroom settings in order to fine tune and further increase the capabilities of educational scenarios, lesson plans, and related activity environments; it will assess students' learning achievements in general and STEAM deeper learning metrics in particular; it will consider the benefits for educator and it will contribute to the formulation of recommendations for good practices and policies for implementing STEAM education.

The evaluation focusses on the following three aspects:

Technical Usability and Acceptance: By applying a user-centred design and implementation to evaluate (i) the technical performance of iMuSciCA workbench; and (ii) the familiarity of the main stakeholders with its functionalities. The informants are teachers and students.

Pedagogical Fit and Value: By assessing the usefulness, user-friendliness, learnability/adaptability/reusability and efficiency of the suggested Educational Scenarios; by integrating STEAM and related Inquiry Based Learning (IBL) pedagogy into the classroom; by increasing opportunities for collaboration, co-creation and collective knowledge amongst educators. The informants are teachers (Abma and Stake 2001).

Learning Fit and Value: By analysing the ability of the learning environment to personalise learning processes; by investigating the potential to motivate students to learn more and beyond the expected; by increasing the capability to achieve deeper learning competences. The informants are students and teachers.

The selected Educational Scenarios for further implementation, on the one hand, are in line with the National Curricula in the participating countries and, on the other hand, demonstrate the potential of iMuSciCA to cover a wide range of educational needs (e.g. in relation to education systems, STEM subject matters, school settings, and students' age groups) across different countries.

Furthermore, a substantial part of the evaluation will take place in real classroom settings and thus the feedback will be generated directly from end users, i.e. science and music teachers and their students.

iMuSciCA therefore follows a multi-methodological research approach adopting an interpretive paradigm aimed at closely documented experience in a socio-cultural framing (Ryan and Deci 2000) considering three aspects: (i) *personal* (i.e. focus on teachers and students and what they are doing), (ii) *interpersonal* (i.e. focus on interactions between teachers, students and peers), and (iii) *contextual* (i.e. considering institutional factors, teachers' mind sets, students' motivation, available resources, physical arrangements).

The related evaluation instruments entail questionnaires, tests, classroom observation, reflections, behavioural and biometrical data and user analytics.

Questionnaires will collect quantitative data from students and teachers concerning issues of the technical usability and acceptance and pedagogical fit and value. In addition, an attitude questionnaire will be given to students prior to and at the end of iMuSciCA's second phase. This will aim to detect any changes in students' motivation towards STEM and STEAM learning due to the intervention and will be examined in conjunction with the behavioural and biometrical data concerning student engagement.

Tests: In addition to questionnaires at the end of the interventions, students will be administered tests on the STEAM knowledge involved in the lesson plans, before and after each implementation with the aim to measure any changes in student subject knowledge (i.e. learning fit and value) as a result of iMuSciCA's use.

Classroom observation: Observations will mainly focus on issues of technical usability and acceptance and pedagogical fit and value; they will look for interactions between students and teacher and/or between students and the learning environment. It is suggested that mapping, sequential digital images, observation field notes using a timeline and audio recordings are amongst the most appropriate instruments to be applied in classroom observation. User analytics about students' activity are expected to complement qualitative data collected with the other methods.

Reflections: To further complement these observations, a certain level of reflection is required from both the students and teachers in the classroom. It is suggested that the digital images and audio recordings would be an appropriate means of triggering such reflections, and these could be elicited by way of interview and/or focus group discussions. Reflections will mainly address the Pedagogical fit and value and Learning fit and value foci of the evaluation.

Student behavioural and biometrical data: Visual attention and affective behaviour in a learning platform such as iMuSciCA can have both positive and negative effect on students' learning. By investigating student gaze patterns and eye movements when interacting with the iMuSciCA web platform activity environments we can capture precise information about how discoverable or attention-grabbing visual elements such as navigation structures, screen graphics, links, text, or multimedia content are to the participants. Furthermore, confusion, frustration, boredom, as well as other affective states are elicited in response to the students' interaction with the iMuSciCA platform and they are inextricably bound to learning by affecting students' perceptions of the iMuSciCA environment and changing how well they learn from it. Towards this end, in order to assess student behaviour, we shall employ the following monitoring mechanisms.

Eye tracking is the recording of eye position (gaze point) and movement on a 2D screen or environment based on the optical tracking of corneal reflections. Eye tracking reflects visual attention as it objectively monitors where, when, and what respondents look at. Furthermore, eye tracking devices can record the dilation and constriction of the pupil, which has been found to correlate with emotional arousal and cognitive workload (Costa and Rudebeck 2016). Eye tracking therefore can be used to validate and complement GSR measurements.

Facial expression analysis is a non-intrusive method to assess both emotions (subtle movements in face muscles, mostly subconscious) and feelings (accompanied by clearly noticeable changes in facial expression). While facial expressions can measure the valence of an emotion/feeling, they cannot measure the associated arousal (Martinez and Valstar 2016).

Electrodermal activity (EDA), also referred to as galvanic skin response (GSR), reflects the amount of sweat secretion from sweat glands in the skin. Increased sweating results in higher skin conductivity. When exposed to emotional stimulation, people "sweat emotionally"—particularly on forehead, hands, and feet (Boucsein 2012). GSR measurements can be taken with lightweight and mobile sensors, which makes data acquisition very easy.

Electroencephalography (EEG) is a neuroimaging technique that measures electrical activity on the scalp. EEG shows which parts of the brain are active during task performance or stimulus exposure. It analyses brain dynamics of engagement (arousal), motivation, frustration, cognitive workload and other metrics associated with stimulus processing, action preparation, and execution (Chaouachi et al. 2011). EEG tracks stimulus-related processes much faster compared to other biometrics sensors.

User analytics recorded by the iMuSciCA system will provide information about the students' interaction with the learning environment.

7.5.1 Usability Evaluation

The usability testing of the iMuSciCA learning environment aims to direct the user-centred development process of the iMuSciCA workbench activity environments and tools. The process involves both user groups, i.e. teachers and students, and the test goals are related to the users' experience and the examination of certain features of the activity environments of iMuSciCA. In particular, the testing evolves around specifically designed tasks of the activity environments under consideration.

The 5Es criteria (Efficient, Effective, Engaging, Error tolerant, Easy to learn) are used to shape the measurements of the usability studies (Barnum 2011). The 5Es are going to be measured and inferred from the observations and answers to questionnaires using the following techniques:

Efficient: Can users find the information they need to complete tasks without assistance? Measure how long each task takes to be completed. Examine eye-tracking data and look for places where screen layout or navigation makes it difficult for the user.

Effective: Can users perform a process within a predetermined time frame? Go through the results of each task and measure the frequency of accurate and total completion of tasks. Look for specific problems and mistakes made by several users and for any skipped information.

Engaging: Do users rate their experience as satisfying or enjoyable? Do their comments (and body language) suggest that they are having a positive experience? Examine the facial/eye-tracking/GSR/EEG data and look for signs that the screens are confusing or difficult to read. Look for places where the interface fails to draw users into their tasks.

Error tolerant: Do users experience errors? And if they do, do they recover successfully? Create a test case in which technical difficulties are likely to happen/appear and see how well users can recover from these.

Easy to learn: Can users get started right away? Does their ability to perform improve as they become familiar with the system? Does the system architecture match their mental model of how they expect the system to work? Control how much instruction is given to test participants, or ask users to try especially difficult, complex or rarely-used tasks. Look for places where the on-screen text/icons or workflow helps or confuses them.

7.5.2 Evaluation of Initial Educational Scenarios by Teachers and Preliminary Findings

The following educational materials (including educational scenarios, lesson plans, and concrete learning activities on the workbench) have been developed: 1. Sound and Tone; 2. Standing Waves and Resonant Frequencies; 3. Let's Listen to the Thales Theorem; and 4. Investigating the Monochord.

The evaluation of the Pedagogical Fit and Value as well as of the preliminary Learning Fit and Value by of the educational materials primarily aimed at:

- familiarising teachers and students with the aims of the STEAM pedagogy;
- assessing the pedagogic and learning value of the proposed Educational Scenarios and related tools and materials;

- customising the Educational Scenarios according to the needs of educators, students and the curriculum.

Feedback from teachers about the Pedagogical Framework and specific Educational Scenarios has been collected with the help of a dedicated questionnaire. The Initial Scenarios Evaluation Tool for Teachers is structured in four sections:

- *Personal Information*: teachers' personal and professional background; previous experience in teaching; Digital Literacy and familiarity with Technology Enhanced Learning and Teaching (TEL&T); ability to connect the teaching of STEM with Music;
- *Role of Educational Scenarios*: concerning the understanding of the pedagogical framework; the implementation of IBL and interdisciplinary approaches in class;
- *Success Criteria of Educational Scenarios*: relevance to curriculum; achievement of declared objectives; usability in real classroom settings; increase in interest and improvement of student's STEM performance;
- *Evaluation of concrete Educational Scenarios*: positive aspects; suggestions for improvement; rating.

The sections combined statistical ratings with open-ended questions requesting either written explanations for the quantitative answers or concrete suggestions about the strengths and weaknesses of the educational materials.

In turn, feedback from students was primarily obtained through Focus Groups placed at the end of learning activities or longer sessions of exploration of iMuSciCA Educational Scenarios. The Focus Groups included aspects such as understanding of the lesson content, clarity of educator's instructions, experience with Educational Scenarios and concrete learning activities within, performance and helpfulness of the iMuSciCA portfolio for the individual and group learning experience and the interaction between as well as the support received by teachers and students. Finally, students were asked to describe positive aspects of the sessions and suggest improvements for the learning and teaching iMuSciCA environment.

Next, we report preliminary findings of this evaluation process. The majority of the 38 participating Science and Music Teachers were Science or Mathematics teachers, around 55% of whom have a teaching experience of more than ten years. More than 80% of all teachers describe themselves as relatively experienced in applying Information and Communication Technologies (ICTs) and e-Learning applications in class. On the flipside, the participating teachers were at large not experienced in connecting STEM education with Music.

Overall, the initial Educational Scenarios were evaluated as positive; however, the Scenario on Standing Waves and Resonant Frequencies gained slightly lower scores since teachers perceived the concept as too sophisticated to be applied easily with students in junior high schools.

Experimenting with the Educational Scenarios clearly helped teachers in understanding iMuSciCA's pedagogical framework better. Furthermore, they are perceived of having high potential to improve the students' STEM performance. Moreover, the Scenarios are helpful to (i) increase students' interest in STEM; (ii) implement IBL and (iii) bring interdisciplinary approaches in the classroom. Thus, the majority of educators are planning to use the teaching and learning environment as well as the educational materials in their daily teaching in the future.

However, the achievement of their educational objectives and their relevance for the curriculum and beyond (e.g. through extra-curricular student clubs or summer camps) should be further improved and reflected in the refined versions of the Educational Scenarios. During the refinement phase, the authors of scenarios (i.e. iMuSciCA experts) will be supported by High School teachers and external experts. The authoring teams are encouraged to pay special attention to express more accurately the educational objectives of each Scenario. In addition, the language should be simplified, and the educational content should be better adapted to the specific age group of students. It was also recommended to follow an inquiry-based approach to teaching and learning more closely.

Finally, a highly diverse range of activity environments have been successfully integrated within individual Educational Scenarios and the workbench, both positively affecting the teachers' satisfaction in using the iMuSciCA service portfolio.

In general, students found the possibility to be working in a digital environment exciting. This is a well perceived change from the more classical, transmissive Educational Scenario involving student, teacher, pen, paper and blackboard.

The animations provide a good alternative for them to visualize certain properties compared to more traditional drawings, which in certain cases have limitations as they cannot show what is really happening. During students' Focus Groups it became clear that the general ideas and concepts of STEAM and IBSE were understood and perceived positively. Students were also able to explain in simple words scientific concepts as presented in the Educational Scenarios.

'Hands on materials' are still considered as a good complement to the proposed activities on the iMuSciCA workbench. They lift students' spirits and may serve as a wake-up call when their attention is dwindling. Whilst many instruments and experiments can be digitalised, having the actual item or performing the experiment in real life creates an alternative and complementary way of learning: the interaction with real instruments sometimes offers something that cannot be achieved by looking at an animation or digital performance only.

Overall, the iMuSciCA services and tools helped students to meet the objectives of the prescribed Educational Scenarios, while their interaction with both teachers and classmates was described as enjoyable and supportive.

7.5.3 Deeper Learning Approach for Learners

The iMuSciCA evaluation metrics was developed to collect "responsive" feedback from users (Youker 2005; Abma and Stake 2001), i.e. teachers and students, concerning the iMuSciCA's STEAM pedagogy, so that it can be further improved, along with the workbench, the scenarios and the lesson plans. In order to reach the desired results, the evaluation process focuses on the achievement of students' *deeper*

Table 7.5 Deeper learning competencies as used by iMuSciCA (adapted, based on National Research Council of USA)

Cognitive (thinking and reasoning)	**Interpersonal** (expressing information to others and interpreting others)	**Intrapersonal** (self-management to reach goals)
Thinking critically Mastering rigorous academic content	Working collaboratively Communicating effectively	Learning to learn Developing academic mindsets

learning competencies, as opposed to superficial or 'thin' learning (Jensen and Nickelsen 2008). In particular, iMuSciCA uses the deeper learning framework proposed by the Hewlett Foundation.[5] In view of the iMuSciCA evaluation methodology and for practical reasons, the Hewlett competencies were classified in the groups shown in Table 7.5.

According to the Hewlett Foundation, each of the above competencies includes a series of related outcomes which refer to what "graduate students from high school should be equipped to". As iMuSciCA does not deal with graduates, but with younger students (aged from 10 to 18), the evaluation framework focuses on a selection of these outcomes fitting this target group. The evaluation metrics have also been developed as follows.

Cognitive and interpersonal competencies

For the evaluation of these competences, the following tools were developed, which can be implemented after each lesson focusing on one iMuSciCA scenario:

i. Tools for observation including a set of criteria for teachers or external observers.
ii. Guiding questions to lead a students' focus group.
iii. A short summary report by teachers about the observation and the results of the focus group.
iv. For the cognitive part: Students' questionnaires in the form of a test, including a short self-evaluation by students on content knowledge: the results of the test can be compared to those of the self-evaluation.
v. For the interpersonal part: Students' reflection questionnaire with questions for students that are very similar to those for observers to make comparison possible.

Intrapersonal competencies

The evaluation tools for interpersonal competencies are applied as a pre- and post-questionnaire, before and after implementing a series of scenarios in a specific class (about 8 school hours). Tools similar to those described in points (i) to (iv) of intrapersonal competencies were developed. In addition, a specific students' motivation questionnaire was included, based on the 'Measurement of Motivation with Science Students' (Mubeen and Reid 2014).

[5] Source: Hewlett Foundation (https://www.hewlett.org/strategy/deeper-learning/).

7.6 Conclusion

In this Chapter, we present current developments of the iMuSciCA project, which proposes a combination of an innovative pedagogical framework and cutting-edge technologies integrated in a web-based workbench that is addressed to secondary school students to carry out STEAM learning activities. At the same time, it provides teachers with modular scenarios that can be adapted to the needs of their students. The overall approach involves a user-centred development of integrating cutting-edge technological tools in novel activity environments, innovative pedagogy, educational scenarios and lesson plans. Learners and teachers are actively involved in assessing the development of the various facets of iMuSciCA in an interactive way. In addition, the iMuSciCA evaluation framework includes the application of deeper learning competencies of students involved in the pilot testing.

The iMuSciCA workbench will be continuously updated with newer versions of the activity environments and core enabling technologies until the end of the project. Moreover, further pilot testing will take place in various settings in secondary schools in the three countries aiming at measuring the educational impact of iMuSciCA on students implementing specific educational scenarios. The final version of the iMuSciCA workbench will be publicly available to schools and educators. In addition, the iMuSciCA project will provide professional development material for teachers and educators for adopting innovative STEAM teaching methodology.

Acknowledgements The iMuSciCA project has received funding from the European Union's Horizon 2020 research and innovation programme under grant agreement No 731861.

References

Abma TA, Stake RE (2001) Stake's responsive evaluation: core ideas and evolution. New Dir Eval 92:7–22

Barnum CM (2011) Usability testing essentials: ready, set…test! Morgan Kaufmann of Elsevier Inc., USA. ISBN: 978-0-12-375092-1

Bartos SA, Lederman NG (2014) Teachers' knowledge structures for nature of science and scientific inquiry: conceptions and classroom practice. J Res Sci Teach 51(9):1150–1184

Bevan B, Gutwill JP, Petrich M, Wilkinson K (2015) Learning through STEM-rich tinkering: findings from a jointly negotiated research project taken up in practice. Sci Educ 99(1):98–120

Boucsein W (2012) Electrodermal activity. Springer Science & Business Media, USA. ISBN: 978-1-4614-1126-0

Chaouachi M, Jraidi I, Frasson C (2011) Modeling mental workload using EEG features for intelligent systems. In: Konstan JA et al. (eds) UMAP 2011. LNCS, vol 6787, pp. 51–61. Springer-Verlag

Costa VD, Rudebeck PH (2016) More than meets the eye: the relationship between pupil size and locus coeruleus activity. Neuron 89(1):8–10

Csikszentmihalyi M (2008) Implications of a systems perspective for the study of creativity. In: Steinberg RJ (ed) Handbook of creativity. Cambridge University Press, New York, NY, pp 313–335

Czerniak CM, Johnson CC (2007) Interdisciplinary science teaching. In: Handbook of research on science education, pp 537–559

Dougiamas M, Taylor PC (2003) Moodle: using learning communities to create an open source course management system. In: Proceedings of the EDMEDIA 2003 conference, Honolulu, HI
Dweck C (2000) Self-theories: their role in motivation, personality, and development (essays in social psychology). Psychology Press, Philadelphia, PA
Frans R, Clijmans L, De Smet E, Poncelet F, Tamassia L, Vyvey K (2013) Vakdidactiek Natuurwetenschappen
Fogarty R, Perkins D, Barell J (1992) How to teach for transfer. Skylight Publishing, Palatine, IL
Hélie T, Picasso C (2017) The Snail: a real-time software application to visualize sounds press. In: The proceedings of the 20th international conference on digital audio effects (DAFx-17), Edinburgh, UK, 5–9 September 2017
Honey M, Kanter DE (2013) Design, make, play: Growing the next generation of science innovators. In Honey M, Kanter DE (eds) Design. Make. Play. Growing the next generation of STEM innovators. New York, NY, Routledge, (pp. 1–6)
Honey M, Pearson G, Schweingruber H (eds) (2014) STEM integration in K-12 education: status, prospects, and an agenda for research. National Academies Press
Jensen E, Nickelsen L (2008) Deeper learning: 7 powerful strategies for in-depth and longer-lasting learning. Corwin Press
Kearney C (2016) Efforts to increase students' interest in pursuing mathematics, science and technology studies and careers, national measures taken by 30 Countries – 2015 Report, European Schoolnet, Brussels
Kim Y, Park N (2012a) Development and application of STEAM teaching model based on the Rube Goldberg's invention. Computer science and its applications. Springer, The Netherlands, pp 693–698
Kim Y, Park N (2012b) The effect of STEAM education on elementary school student's creativity improvement. Computer applications for security, control and system engineering. Springer, Berlin Heidelberg, pp 115–121
Kirschner PA (2001) Using integrated electronic environments for collaborative teaching/learning. Res Dialogue Learn Instr 2(1):1–10
Kirschner PA, Sweller J, Clark RE (2006) Why minimal guidance during instruction does not work: an analysis of the failure of constructivist, discovery, problem-based, experiential, and inquiry-based teaching. Educ Psychol 41(2):75–86
Lederman NG, Niess ML (1997) Editorial. School Sci Math 97(7):341–344
Martinez SL, Stager G (2013) Invent to learn: A guide to why making should be in every class. Constructing Modern Knowledge Press, Torrance, CA
Martinez B. Valstar MF (2016) Advances, challenges, and opportunities in automatic facial expression recognition. In: Advances in face detection and facial image analysis, pp 63–100
Matthews MR (1994) Science teaching: the role of history and philosophy of science. Psychology Press
Mubeen S, Reid N (2014) The measurement of motivation with science students. Eur J Educ Res 3(3):129–144
New Cabri authoring tool, (version 3) [Computer Software]. Grenoble, France, Cabrilog
Organization of Economic Cooperation and Development (2009) Creating effective teaching and learning environments: first results from TALIS. ISBN: 978-92-64-056
PISA (2012) Assessment and analytical framework: mathematics, reading, science, problem solving and financial literacy. OECD Publishing
PISA (2012) Results: what students know and can do—student performance in mathematics, reading and science (vol I, Revised edn, February 2014). PISA, OECD Publishing
Perkins DN (2010) Making learning whole: how seven principles of teaching can transform education. Jossey-Bass, San Francisco, CA
Perkins DN, Grotzer TA (2008) Dimensions of causal understanding: the role of complex causal models in students' understanding of science. Stud Sci Educ 41(1):117–165

Pedaste M, Mäeots, M, Siiman, LA, de Jong T, van Riesen SAN, Kamp ET, Manoli CC, Zacharia ZC, Tsourlidaki E (2015) Phases of inquiry-based learning: definitions and the inquiry cycle. Educ Res Rev 14:47–61

Quigley CF, Herro D, Jamil FM (2017) Developing a conceptual model of STEAM teaching practices. School Sci Math 117(1–2):1–12

Robinson K (2001) Mind the gap: the creative conundrum. Crit Q 43(1)

Ryan RM, Deci EL (2000) Self-determination theory and the facilitation of intrinsic motivation, social development, and well-being. Am Psychol 55(1):68

Saavedra AR, Opfer VD (2012) Learning 21st-century skills requires 21st-century teaching. Phi Delta Kappan 94(2):8–13

Salomon G, Perkins D (1989) Rocky roads to transfer: rethinking mechanism of a neglected phenomenon. Educ Psychol 24(2):113

Schwartz M, Fischer K (2006) Useful metaphors for tackling problems in teaching and learning. About Campus 11(1):2–9

Sternberg RJ (2006) The nature of creativity. Creat Res J 18(1):87–98

Tamassia L, Frans R (2014) Does integrated science education improve scientific literacy? J Eur Teach Educ Netw 9:131–141

Tiberghien A (2000) Designing teaching situations in the secondary school. In: Millar R, Leach J, Osborne J (eds) Improving science education: the contribution of research. Open University Press, Buckingham, UK, pp 27–47

Tillett J (2012) Project Tin can—the next generation of SCORM. Project Tin Can—The Next Generation of SCORM. Float Mobile Learning

Tsupros N, Kohler R, Hallinen J (2009) STEM education in Southwestern Pennsylvania: report of a project to identify the missing components. Center for stem education and Leonard Gelfand center, Carnegie Mellon University

Wagner T (2008) The global achievement gap: why even our best schools don't teach the new survival skills our children need—and what we can do about it. Basic Books, New York, NY

Workshop Summary Report, Workshop Education for innovation: the role of arts and STEM education, France, p 8. https://www.oecd.org/edu/ceri/48252279.pdf. Accessed on 23–24, 2011

Youker BW (2005) Ethnography and evaluation: their relationship and three anthropological models of evaluation. J Multidiscip Eval 2(3):113–142

Chapter 8
A Case Study of Peer Feedback as a Continuous Assessment Tool for Transversal Competencies

Mirjam Neelen, Evangelos Kapros and Eddie Walsh

Abstract This paper describes a mobile application that functions as a professional development tool by leveraging peer feedback in corporate environments. Specifically, the focus has been on feedback about specific events where a behaviour around transversal competencies was evident. The design of the application and the analytics made the attempt to emphasise the professional development dimension of peer feedback, as opposed to merely a quantitative performance management one, and the appropriate aggregation of any analytics so as to avoid any inappropriate employee "surveillance" effects. Moreover, the paper presents results of three trials with employees and line managers in corporate environments. The trials confirmed the hypothesis that our method and application would function positively in combination with or as an improvement upon traditional performance management methods and tools, such as annual performance reviews or 360° feedback, assuming there is feedback culture and institutional support in the organisation.

8.1 Introduction

Contemporary organisations are changing and becoming more agile to address modern business needs. As a consequence, employees are also affected and respond to this change, thus becoming at the same time a vehicle for change. Transversal competencies, such as communication and collaboration are critical to move across this fast-paced and continuously evolving work environment. This change is ongoing

M. Neelen
Accenture, Dublin, Ireland
e-mail: neelenm@gmail.com

E. Kapros (✉)
Science Gallery Dublin, Trinity College Dublin, Dublin, Ireland
e-mail: ekapros@tcd.ie

E. Walsh
Learnovate, Trinity Technology & Enterprise Campus, Dublin, Ireland
e-mail: eddie.walsh@learnovatecentre.org

E. Kapros and M. Koutsombogera (eds.), *Designing for the User Experience in Learning Systems*, Human–Computer Interaction Series,
https://doi.org/10.1007/978-3-319-94794-5_8

and has been perceived already in 1999, when it was understood that training would need to reflect these changes, in what was called "21st Century Skills for 21st Century Jobs" (Stuart 1999). While competency-based-education is not a new concept[1] (Spady 1977), the reappearance of the need to explore it has created opportunities to re-surface much desirable student-centred pedagogies (Rotherham and Willingham 2009).

Our industry partners[2] have expressed the challenge to capture and objectively assess, analyse, and visualise employees transversal competencies as performed on the job. Previous research has demonstrated that current approaches, such as talent and performance management systems—standalone or integrated into LMSs—and 360° feedback generally lead to insufficiently accurate data about day-to-day employee performance (Akram et al. 2014; Aguinis et al. 2012; Saba 2015).

Assessing transversal competencies is complex for many reasons. For example, in order to get accurate insight in these competencies, they need to be assessed through a process that is integrated in the natural workflow. Currently, that is commonly done through periodic self-rating and rating by others. One of the problems with rating is that it can be quite subjective. For example, a '3' on a 1–5 Likert scale, or labels such as 'Strongly Agree' or 'Seldom' are open to wide-ranging interpretations.

Transversal competencies are also particularly complex to assess because the behavioural elements are more prevalent than the concrete expertise elements and these are simply harder to assess as they are often more nebulous and prone to subjectivity.

In addition, supporting employees in the development of their transversal competencies is complex as well as they are difficult to acquire and change. One reason is that transversal competencies mean different things depending on the context (Robles 2012). Furthermore, Eraut (2004) points out that they cannot likely be learned in formal training settings.

We have designed, built, and evaluated a mobile application for peer feedback and analytics visualisations that try to address some of the above issues. The application was evaluated in various authentic workplace environments. The following sections of this paper describe the design process, the mobile application's functionality, and the evaluation as well as its results to date.

8.2 Design Considerations

8.2.1 Iterative Design Process

The design process was highly iterative, and we validated our design with approximately $n \approx 80$ participants in total. Various methods were used for validation,

---

[1]Papers from the 70s go so far as mapping U.S. efforts to capture competencies during the 20s and 30s back to the operationalisation of WWI (Callaghan 1962; Davies 1976; Neumann 1979).

[2]http://www.learnovatecentre.org/membership/our-members/.

depending on the stage of the design or development. Throughout the design and development process we iteratively ran two functional tests (with 6 and 20 participants respectively) and four focus groups (varying from 2 to 8 participants each).

The team[3] has also conducted research using the Q methodology to evaluate an early version of the prototype (with 6 participants). The statements in the Q-set were formed by designers' intentions, in this case by the authors. End-users test the application and rank the statements, according how well they think the statement is realised in the corresponding feature. Results show different points of view. This methodology helped the team to understand which features were best—and worst—implemented and why, and also which features were seen as more critical by users. These insights facilitated prioritisation in following design iterations.

We have set up several trials to evaluate our designs and hypotheses. One functional trial (to ensure that everything is technically ready for full trials) and two full trials have been conducted so far (with approx. 12 participants each). Since our trials include human participants, our team completed a Research Ethics Approval process with the School of Computer Science and Statistics in Trinity College, the University of Dublin.

Process aside, the design was additionally informed by the limitations described below.

8.2.2 Limitations

Some limitations were imposed to the app during the implementation phase due to technical issues. For instance, since this was the first version of the software application, we decided to limit ourselves to a mobile app; however, we do plan to better integrate the tool with employees' workflows in the future, either as a browser plugin, or as an extension to collaboration software. Similarly, in this first version of the project we offer no calendar or contact-list integration. While these limitations may reduce the usability of the app, we anticipate that they do not affect the validation of the concept by our end users for the purposes of our trials.

Moreover, the application to date allows for feedback to/from one person at a time, about one competency at a time. While this may seem limiting with regard to the functionality and usability of the app, as it is not possible to send a common piece of feedback to a group about a specific event, it helped the researchers to evaluate the basic premises of the app. Allowing for multiple people or events would affect the app design in various ways which are described in the following section.

Another limitation concerned various ethics considerations around feedback in the workplace. These considerations are twofold: on the one hand the existence of the phenomenon of the "toxic worker" (Housman and Minor 2015) who may use peer feedback opportunities to harm rather than improve their workplace, and the use

[3]The Q methodology team consisted of Stéphanie Gauttier in addition to the authors.

of performance management as "surveillance" by abusive powerful roles within the organisation (Ajunwa et al. 2017). A feedback app could potentially facilitate such behaviours.

The following section describes design decisions which were made in response to the considerations in this and the previous section.

8.2.3 Design Decisions

The first main design decision that was made was to design and build our peer feedback professional development tool as a mobile software application (mobile app). While mobile phones are not always integrated in workplace workflows, they are practically ubiquitous in organisations where workers would typically undertake a periodic performance review or a 360° feedback process.

The app has two main user interaction paths: (a) send/receive feedback (unsolicited), (b) send/receive requests for feedback (solicited). In addition, it offers a view to analytics around the feedback.

Unolicited Feedback:

In what is the most straightforward usage scenario of the app, a peer should be able to send a piece of feedback to another peer.

To keep feedback actionable, it should be specific and timely, so the design decision was made that the peers should give feedback about a specific event to another peer. The recipient can acknowledge they received feedback or reply with another piece of feedback, but we avoided notes, comments, or any other type of bi-directional annotation of the feedback, as this feature might result in non-productive discussions around semantics rather than actual feedback. While there is room for discussion about semantics, there is no reason why our feedback app is a more appropriate place for such discussions than traditional organisational communications channels.

Solicited Feedback:

Moreover, a peer has to be able to request a piece of feedback from another peer. As above, in order to allow for actionable feedback, the requests are sent to a specific peer, and are about a specific event. In this version of our design, requests do not have a time-out window and can be acted upon anytime. Also, all requests are received and can be acted upon or not, but no ignoring mechanism is put in place either for an individual request or a sender.

Competencies Analytics:

The feedback generated from the app is mapped by the peers with specific behavioural statements. To date we use anchors related to UC Berkeley Core Competencies.[4] We have fully deployed 5 Competencies and the corresponding behaviours and anchor statements, but in principle any equivalent framework could be used in our design.

[4]http://hr.berkeley.edu/development/learning/uc-berkeley-competencies.

Moreover, a different set of aggregated feedback analytics are visualised for team leads and managers; there is no requirement that these be in the mobile app: in our case, we developed a web-based application for these other roles. These roles do not have access to the peer feedback text itself, but they do have access to the competencies, behaviours, and anchor statements around said feedback.

Social Messaging Settings:

In this version of the app we decided to exclude features such as blocking all feedback from a specific peer, or sending a piece of feedback anonymously. Our intention was to allow for accountability for and ownership of the sent feedback, and also observe if the social network of the feedback senders and receivers will isolate some individuals who may have been "toxic" in their feedback.

8.3 The Peer Feedback App

8.3.1 Use Within an Organisation

Our mobile peer feedback app facilitates an agile peer feedback process that allows for continuous formative peer assessment of transversal competencies based on near to real time on-the-job performance.

The process fits into current workflows and supports more evidential feedback methods to reduce subjectivity in the data. This is achieved through a *flipped competency capture* process where one can map feedback about day-to-day activities to behaviours, which are then mapped to competencies. The app uses *behavioural anchors* instead of more subjective ratings, ensuring more objective peer assessment (see e.g. Table 8.1). More truthful data on transversal competencies are not only helpful for employees but also delivers more accurate data to organisations. Through the feedback, competency data is captured regularly, analysed and visualised and gives relevant, timely, and actionable insights to the employee (see Fig. 8.1).

Our mobile peer feedback app truly supports *informal social learning*, critical in todays agile workplace. It also acknowledges that this type of learning is highly contextualised (Tynjälä 2008; Eraut 2004; Eraut and Hirsh 2007) as the feedback is

Table 8.1 Example of triads 'Competency-Behaviour-Anchor Statement' for a specific behaviour (sharing information with others). These triads help describe behaviours objectively and can thus improve feedback

Competency	Behaviour	Anchor statement
Communication	Sharing information with others	Shared accurate, timely information with appropriate colleagues in the right format
Communication	Sharing information with others	Did not share information with others when needed, which often created problems with the team

Fig. 8.1 High level use case diagram of the mobile peer feedback app. Employees, depicted in a circle, use the mobile app, which sends data to an analytics platform. The analytics platform offers output at different levels of granularity, so as to offer aggregate context to an, e.g., manager, while protecting the personal feedback of individual employees

always event-based; for example it can be based on a meeting or presentation that just took place.

Peers can request feedback from and offer feedback to each other. The in-app feedback process acknowledges the many ways employees might (want to) develop their competencies. For example, they might want to focus on certain competencies for a certain period of time and request very focussed feedback on those. On the other hand, they might have strengths or weaknesses that they are not aware of. Peers can offer feedback at their own initiative to increase that awareness.

Peers explain what their team member did well or could improve in a free text field. This makes feedback more concrete and transparent. It supports an open learning culture. The app also includes a *scaffolding model* to support effective feedback. After all, feedback needs to be done 'right' to help someone learn and improve (Hattie and Timperley 2007).

8.3.2 Benefits for Organisations

We have concluded thus far that a mobile peer feedback app used within functional and/or cross-functional teams supports employee transversal competency assessment and development and provides accurate business performance analytics.

A mobile peer feedback app recognises the social significance of learning from your peers in the workplace (Eraut 2004). That is provided that an organisation supports an open feedback culture and allows the individual employee to own their feedback data so that they will be more open to improving their performance. This is a critical assumption for our trials.

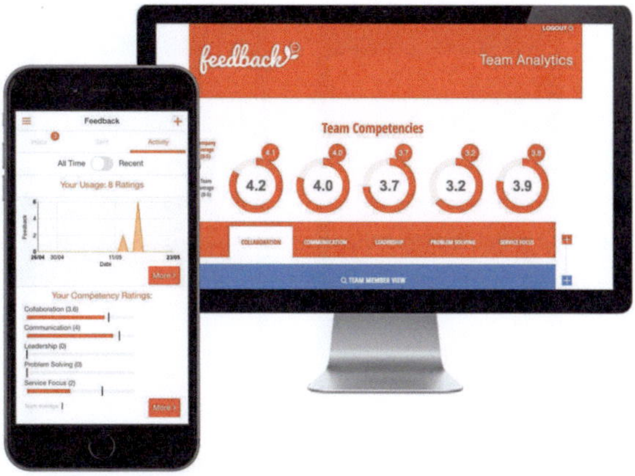

Fig. 8.2 Analytics are tailored for each user type. The emphasis on usage statistics is intended to help the users focus on the context of their received feedback and, thus, on professional development, rather than on quantifying the results

Because this is not just about the individual's transversal competency assessment and development but also about business performance analytics, we have identified three user types with different needs. They will therefore receive different types of analytics (Fig. 8.2).

Employees need to be able to improve their performance based on peer feedback. Therefore, they need detailed insights into the feedback they receive with regards to their behaviours. **Team leads** need to be able to act on identified competency gaps within their team and therefore need analytics on their team's competencies. The **business unit owner** (e.g. HR) needs to see organisational competency patterns and gaps.

The app also offers analytics to support conversations, for example between team members and their team lead. Because the feedback is highly contextualised, there should never be a focus on 'numbers' only.

The quantity and quality of the data is increased by flipping competency capturing (feedback about day-to-day events or activities is mapped to behaviours, behaviours are mapped to competencies) which reduces subjectivity and acknowledges the context dependent nature of feedback. The app, within the limitations described in previous sections, wishes to deliver high quality UX/UI to support more continuous use as well as an in-app scaffolding model to support effective feedback. This model, as well as the open and transparent feedback process support an open learning culture (Fig. 8.3).

8.4 Impact and Results

Participants from the trials have completed a pre-trial survey, and we also conducted post-trial semi-structured interviews (4 team members, 4 team leads) with the completed-trial organisations. Preliminary findings around the impact of using

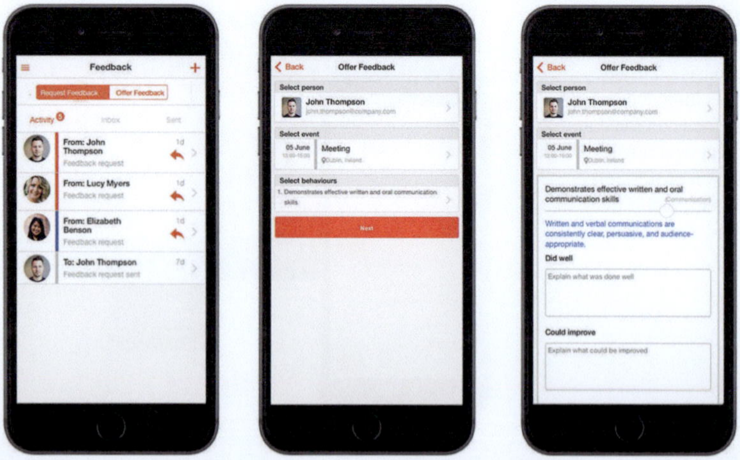

Fig. 8.3 Screenshot of the feedback app. The users select one person to give feedback to, about a specific event, and then they select an anchor statement that describes the behaviour through a slider UI component. Finally, through the open text the users can describe the behaviour, either positively or constructively. Scaffolded helpful information can assist users with how to give useful feedback

the Feedback app were positive and favourable in regards to the design premise. More specific initial results on learning and performance improvement and feedback perception are outlined below.

8.4.1 Pre-trial

8.4.1.1 Learning and Performance Improvement

In the pre-trial surveys the majority of team members (2 different organisations) indicate that the current performance review process does not help them to understand their strengths and weaknesses. One of the team leads in the post-trial interview confirms this. He indicates that current performance reviews are basically salary reviews; there is no support for professional development or performance improvement. Both team leads see the feedback app as an opportunity to move from task- and results-oriented feedback to behaviour-focussed feedback. They believe that the app can function as a catalyst for conversations between peers on their competencies and that it will be an enabler for having accurate and focussed discussions on professional development opportunities. However, all interviewees interpret the feedback app more as a performance review tool than as a learning and development tool.

8.4.1.2 Feedback Perception

Both pre-trial surveys indicate that the current feedback process is perceived as unstructured and team members do not give each other focussed feedback. The majority of team members indicate that they feel capable giving peers feedback and almost everyone likes receiving it. All interviewees strongly felt that the feedback app would work in their culture of speaking up and helping each other. They also said that the app is very quick and easy to use so it will not distract for day-to-day activities. They indicated that the structure of the app made it easy to use and made them feel more comfortable giving the feedback.

The pre-trial surveys to the 3 participating organisations are presented below. Out of the 33 collected responses 32 were complete sets and were used in the analysis. A summarisation visualisation can be seen at Fig. 8.4 and a correlation matrix of the responses at Fig. 8.5.

The summary of the survey results clearly demonstrates a dissatisfaction with current feedback practices. Participants felt that in their organisations they either do not have a feedback process, or it is not very structured. In addition, the responses indicated that feedback is sparsely sought or given. However, the participants claimed to be capable of giving feedback to their peers, and even claimed that they would *like* to do so.

Concerning the correlations between the answers, the following were observed. The Pearson Coefficient r was calculated for the survey $(df = 30, \alpha = 0.5 : r = 0.349, \alpha = 0.1 : r = 0.449)$ and statistically significant results were found for some pairs of questions. Specifically, the questions about the sentiment towards the existing processes present a statistically significant positive correlation, as do the ones about the comfort, capability, and desire to give/receive feedback.

There is a statistically significant negative correlation in the questions regarding the frequency of feedback as opposed to either the rating of the current processes, the

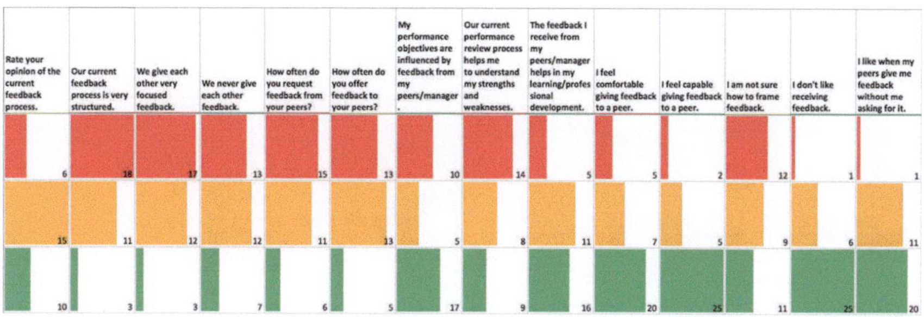

Fig. 8.4 Survey responses for all 3 organisations. Answers are on a Likert scale 1–5 where 1 are negative answers and 5 are positive answers. Here they are grouped into *negative*, *neutral*, and *positive* responses (top, middle, and bottom row, respectively). Positive answers here sometimes differ to *yes*, as in the negatively phrased question *I do not like receiving feedback* we take the positive answer to be *I like receiving feedback*. One can observe dissatisfaction with current feedback practices

	C	D	E	F	G	H	I	J	K	L	M	N	O	P
	Rate your opinion of the current feedback process.	Our current feedback process is very structured.	We give each other very focused feedback.	We never give each other feedback.	How often do you request feedback from your peers?	How often do you offer feedback to your peers?	My performance objectives are influenced by feedback from my peers/manager.	Our current performance review process helps me to understand my strengths and weaknesses.	The feedback I receive from my peers/manager helps in my learning/profes sional development.	I feel comfortable giving feedback to a peer.	I feel capable giving feedback to a peer.	I am not sure how to frame feedback.	I don't like receiving feedback.	I like when my peers give me feedback without me asking for it.
C to everything		0.544013515	0.605144513	-0.364527475	0.181957449	0.0020536	0.113496667	0.520303025	0.230184221	-0.004132373	-0.158647728	-0.054181233	-0.257147817	-0.436974793
D to everything	0.544013515		0.390574604	-0.111623533	-0.075878215	-0.261585081	0.333014767	0.434079068	0.139033524	-0.250504791	-0.348865163	-0.305309711	-0.260141073	-0.265522445
E	0.605144513	0.390574604		-0.409379326	0.441187515	0.229426139	0.216109104	0.272169959	0.181959705	0.035624362	-0.160759927	0.031509198	-0.142373699	-0.231433792
F	-0.364527475	-0.111623533	-0.409379326		-0.358180191	-0.320227444	-0.213793248	-0.242951776	-0.21841189	-0.444578954	-0.120047436	-0.057032375	0.040689423	-0.106135133
G	0.181957449	-0.075878215	0.441187515	-0.358180191		0.587692091	-0.093657123	-0.164918189	-0.331201477	0.341370048	0.03371127	0.374765448	0.143970762	-0.123623756
H	0.0020536	-0.261585081	0.229426139	-0.320227444	0.587692091		-0.173490197	-0.015437779	-0.025649459	0.3869726	0.233293458	0.10681593	0.051430285	0.203235695
I	0.113496667	0.333014767	0.216109104	-0.213793248	-0.093657123	-0.173490197		0.21158318	0.314867511	-0.059892319	0.059328106	-0.321719121	-0.017514236	-0.07349245
J	0.520303025	0.434079068	0.272169959	-0.242951776	-0.164918189	-0.015437779	0.21158318		0.446390939	0.084565252	-0.086894125	-0.226279542	-0.189884706	-0.221051208
K	0.230184221	0.139033524	0.181959705	-0.21841189	-0.331201477	-0.025649459	0.314867511	0.446390939		0.161670831	0.304911	-0.183851168	0.063902148	0.113538163
L	-0.004132373	-0.250504791	0.035624362	-0.444578954	0.341370048	0.3869726	-0.059892319	0.084565252	0.161670831		0.672149206	0.219967463	0.562988918	0.461126939
M	-0.158647728	-0.348865163	-0.160759927	-0.120047436	0.03371127	0.233293458	0.059328106	-0.086894125	0.304911	0.672149206		0.175328767	0.519040446	0.430637854
N	-0.054181233	-0.305309711	0.031509198	-0.057032375	0.374765448	0.10681593	-0.321719121	-0.226279542	-0.183851168	0.219967463	0.175328767		0.202870556	0.106670987
O	-0.257147817	-0.260141073	-0.142373699	0.040689423	0.143970762	0.051430285	-0.017514236	-0.189884706	0.063902148	0.562988918	0.519040446	0.202870556		0.652105174
P	-0.436974793	-0.265522445	-0.231433792	-0.106135133	-0.123623756	0.203235695	-0.07349245	-0.221051208	0.113538163	0.461126939	0.430637854	0.106670987	0.652105174	

Fig. 8.5 Survey response correlations for all organisations. Answers are on a Likert scale 1–5 where 1 are negative answers and 5 are positive answers. Statistically significant values of the Pearson Coefficient r are highlighted $(df = 30, \alpha = 0.5 : r = 0.349)$

focus of feedback, or the comfort in giving feedback. Moreover, the pair of questions regarding the opinion of the current process and liking unsolicited feedback similarly demonstrates a statistically significant negative correlation.

Apart from the correlation matrix for all the participants, individual matrices for each organisation were calculated (see Fig. 8.6). The organisation matrices yielded different patters than the overall matrix, notwithstanding their similarities as they contributed to the latter.

From these matrices one can clearly see that especially the bottom-right matrix is quite different in the correlations at replying the survey questions. The difference in correlation patterns, especially for this organisation is a clear indicator for **cultural**

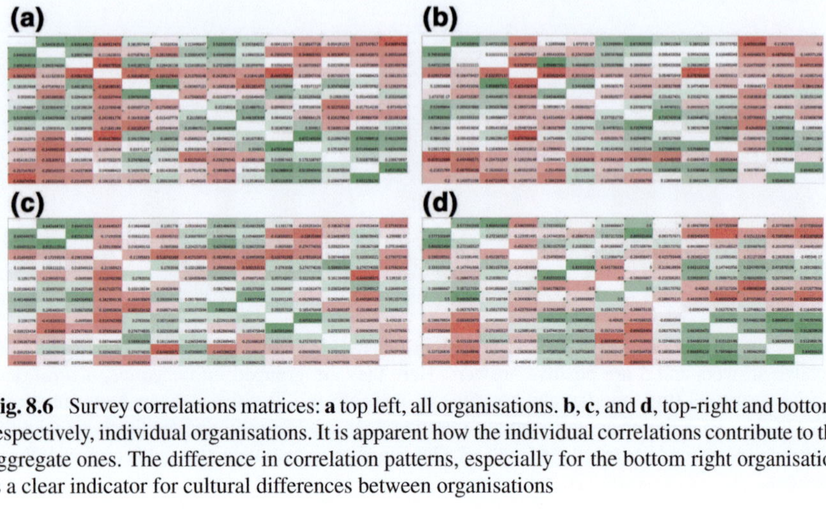

Fig. 8.6 Survey correlations matrices: **a** top left, all organisations. **b**, **c**, and **d**, top-right and bottom, respectively, individual organisations. It is apparent how the individual correlations contribute to the aggregate ones. The difference in correlation patterns, especially for the bottom right organisation is a clear indicator for cultural differences between organisations

differences between organisations with regard to how they understand and treat feedback.

8.4.1.3 Envisaged Impact by Industry

We have asked our trial partners to share their vision on the envisaged impact of the peer feedback app on individual employees, organisational performance, and the learning culture.

— *What impact do you expect the mobile peer feedback app to have for individual employees?*

> We want to move from results-oriented feedback to behaviour-focussed feedback so that we can have accurate conversations about performance. (*Team Lead 1*)

> We think this app can help create an open and honest feedback culture, which can increase an individual employee's learning. (*Team Lead 2*)

— *What impact do you expect the mobile peer feedback app to have for organisational performance?*

> Instead of doing performance reviews that don't usually offer true data, you can spend less time on this app and get more accurate data. Win-win. (*Team Lead 1*)

> Using the feedback app, we expect to improve team communication, collaboration, and build leadership skills – all of which are essential in a fast-paced agile environment. (*Team Lead 2*)

— *How do you envision that the mobile peer feedback app will help to create or enhance the overall learning culture?*

> The continuous and seamless nature of the app will help the learning culture without putting strain on individuals. (*Team Lead 1*)

> With this app, we will have an implicit focus on professional development which will help us to have a learning culture without spending the time explicitly. (*Team Lead 2*)

8.4.2 Full Trials

Our full trials were conducted in authentic business environments, and lasted from 24 to 66 days, depending on the organisation. In addition to research on the app usability, the trials intend to determine temporal or usage patterns, or networking effects throughout the usage of the app. Furthermore, we want to explore if the app helps to gain more insight in behaviours/competencies and can support performance improvement. Last but not least, we research if team members perceptions on giving and receiving feedback change over time when they regularly use the feedback app.

We use a combination of qualitative (pre-trial competency assessment; pre-trial/post-trial surveys; and post-trial interviews) and quantitative (in-app usage) data methods to ensure a complete capturing of various aspects of the app usage.

8.4.2.1 Usage and Usability

The usage activity from trial 1 has shown that the team of 11 participants generated 89 items of feedback during the 66 working days, while trial 2 of 10 participants generated 19 items of feedback in 24 working days ($average_1 = 1.35$ and $average_2 = 0.8$, respectively; total $average = 1.2$ feedback items per day).

The breakdown of individual users show a wide distribution of activity between different team members. The 3 most active users sent 15–20 items of feedback, averaging approximately 1–2 times a week which is a significant increase of feedback frequency. The 3 least active users sent 6 or fewer items of feedback. As this was a trial in a real-world business setting, there was some change in roles and personnel within the team which will likely account for some of the least active users.

The overall amount of text feedback was weighted significantly in favour of positive over constructive with 56 positive statements and 10 constructive statements. The popularity of the competencies was as follows: *Communication*: 35.71%, *Collaboration*: 22.22%, *Problem Solving*: 19.84%, *Leadership*: 12.7%, *Service Focus*: 9.52%. With regard to the UC Berkeley anchors, even though they do not directly represent a progression on a scale, for the sake of simplicity we have coded them with values from 1 to 5; their usage popularity within the app was: $anchor_4$: 58.73%, $anchor_5$: 24.6%, $anchor_3$: 14.29%, $anchor_1$: 1.59%, and $anchor_2$: 0.79%.

Concerning usability, the team-lead analytics dashboard's SUPR-Q (Sauro 2015) score[5] is 78.5%, and the scores for the attributes represented by clusters of questions are: Usability 77.5%, Credibility 70%, Appearance 80% (Loyalty is out of scope in this context of a short-term trial). The SUS score for the app is 69.7, which, according to the adjective scale described in Bangor et al. (2009), is characterised as 'Good'.

8.4.2.2 Social Network Analysis

This usage was analysed with regard to its distribution and density per user. Since this is a peer-feedback tool, the first way this analysis was conducted was by analysing the networks that were formed when giving and receiving feedback. The density is 0.29, and the average clustering coefficient is 0.318, showing that the participant connections percentage and extent of interactions is approximately 1 out of every 3 possible interactions.

Three main findings can be reported from the network analysis. First, despite the small sample, there seems to be a clustering effect. Apart from the clustering coefficient value of 0.318 which, given that it is the global variable, shows a fair amount of clustering, one can see in Fig. 8.7 the existence of clusters. These can be either completely separate sub-groups, such as in the organisation labelled *team*3, or clusters that have no immediate neighbours, but are eventually separated after a

[5]As SUPR-Q is a percentile scoring system, these scores mean that the score is higher than the 78.5% of the benchmarked websites at Sauro (2015).

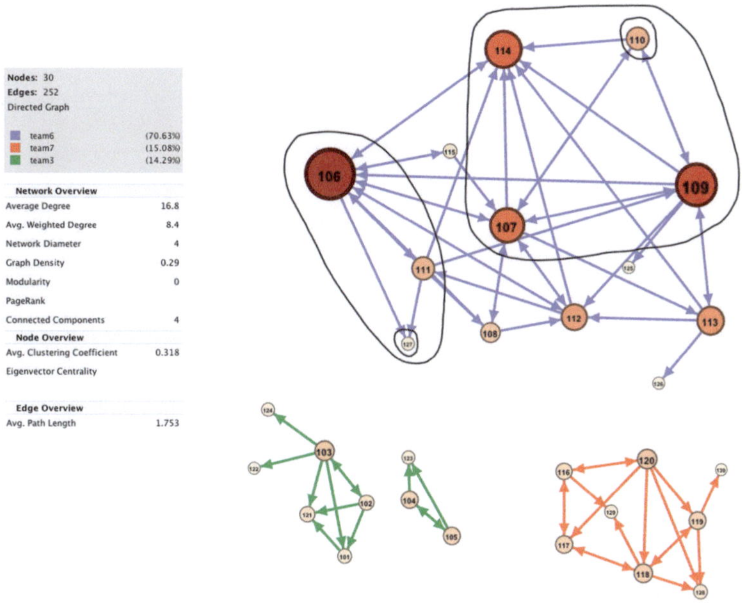

Fig. 8.7 Network analysis diagram of the mobile peer feedback app. Node size/colour show the degree. Even though the sample size was quite small, team6 and team3 formed clans, either strong ones in team3 or looser ones in team6 (i.e., nodes 110 and 127 have no common direct neighbours)

degree of edge traversals. An example of the latter behaviour is the formation of separate groups with no immediate neighbours for nodes 110 and 127 in *team*6 (sub-groups circled in black in Fig. 8.7). This is a significant finding given that this is a peer feedback tool, therefore edge transversal does not necessarily imply carrying information: i.e., nodes 106 and 109 independently communicate with 107, but not necessarily about the same behaviour or attribute; in addition, these communications do not help node 110 and 127 to independently communicate.

Secondly, despite the popularity of some competencies against others, individual users can be seen to express different preferences in how they gave or requested feedback. Some focused on only a few competencies, while others had a more diverse range of feedback giving. For example, in Fig. 8.8 node 106 can be seen to have focused on only two competencies, while 107 on all of them. Similarly, 108 and 110 demonstrate the respective behaviours, thus showing that the diversity in behaviour is not specific to nodes with either high or low degree.

Finally, the same can be said about the anchor selections. Individual preference seems to be the main factor in the selection of anchor statements when giving feedback.

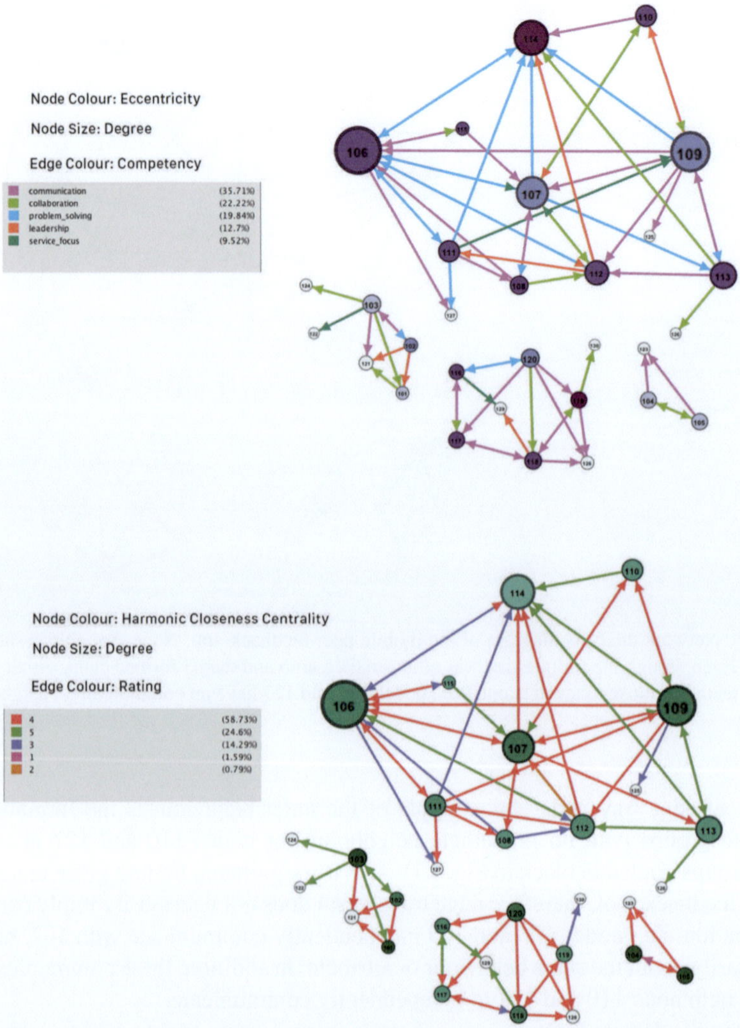

Fig. 8.8 Network diagram for different metrics of the mobile peer feedback app. Personal preference seems to affect the selection of competencies and anchor statements

8.4.2.3 Post-trial Surveys

The participants in trial 1 were asked to complete a survey post-trial. Due to some change in the composition of the team during the course of the trial, 7 responses were gathered from the participants. As shown in Fig. 8.10, the majority of the participants had a good opinion of the feedback process delivered in the app. In the pre-trial survey shown in Fig. 8.9, the trial 1 participants expressed an equal number of Poor, Fair and Good responses with regard to their current feedback process. In general, the app's approach was received better than any current approach to feedback and the

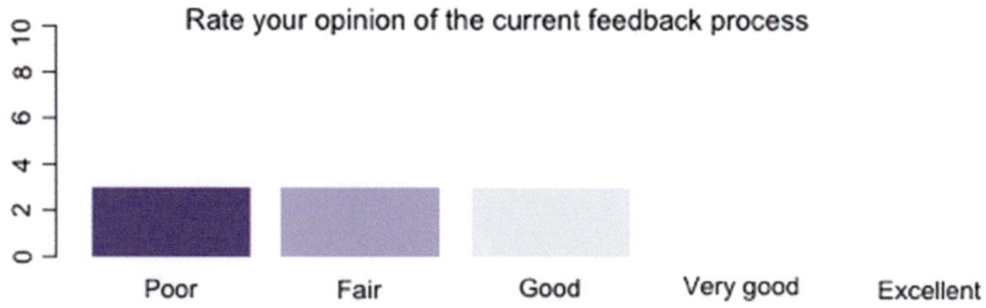

Fig. 8.9 Pre-trial

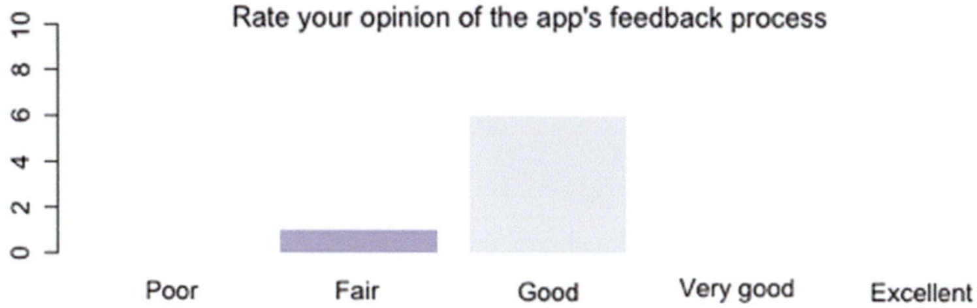

Fig. 8.10 Post-trial

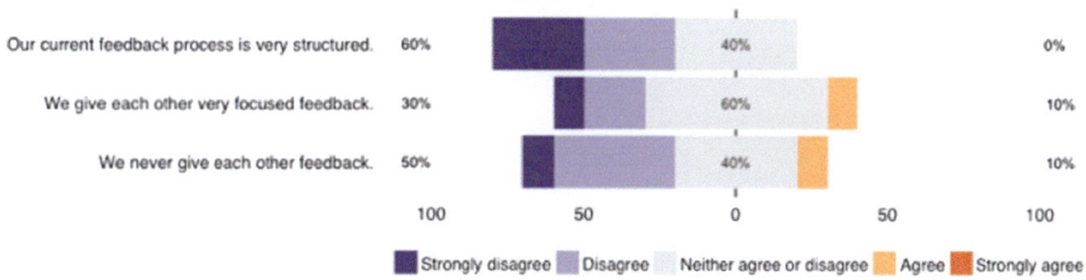

Fig. 8.11 Pre-trial

participants responded well to the new, unfamiliar concept of continuous, event-based feedback.

Figure 8.12 shows that participants agreed that app allows them to give more structured, focused feedback. Again, when examining the similar pre-trial questions shown Fig. 8.11, there were more neutral and negative responses with regard to structured and focused feedback in their existing processes (Fig. 8.13).

Figure 8.14 shows the participants were unsure if the app helped with their performance objectives or learning and development. There could be several reasons for this. The trial ran for a relatively short timeframe in the context of setting learning and performance objectives which are typically more long-term. Also, as expressed by the participants in the surveys and interviews, there was a lack of existing support framework for this within the trial company. At present, the app does not explicitly support the setting of organisational learning and performance objectives. More structured support for allowing team members and managers to define objectives

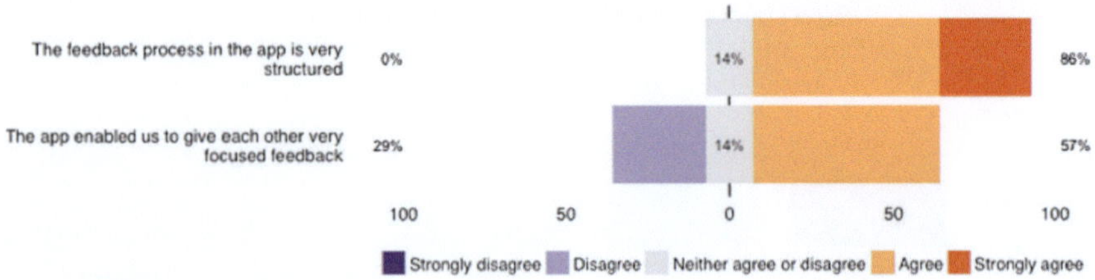

Fig. 8.12 Post-trial

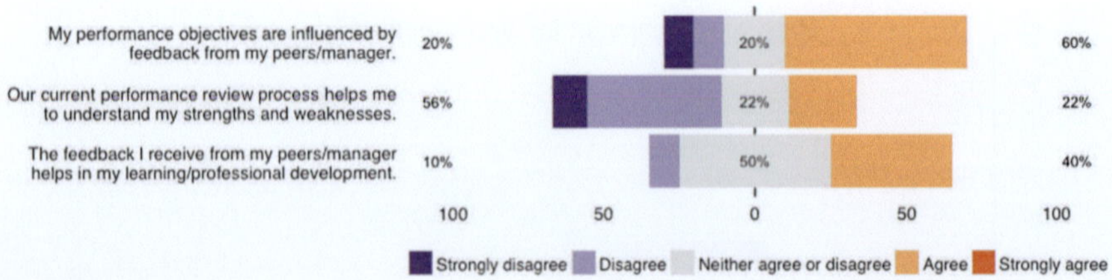

Fig. 8.13 Pre-trial

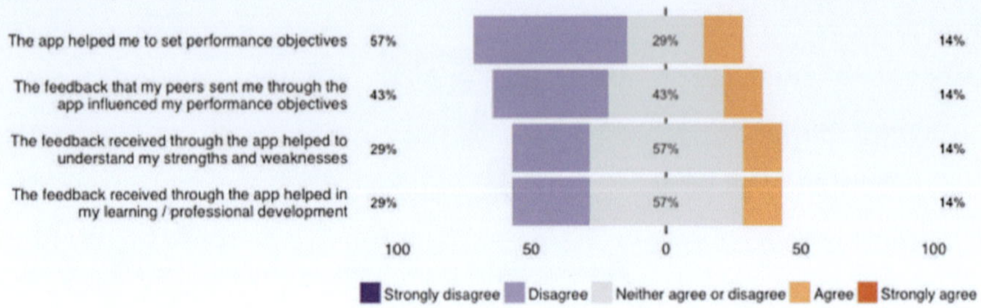

Fig. 8.14 Post-trial

could potentially help with giving the users more support and guidance in these areas.

The participants' general perception of giving and receiving feedback remained largely positive post-trial. In the pre-trial survey, participants expressed positive sentiment regarding feedback however, this was largely based on infrequent feedback given in face-to-face, informal interactions. For many, the usage of the app was a major change to a documented, continuous peer-to-peer feedback process. That largely positive responses were recorded post-trial suggests that this method did not impact on the participants' willingness to give and receive feedback on a regular basis. When comparing Figs. 8.15 and 8.16, it shows that participants seemed to be more aware if they are capable of giving feedback after using the app during the trial than before using it.

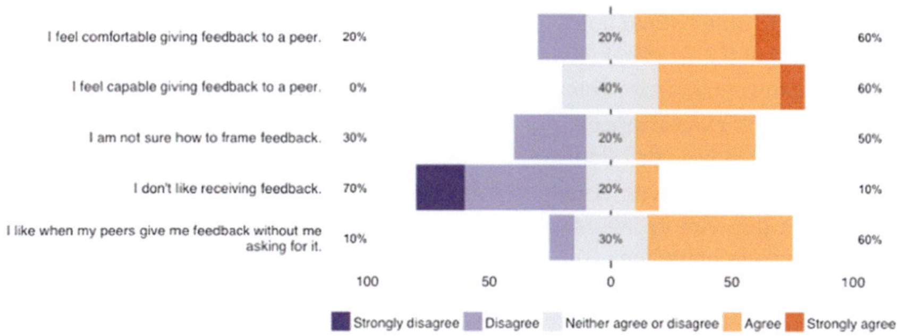

Fig. 8.15 Pre-trial

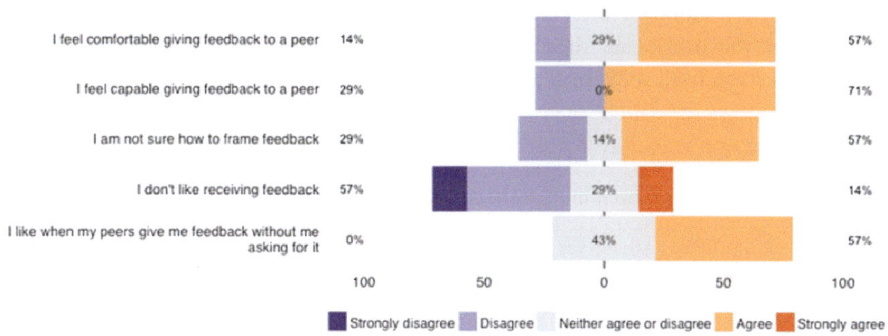

Fig. 8.16 Post-trial

8.4.2.4 Text Analysis

With regard to the actual open text of the feedback, the following were observed. The feedback consists of 1379 words in 64 sentences, with an average of 12.7 words per sentence. It consists of 12% passive sentences, and it has an overall Flesch Reading Ease of 54.5 (out of 100), and a Flesch-Kincaid Grade Level of 8.8, which indicates that a ninth-grader should understand the text.

With regard to following the examples about how to give feedback, some did, i.e.:

— Positive Feedback:

> You provided a lot of details through each stories which was great info for the team.

— Constructive Feedback:

> You were going fairly fast and maybe allow a pause time for the listener to be able to digest the information you provided.

While others did not:

— Positive Feedback:

> Open badges integration.

The latter comment did not follow the examples, as beyond giving a status update on an item that the feedback giver appreciated, the nature of this appreciation is not explained, thus making it unclear to the feedback recipient if it was positive that the said integration even happened, or if it was masterfully executed, or if it was the process of it that was well done as opposed to just the final artefact.

This ambivalence with regard to following the examples could be related to a playfulness that can be observed when using the feedback tool, as there were 7 occasions where emoticons (such as :-)) where used to display emotions.

8.4.2.5 After-Trial Interviews

The team also conducted interviews in all 3 organisations that participated in the pre-trial and the trial, after these were terminated. Interviews were taken from 8 individuals, from both roles of team member and team lead.

The interviews identified several common threads across teams and organisations. Overall the app was usable and many users commented on it as being intuitive:

— the whole layout and everything makes a lot of sense to me I mean it is very intuitive

— Easy enough to use - sliders very handy - picking the actual things you are giving feedback on or asking for feedback on different criteria like comms collab and all those; clear enough

However, due to limitations of resources and as this is a trial software for a research project, there were also limitations, especially with having a mobile-only implementation:

— mobile device is not the easiest thing to be jotting down long paragraphs on

— Asking contract engineers or employees…to implement and install applications on their own private hardware, that did come up…with more than one individual.

Concerning the actual feedback within the app, some indicative comments from the interviews were as follows:

— Managers need to be trained in soft skills so that they know better how to give feedback. We are not prepared for some aspects of our role.

— because of the behaviours you are not going to be overly hurtful or critical. You know, you do not feel like you are abusing somebody by giving feedback. It is constructive, so. There is nothing really stopping you in that regard.

With regard to how the tool compares to a traditional performance review, there was also a variety in responses:

— I really think people would benefit from it (feedback app), because we do not sit down and talk about behaviour, and the annual review is not about behaviour, it is task driven.

— So in terms of, was it evaluating me, I am not so sure, not within the trial period. I would not have felt that so much.

— Not just the annual appraisals that it feeds into. In general you would have your set team 1-to-1s, weekly, bi-weekly or monthly, different teams do it differently. Those bits of information are also very useful for a manger of a resource going into those.

Finally, about the relation to professional development:

— People saw value in learning competencies/skills, got team members learning that what they do relates to competencies/skills, helps me to change my language when I talk to my team about these things, do not think it was used to drive behaviour change

— Originally, it was to look at finding out which area I need to improve on but, with my ego talking, to tell other people what they are not doing right. It can be weapon as much as a tool for growth depending on the frame of mind you are at at the time. None of us went back and asked questions about feedback, it was I have to do this, just tick the box and I've done it. I gave a little bit of feedback about what went well but it was not really taken on board.

8.5 Discussion

Overall, the results presented above indicate an ambiguity around using feedback in an organisation: on the one hand some responses demonstrated great variation, but on the other hand some patterns do exist in replies and behaviours.

Firstly, the design of the app did not seem to affect the outcome of the trial, as the interviewees found it in general intuitive and the usability score it received was high. Therefore, despite the fact that some users were reluctant to install it on their mobile device (which was a known limitation of the trial as opposed to oversight), the ones who did install it did not report any serious issues.

Moreover, the usage was satisfactory, as there was more than one feedback item per day on average, and the reading level was adequate. This shows that the users were committed to this usage and did not take the tool lightly.

From the social network analysis and the interviews it can be seen that managers may require support in successfully setting up teams for feedback, as they often operate in an organisation with little to no prior feedback culture, and thus they may fail to motivate the team to use the tool, or strong clans may develop. However, the formation of clans in the network cannot be considered an outright negative outcome, as it may be the case that some teams are structured in a way that facilitates it. Moreover, the existence of clans is enhanced by our design decision to be able to give feedback to only one person at a time.

Having said that, the managers may not be the only ones who need support, as the team members often linked the current inadequate, in their opinion, feedback processes to their inability to effectively give feedback. A drop in the perceived comfort in and capability of giving feedback is noted between the pre-trial and after-trial periods. This is not to say that the app had a negative effect in feedback-giving, but rather that it increased awareness around peer rating and feedback as a vehicle for both performance management and professional development.

Finally, the diversity of opinion in the interviews and of behaviours in the social network analysis can be attributed to the lack of a unified organisational culture on these matters, a lack which allows for individual differences to flourish. This view is enhanced by the otherwise strong correlations we see in the survey results, where several statistically significant relations appear, despite the small sample. If the individual differences were not related to organisational culture, then they would have most likely also prevailed at the survey, and the identification of cultural patterns per organisation would have been impossible.

Thus, it is with the combination of the above points that it seems evident that (a) feedback can potentially support the performance management and professional development needs of an organisation, (b) but only given the appropriate institutional support, in both *cultivating and encouraging a feedback culture* overall and *supporting individuals in their learning and performance paths*, either as team members or as managers.

8.6 Conclusions

Modern organisations are becoming more agile to address modern business needs. To be able to move across this continuously evolving work environment, employees need to develop and apply their transversal competencies more intentionally and effectively. Employees need regular and contextualised insights into their strengths and weaknesses so that they can track their competency development on an ongoing basis. Employee competency analytics are also critical for managers in order to improve performance and facilitate a culture of learning and development within their teams. This paper has explored some of the challenges of assessing transversal competencies in the workplace. Transversal competencies are particularly complex to assess because behavioural elements are more prevalent than expertise elements and these are often more nebulous and prone to subjectivity. Currently, the most common approach to assessing transversal competencies is through ratings in performance management systems, for example through 360° feedback. However, these approaches are often infrequent and lead to ad-hoc, decontextualised, and subjective evidence of an employee's transversal competency proficiency levels.

In exploring these issues, this paper has presented a novel approach to assessing transversal competencies through event-based, continuous peer feedback. The feedback process supports more evidential feedback methods by using behavioural anchors to reduce subjectivity in the data. The approach also allows for subjective free text feedback, which is supported by a scaffolding model to facilitate effective feedback. Through the peer feedback, competency data is captured regularly, analysed and visualised to provide regular insights into abilities and performance for team members and team managers. The paper has demonstrated how this approach has been implemented and trialled in real-world settings with existing teams in multiple companies and presented the findings from this evaluation.

The results demonstrate that team members and team managers alike perceive continuous peer feedback as an improvement upon existing performance management methods. However, interestingly they do not necessarily perceive the app as a performance improvement or learning tool. However, the results of this case study indicate that there are conditions under which this approach functions successfully, and these lie within the organisation itself as they need to actively pursue cultivating a feedback culture in order to avail the benefits in performance improvement.

Some limitations in the evaluation to date give opportunities for further improvement of the approach. The communication of learning analytics related to the feedback to different stakeholders, and the exploration of different delivery mechanisms and platforms for the feedback and the analytics are some future steps for this project.

Acknowledgements This research is supported by the Learnovate Centre at Trinity College, the University of Dublin. The Learnovate Centre is funded under the Technology Centre Programme through the Government of Ireland's state agencies Enterprise Ireland and IDA Ireland.

Part of this work has received funding from the European Union's Horizon 2020 research and innovation programme through the DEVELOP project, under grant agreement No 688127.

References

Aguinis H, Gottfreson RK, Joo H (2012) Using performance management to win the talent war. Bus Horiz 55:609–616

Ajunwa I, Crawford K, Schultz J (2017) Limitless worker surveillance. Calif Law Rev 105:3

Akram AA, Cascio WF, Paauwe J (2014) Talent management: current theories and future directions. J World Bus 49:173–179

Bangor A, Kortum P, Miller J (2009) Determining what individual SUS scores mean: adding an adjective rating scale. J Usabil Stud 4(3):114–123

Callaghan RE (1962) Education and the cult of efficiency. Chicago University

Davies I (1976) Objectives in curriculum design. McGraw Hill

Eraut M (2004) Informal learning in the workplace. Stud Contin Educ 26:247–273

Eraut M, Hirsh W (2007) The significance of workplace learning for individuals. Groups and Organisations, SKOPE 9, pp 1–97

Hattie J, Timperley H (2007) The power of feedback. Rev Educ Res 77:81–112

Housman M, Minor D (2015) Toxic workers. Harvard Business School, Working Paper 16-057

Neumann W (1979) Educational responses to the concern of proficiency. In: Grant G (ed) On competence: a critical analysis of competence based reform in higher education. Jossey Bass

Robles MM (2012) Executive perceptions of the top 10 soft skills needed in today's workplace. Bus Commun Q 75:453–465

Rotherham AJ, Willingham D (2009) 21st century skills the challenges ahead. Educ Leadersh 67(1):16–21. ASCD

Saba (2015) winning your workforce: the essential guide to improving retention and employee performance. Saba eBook

Sauro J (2015) SUPR-Q: a comprehensive measure of the quality of the website user experience. J. Usabil Stud 10(2):68–86

Spady WG (1977) Competency based education: a bandwagon in search of a definition. Educ Res 6(1):9–14

Stuart L (1999) 21st century skills for 21st century jobs. A Report of the U.S. Department of Commerce, U.S. Department of Education, U.S. Department of Labor, National Institute for Literacy and Small Business Administration. U.S. Government Printing Office

Tynjälä P (2008) Perspectives into learning at the workplace. Educ Res Rev 3:130–154

Chapter 9
Constructive Learning by Teaching: Flip-Flop, Peer Evaluation, and Agile Tooltip: Making and Taking Peer Quizzes Synchronized with Lecture Screencasts

Jan Stelovsky, Michael-Brian Ogawa, Branden Ogata and Umida Stelovska

Abstract We are introducing the Constructive Learning instructional methodology, where students' comprehension is augmented by active creation of teaching materials. The premise is that as students create quizzes with questions, correct and incorrect answers, hints and hint links that lead to relevant resources, they get in depth understanding of the content presented in a lecture screencast and thus learn through creating resources for peers and learn from resources their peers created. Our Flip-Flop online web set of tools supports students in creating quizzes directly synchronized with lecture screencasts and facilitates instructors' chores when defining peer groups and scheduling their quiz-creating and quiz-taking activities. Peer evaluation is also an integral part of this methodology. In addition, we are introducing new concepts: the Peer Improvement methodology where learners can suggest—and are rewarded for—changes to a quiz they just took. Moreover, the Agile Tooltip component solicits additional feedback from the learners. The collected data can be used for grading and as a resource pool for future quizzes. We describe a pilot test of Flip-Flop that showed promising results which included a statistically significant increase in task performance and greater engagement in passive homework assignments including watching videos to prepare for in-class sessions. Finally, we highlight the vision of how plethora of online quizzes accompanying any textbook, journal, or lecture may change our concept of education in the future.

J. Stelovsky (✉) · M.-B. Ogawa · B. Ogata
Department of Information and Computer Sciences, University of Hawaii at Manoa,
1680 East-West Road, Honolulu, HI 96822, USA
e-mail: janst@hawaii.edu

M.-B. Ogawa
e-mail: ogawam@hawaii.edu

B. Ogata
e-mail: bsogata@hawaii.edu

U. Stelovska
parWinr Inc., 1291 Ayala Dr. Suite 2, Sunnyvale, CA 94086, USA
e-mail: umida@parwinr.com

E. Kapros and M. Koutsombogera (eds.), *Designing for the User Experience in Learning Systems*, Human–Computer Interaction Series,
https://doi.org/10.1007/978-3-319-94794-5_9

9.1 Introduction

Learning by teaching has been generally accepted one of the best ways for students to learn for centuries. As of this writing, Google Scholar lists over 7,030 entries for a search on this topic, which is 1,390 more than in two years ago when our first article about Flip-Flop was published (Stelovska et al. 2016). A yearly increase of almost 10% in scholarly publications clearly shows that the interest in this arena continues unabated and there is and will be increased demand for practical applications that support this idea. Many sources (Duran 2016; Hanke 2012; Goodlad and Hirst 1989; Biswas et al. 2015; https://en.wikipedia.org/wiki/Learning_by_teaching) discuss the various pros and cons of *learning by teaching*: students benefit not only in quantity of learning in terms of the amount of knowledge gained, but also in the degree to which they understand the material.

As the theory of *learning by teaching* proposed the concepts of *Active Learning* (https://en.wikipedia.org/wiki/Active_learning; Bishop and Verleger 2013) and *Constructivist Learning* (Vygotskii 1978; https://en.wikipedia.org/wiki/Constructivism_(philosophy_of_education), these approaches have also seen widespread acceptance and integration into curricula. Both of these methodologies prioritize actively involving students in their own education rather than passively absorbing lectures. These concepts in general and our approach in particular satisfy most of the levels in all the dimensions of the Bloom's *Taxonomy of Educational Objectives* (https://en.wikipedia.org/wiki/Bloom%27s_taxonomy).

In the traditional model of instruction, students attend lectures in person while working on assignments at home. The *Flipped Classroom* (Bishop and Verleger 2013; https://en.wikipedia.org/wiki/Flipped_classroom) builds on these concepts and reverses this model: students watch lecture videos before class sessions, then work on exercises and ask questions in class where the instructor is available to assist them.

While *Massive Open Online Courses* (MOOC) (Baggaley 2013; Christensen et al. 2014; https://en.wikipedia.org/wiki/Massive_open_online_course; Vardi 2012; Hartnett 2013) are often regarded only as means of replacing classroom lectures by learning from screencasts and lecture recordings on a larger scale, e.g. allowing students to watch and listen to lectures from around the globe, such resources can obviously be used in flipped classrooms as well.

The flipped classroom depends on students actually learning the material presented in the lecture videos. Even if students do watch the videos, there is no guarantee that they do so attentively: they may view the lectures in an environment with distractions or listen to the lecture in the background as they work on other tasks. If students do not understand the concepts covered in the screencast at home, their ability to participate in problem solving during the classroom session is constrained and therefore they learn less from those exercises as well.

The same problems arise in MOOC context: while the students can easily re-watch a section of a lecture video, how do they know whether it is necessary—whether they understood it or not? Here, an immediate feedback via test questions synchronized at crucial points within the screencast is an obvious remedy. But even if creating such quizzes is supported in within the supporting technology, it is unlikely that most of the instructors will embrace additional quiz-authoring chores.

Therefore we propose that the student peers construct quizzes synchronized with lecture videos and take the quizzes their peers constructed while watching screencasts. Our Flip-Flop methodology allows to conduct these activities in a well-organized fashion during the entire length of the course and offers a complete set of supporting online tools. In particular, we introduce Peer Improvement, a component of Flip-Flop that allows the student who just took a quiz to suggest improvements to all the quiz tasks and their elements.

According to the most recent Fall 2017 report by Hill (2017), 87% of institutions of higher learning and 91% of student enrollments rely upon a learning management system (LMS) such as Blackboard (http://www.blackboard.com), Canvas (2018), Moodle (https://moodle.org), or D2L Brightspace (https://www.d2l.com). None of these popular school-wide 'big four' LMS's offers quiz editing features for the students, records the authored quizzes, or allows taking peer quizzes. While the name of Quizlet (https://quizlet.com)—another recent commercial LMS—seems to indicate that quizzes are its core essence, it mainly supports creating study plans, scheduling study sessions, or taking short quizzes to measure progress, and does not focus on creating peer quizzes. Moreover, Quizlet does not target educational institutions, and is used almost exclusively in the language learning community. Quiz It!, another interesting framework that recently won "Best Education Hack" as well as "Best Google Cloud Platform Hack" prizes (https://devpost.com/software/quiz-it) attempts to create quizzes automatically using artificial intelligence to analyze the underlying resources. While quiz-making is offered by some based on video lectures—e.g. Kahoot (https://kahoot.com), none of these platforms feature the comprehensive set of features that our methodology proposes. In particular, the Peer Improvement component mentioned above is not available in any of the aforementioned environments.

The remaining sections of this article are organized as follows: while Sect. 9.2 introduces the general principles of Flip-Flop, Sect. 9.3 describes the technology framework that supports these principles. Section 9.4 then describes a study evaluating the principles behind the Flip-Flop methodology and showcases the quizzes that students created. Finally, Sects. 9.5 and 9.6 discuss planned improvements to the existing software implementation, offer a glimpse of upcoming data analysis efforts, and highlight the potential impact on education and knowledge acquisition per se.

While this article is mainly based on our contributions to the HCII 2018 conference (Stelovsky et al. 2018; Ogawa 2018), several sections—in particular Sect. 9.6. The Vision—cover new ground.

9.2 Flip-Flop Concepts

While the Flip-Flop approach was devised primarily with the Flipped Classroom methodology in mind, it can also enhance any MOOC-type of instruction as it adds a "flop" component to any lecture videos: learners construct quizzes synchronized with educational screencasts.

In order to create quality quizzes, students must understand the material in the lecture video. Even when constructing a simple multiple-choice task, the quiz author has to think of a question that is relevant for the specific screencast segment along with answer choices whose correctness is not too easy to guess or too hard to answer. Finding the correct answer is typically straightforward once the student has decided on a question. However, developing incorrect answers is non-trivial: these incorrect answers must be incorrect but not obviously so.

Even multiple-choice quizzes can offer features that while being more informative for the quiz-taking student are more challenging and therefore can bring more educational benefit to the quiz author. For instance, we propose that each answer can be accompanied by a feedback that can explain why the answer is correct or incorrect. In particular, the feedback for an incorrect answer can indicate the likely misconception that often leads to such incorrect choice. Thinking in terms of answer feedbacks and how to formulate them concisely brings additional benefits not only to the quiz author, but demonstrates the pros and cons of the author's approach to the peers who take the quiz.

Furthermore, we propose that the author can append a short hint phrase as well as a hint link to any question. Formulating a concise hint is quite challenging as the author should only point the quiz taker in the right direction without giving away the entire correct answer. The hint link also challenges the author to find the most appropriate web page online that explains the topic well enough to answer the corresponding question.

In our version of *Flip-Flop*, the answer feedbacks, hints, and hint links are optional. However, the quiz templates that are automatically added to authors' channels to assist with their initial editing chores include several dummy answers each with a default dummy feedback, a default hint as well as a dummy hint link. While these dummy elements seem to simplify the student's work, they need to be deleted if the author decides to omit them and thus serve as a reminder that it would be more appropriate to replace them with some substantial content.

When synchronizing tasks with the video, the author can simply opt to limit the response time to the duration of the corresponding video segment or choose to pause the video and give the quiz taker a specific time limit to choose an answer. He or she can also choose whether to show the correct answer after an incorrect answer was selected.

In addition to multiple-choice questions, we support poll tasks—where there is no distinction between correct and incorrect answers—as well as "pinboard tasks" where the author displays text or an image and optionally a link to an external web page and the quiz-taker does not need to take any action except possibly to click on the

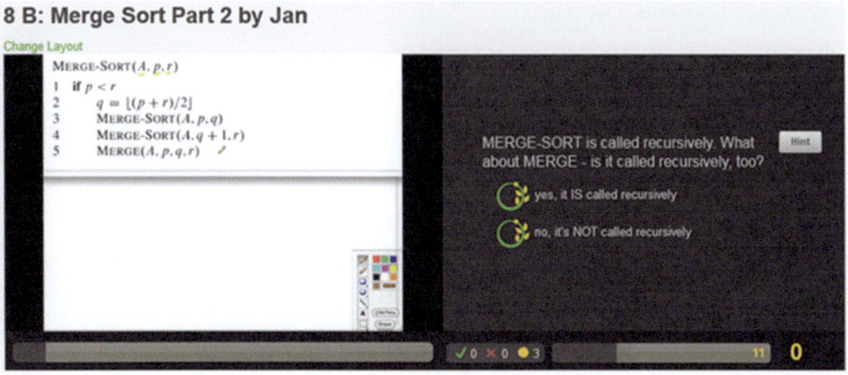

Fig. 9.1 Taking a quiz: question and answers

link to view such a page. Since the author of the quiz can specify the maximum points per task and whether the number of possible points decreases with time, correctly answered questions increase the total score for this quiz and consequently motivates and rewards students for positive performance.

Since the students also take peer-generated quizzes in conjunction with creating quizzes, each student has multiple opportunities to engage with the material and thus assess themselves whether they understand the content.

Since the tightly structured and systematic approach of Flip-Flop does not explicitly fit other well-documented and researched educational methodologies, we propose the term *Constructive Learning* for approaches and technologies that require the students to construct teaching materials based on and synchronized with recordings of educational lessons.

9.3 Flip-Flop Technology

9.3.1 Taking Quizzes

To take a quiz, a student may either navigate directly to a quiz through a notification email or find the quiz in the list of quizzes that peers have created. A sample Flip-Flop quiz is shown in Fig. 9.1.

If the quiz taker selects the correct answer, he or she sees feedback indicating that the choice was correct (see Fig. 9.2).

If the selected answer is incorrect, the feedback will indicate this as well, hopefully identifying the misconception that the student has made and suggesting how to correct this mistake (shown in Fig. 9.3).

The question in Fig. 9.4 also has a hint for the quiz taker to look at.

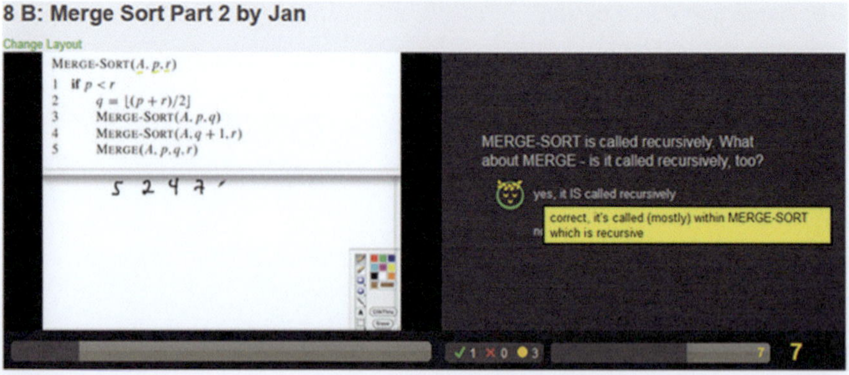

Fig. 9.2 Taking a quiz: selecting a correct answer

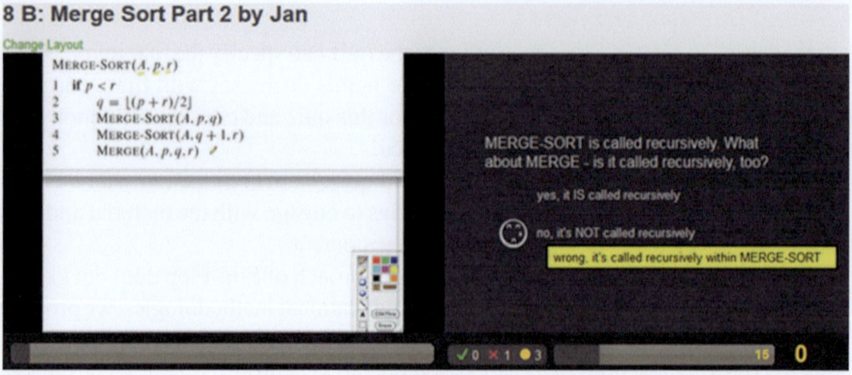

Fig. 9.3 Taking a quiz: selecting an incorrect answer

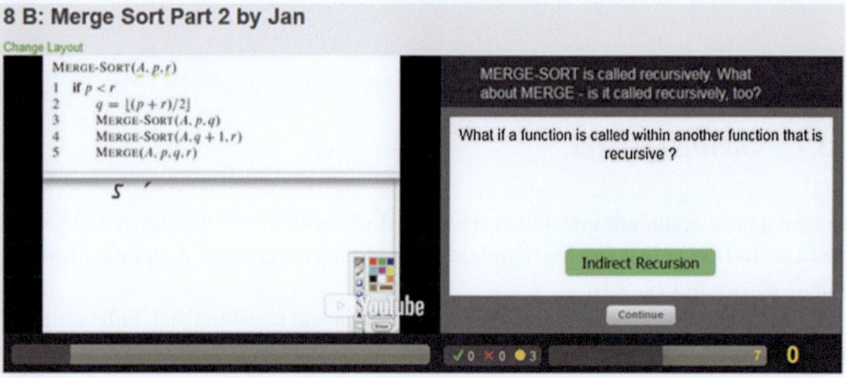

Fig. 9.4 Taking a quiz: viewing a hint

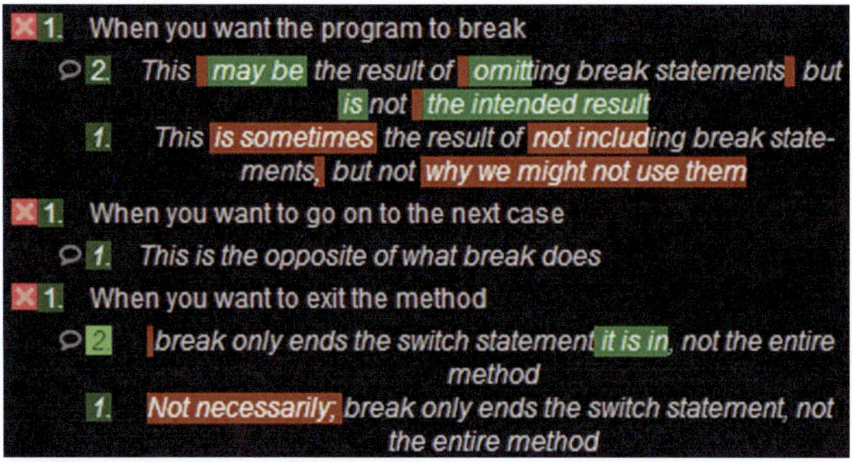

Fig. 9.5 Peer improvement: suggested improvements

9.3.2 *Peer Improvement*

Once the student has finished taking the quiz, he or she enters an editing suite where he or she can page through every task of the quiz just taken and suggest an improvement to every task component. For instance, clicking on the question for the task displays an editing field where the student can change the wording or type an entirely new question text. Similarly, the student can change each of the answers and modify the feedback for each of the answers, the task's hint text, and hint link. Figure 9.5 shows the editing field where the question has been reworded. Notice that the differences between the original and the edited text of the question are depicted in red and green colors.

The editing facilities do not stop at just editing the texts. Students can suggest that another answer is correct rather than the one that the author selected simply by clicking on its red "x" sign. (Obviously, a green check mark will now indicate the answer deemed correct.)

Notice that once one or more students take the quiz and suggest improvements, the next student can select any of the previous improvements (as well as the original item) and improve it again. Alternately, the student can just click on the check mark to indicate that he or she approves of that particular item. Such an approval earns this suggestion item a '+'. As Fig. 9.6 shows, the '+' stars appear next to the ID of the student who suggested the improvement.

We also automatically feature an evaluation page where the quiz taker clicks on the star rating for each of the essential quiz components as depicted in Fig. 9.7.

Peer Improvement has numerous advantages. The learner who just took the quiz and has its tasks fresh in memory can immediately change all the items he or she found problematic or even judges as incorrect. Note also that only one feedback—the

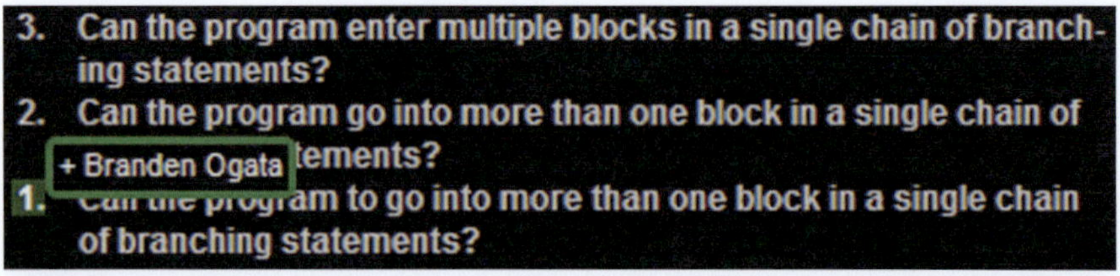

Fig. 9.6 Peer improvement: approval

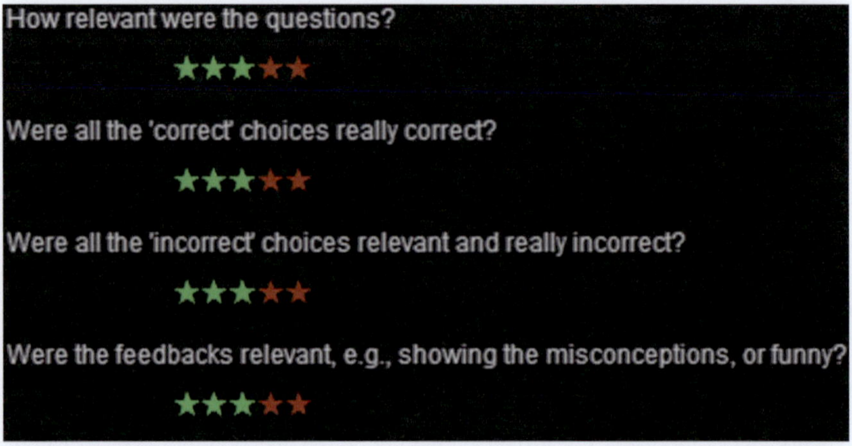

Fig. 9.7 Peer evaluation: star ratings

one associated with the selected answer—is shown during the quiz taking session. In contrast, all the feedbacks are shown during the *Peer Improvement* session. Since we encourage the authors to provide additional information within the feedbacks such as an indication of what misconception might have led to an incorrect answer, the student can even learn more in-depth aspects of the subject. Similarly, the *Peer Improvement* framework presents all the hints and the hint links which were not unless the student clicked on the "Hint" button during the quiz, enabling the student to follow the hint links and learn from these additional resources.

Peer Improvement is also likely to increase the motivation of learners. After all, improving and even suggesting additional improvements to already posted ones can be perceived as a challenging opportunity to showcase mastery of the subject. Collecting '+' from the peers only adds to the motivation of the student.

Last but not least, the instructor naturally benefits from the *Peer Improvement* methodology as the improvements can be showcased in the order of most '+' scores earned. This makes it easy to incorporate Flip-Flop methodology into grading, to build a prioritized database of quiz tasks that can be used in future tests, and to promote the applications of online tasks discussed in the Conclusions section below.

9.3.3 Creating Quizzes

In order to create a quiz with the Flip-Flop authoring tool, a student must first log into his or her channel—currently on slippah.com—and select the quiz she needs to create. The initial quiz authoring page is shown in Fig. 9.8.

The left half of the page contains the video and segments for the quiz. The gray anchors below the video indicate the start and end points of the quiz; this particular quiz covers the second quarter of the lecture. Between those anchors, green and yellow rectangles represent individual question segments: the question will be displayed on the screen during that portion of the video. The student may change the quantity, placement, and duration of these segments to ensure that the application displays quiz questions during relevant portions of the video.

The right hand side of the page shows the currently selected question (highlighted in green below the video), up to five answers with radio buttons to indicate the correct choice, as well as feedback for each of the answers that can be expanded or hidden using the text bubble to the right of each answer.

Clicking the light bulb to the right of the question reveals the hint entry with fields where the author can post the hint link and type in the label for the link as shown in Fig. 9.9. Since we observed that some students in the Algorithms CS course often wanted to formulate quiz content with special math symbols and Greek letters used in the textbook, we have now added a special symbol keyboard pane shown on the right.

Fig. 9.8 Creating a quiz: authoring tool

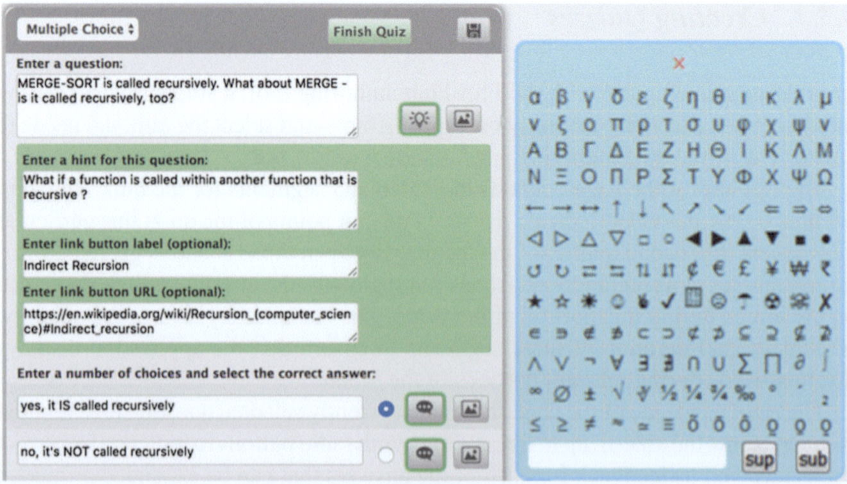

Fig. 9.9 Creating a quiz: editing a hint with hint link and label; symbols pane

9.3.4 Instructor Perspective

Simplifying the chores of the instructors is one of the main objectives of a learning management system. Given that the Flip-Flop method needs specific scheduling facilities that are essential for assigning students quizzes to make and take based on screencasts, a substantial portion of the underlying technology had to be devoted to providing instructors with (1) a tool for easy review of the work from students, and (2) with the scheduling tool that subdivides the students into groups and assigns the quiz authors portions of the corresponding screencasts.

A previous iteration of this application had a standalone website displaying all of the quizzes for the current course. This page (shown in Fig. 9.10) divided the students into groups for each quiz, providing links to the lecture video and notes for students to refer to.

The student assigned to a section of the video is highlighted in blue. Hovering the mouse over the name of a student brought up a menu of choices that allowed the quiz authors to send links to their peers who then took the quizzes through this same interface.

The current version of the scheduling tool helps instructors to define the student groups, determine the quiz author for a particular segment of a screencast and when to generate the corresponding quiz templates, add them to the channel of each student, and remind the author once the template is up as well when his or her quiz is due (see Fig. 9.11).

After students create quizzes, their instructor can easily look through those quizzes for grading. For example, in Fig. 9.12 we can see the contents of the one quiz that Samantha Lewis wrote.

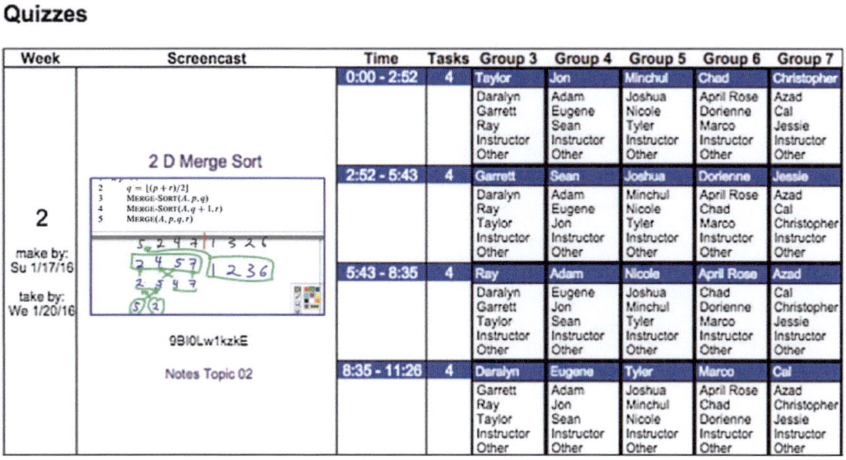

Week	Screencast	Time	Tasks	Group 3	Group 4	Group 5	Group 6	Group 7
2 make by: Su 1/17/16 take by: We 1/20/16	2 D Merge Sort 9BI0Lw1kzkE Notes Topic 02	0:00 - 2:52	4	Taylor Daralyn Garrett Ray Instructor Other	Jon Adam Eugene Sean Instructor Other	Minchul Joshua Nicole Tyler Instructor Other	Chad April Rose Dorienne Marco Instructor Other	Christopher Azad Cal Jessie Instructor Other
		2:52 - 5:43	4	Garrett Daralyn Ray Taylor Instructor Other	Sean Adam Eugene Jon Instructor Other	Joshua Minchul Nicole Tyler Instructor Other	Dorienne April Rose Chad Marco Instructor Other	Jessie Azad Cal Christopher Instructor Other
		5:43 - 8:35	4	Ray Daralyn Garrett Taylor Instructor Other	Adam Eugene Jon Sean Instructor Other	Nicole Joshua Minchul Tyler Instructor Other	April Rose Chad Dorienne Marco Instructor Other	Azad Cal Christopher Jessie Instructor Other
		8:35 - 11:26	4	Daralyn Garrett Ray Taylor Instructor Other	Eugene Adam Jon Sean Instructor Other	Tyler Joshua Minchul Nicole Instructor Other	Marco April Rose Chad Dorienne Instructor Other	Cal Azad Christopher Jessie Instructor Other

Fig. 9.10 Old scheduling tool

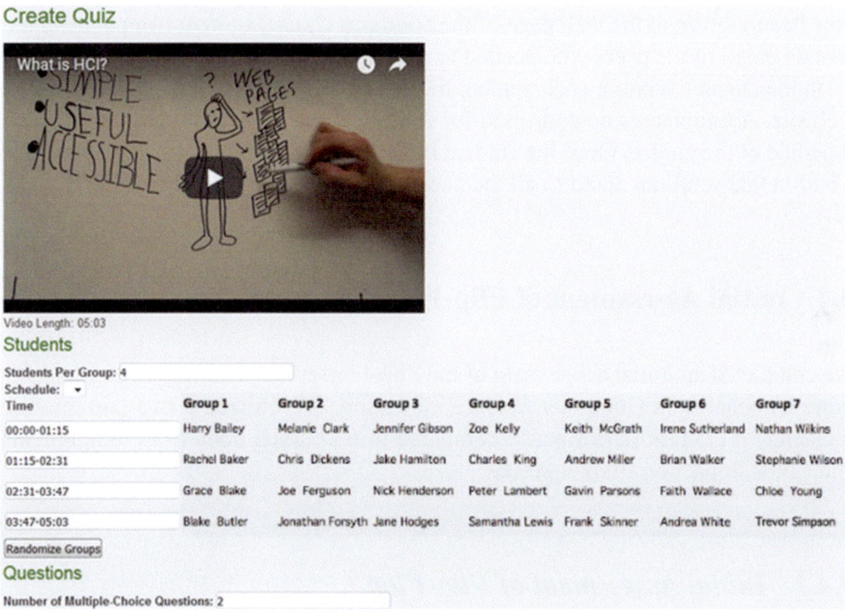

Time	Group 1	Group 2	Group 3	Group 4	Group 5	Group 6	Group 7
00:00-01:15	Harry Bailey	Melanie Clark	Jennifer Gibson	Zoe Kelly	Keith McGrath	Irene Sutherland	Nathan Wilkins
01:15-02:31	Rachel Baker	Chris Dickens	Jake Hamilton	Charles King	Andrew Miller	Brian Walker	Stephanie Wilson
02:31-03:47	Grace Blake	Joe Ferguson	Nick Henderson	Peter Lambert	Gavin Parsons	Faith Wallace	Chloe Young
03:47-05:03	Blake Butler	Jonathan Forsyth	Jane Hodges	Samantha Lewis	Frank Skinner	Andrea White	Trevor Simpson

Fig. 9.11 Instructor perspective: creating quizzes

9.3.5 Channels

In the previous version of our software technology, the students had to download a template of their quiz from the website for the course, integrate it manually within their own web pages, and after they finished authoring the quiz based on this template

- Samantha Lewis
  - Quizzes Created (1)
    - 25 Places You Have To See Before You Die (last modified at 2017-10-30 12:30:03 -1000) - Take Quiz
      - Name the colors in a rainbow in the correct order
        - Answers:
          - Red, yellow, blue
            Feedback: feedback 1
          - Cyan, magenta, violet, gold
            Feedback: feedback 2
          - Blue, purple, red, green, orange, yellow
          - Red, orange, yellow, green, blue, purple ✓
          - Red, yellow, orange, blue, green, purple
        - Hint:
          - Text: Although you'll find gold at the end of the rainbow, you won't find it in the colors of the rainbow.
          - Label: sample hint button label
          - URL: http://www.slippah.com
      - What color shirt are you wearing?
        - Answers:
          - Red
          - orange
          - yellow
          - Green
          - Blue
  - Quizzes Taken (0)

Fig. 9.12 Instructor perspective: viewing quizzes

they had to return to the web page of the course to choose an item from a menu that sent an email to the peers who needed to take this new quiz.

In the current version, each student has his or her own channel on the Flip-Flop web site. A template is now inserted for each new quiz to be authored based on the schedule of the course. Once the student has created the quiz he or she simply clicks a button that sends an email to all the peers announcing that the quiz is ready.

9.4 Initial Assessment of Flip-Flop Conceptual Framework

We conducted an initial assessment of the Flip-Flop conceptual framework to determine its benefits in Computer Science education. We utilized a two-part analysis focusing on (1) task performance compared to traditional homework assignments, and (2) its impact on study methods.

9.4.1 Initial Assessment of Flip-Flop

To evaluate the effectiveness of Flip-Flop, we focused on its impact on task performance and study approach. The frame used for the study was a computer science service course that utilized a hybrid approach that included traditional lectures and online video lectures. Students met in the lecture hall once a week for a 75-min lecture and subsequently watched an approximately 25-min online video developed by a faculty member and completed a 10-question quiz based on the video content. This structure repeated each week with a range of topics including search sets, logic, financial functions, social computing, security, and information management. Students also met in the laboratory with teaching assistants twice a week for hands-on application of the topics covered in the lectures.

9.4.1.1 Data Collection Tools and Procedures

To determine the effectiveness of the Flip-Flop approach, we used an experimental design to test the effectiveness of the Flip-Flop and original approaches. Students who enrolled in at least one upper-division course were invited to participate in the study for extra credit. A total of 14 students participated in the study and were randomly assigned to the control or experimental group. The control group watched the video and completed a twenty minute 10-question quiz about the content, while the experimental group was required to watch the video and develop five multiple-choice questions with time stamps. After completing the initial activity, both groups completed a ten minute 5-question quiz based on the final examination questions as the dependent variable.

After completing the experiment, we conducted two focus group interviews with the participants to determine if the Flip-Flop approach changed the students' study habits. We used a semi-structured interview format to allow the conversation to flow naturally and include follow-up questions based on responses. The following open-ended questions served as the interview guide:

- How did you take notes during the video?
- How did you study for the quiz(zes)?

9.4.1.2 Analysis

A univariate analysis of variance using the final examination questions scores was used to determine the difference in task performance and if the result was statistically significant. The focus group interview data were coded to identify themes among the participants' study habits.

9.4.2 Improving Task Performance with Flip-Flop

A univariate analysis of variance demonstrated a statistically significant difference ($p<0.05$) with $F=6.25$ in final examination questions scores between the control and experimental groups (Table 9.1). The mean for the control group was 80% and the experimental group was 94%. Therefore, participants using the Flip-Flop approach to student performed on average 14% higher than those with the traditional approach.

Table 9.1 Univariate analysis of variance

Source of variation	SS	df	MS	F	P-value	F crit
Between groups	1.785714	1	1.785714	6.25	0.027915	4.747225
Within groups	3.428571	12	0.285714			
Total	5.214286	13				

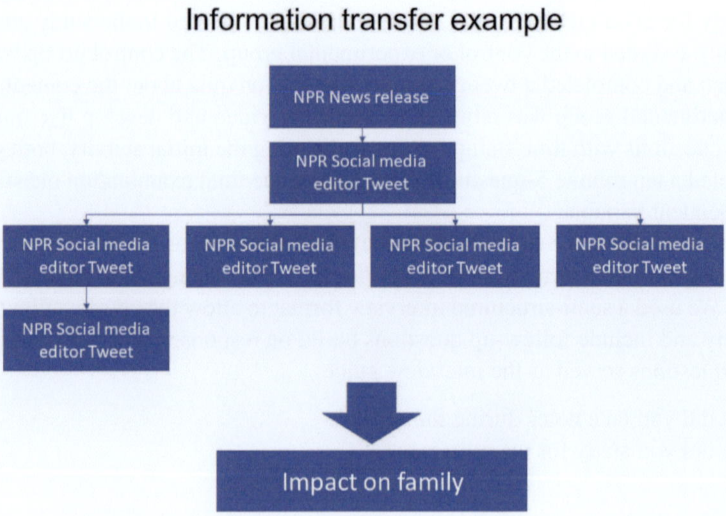

Fig. 9.13 Sample illustration for information transfer

9.4.3 Changing Study Approaches

The control group (traditional approach) included four themes for study habits. Students focused their notes on facts and definitions, copied bulleted lists from slides, scrubbed the video for slides with text (used the navigation slider to select a section of the video), and multi-tasked while they watched the video. Several participants noted that they had the video playing in one window, while they had their email open in another window. Those students stopped working on their email messages when they heard or saw an important point to write as study notes.

The experimental group (Flip-Flop approach) indicated that they also took factual notes. However, they also attempted to understand concepts and develop notes with illustrations to aid in question development. Figure 9.13 includes an example of a student illustration to demonstrate how information was transferred. Since they were required to note the time for each question, their notes were more detailed and included timestamps next to facts and concepts rather than solely including content. This helped them to revisit difficult concepts because they knew the location in the

Table 9.2 Study habits for control and experimental groups

Control (traditional)	Experimental (Flip-Flop)
• Factual notes • Copy bullet points • Scrub for image content • Multi-task during video	• Factual notes • Conceptual notes with illustrations • Thinking about concepts and misconceptions • Single-task during video • Difficulty in creating distractors

video to replay content instead of having to search. The Flip-Flop group also focused on the task because it required an active approach to note-taking as they prepared questions compared to the control group who multitasked while watching the video. Most of the experimental group had difficulty creating appropriate distractor items for questions and noted that writing distractors took more time than the questions. The themes for both groups are summarized in Table 9.2.

The initial benefits of the Flip-Flop model are quite promising, as they improved assessment scores and student note-taking approaches. The students' notes also addressed a typical concern about the focus on multiple-choice questions, which is the importance of developing a conceptual understanding of content. This approach led students to study concepts rather than facts without additional instruction.

9.4.4 Flip-Flop in CS Courses

Until now, Flip-Flop has only been applied in computer science courses at the University of Hawaii at Manoa. It was primarily used in the inverted Algorithms course—ICS 311. We have constructed a web page the showcases the quizzes that students constructed in Fall 2016 when it was in used for the first time (http://honza.epizy.com/slippah/questions.html). Figure 9.14 shows the top of this page and demonstrates that clicking on a question reveals all of its possible answers, their feedbacks, the hint, and the hint link which when clicked opens the target resource in another tab. (The hint to the question currently displayed showcases that some students did take our suggestion seriously that a little humor does not hurt—even within an algorithms quiz.)

As the tiny size of the scroll thumb in the bottom right of Fig. 9.15 indicates, scrolling through all of the pages of 5554 student questions is quite impressive in its own right. However, the reader may appreciate not just the quantity but the quality of the students' contributions as most of the quiz tasks are well conceived, well formulated, and fit well with the screencast topics.

Subsequently, Flip-Flop was also employed in the Algorithms course in Fall 2017 and we are now expanding its use into Data Structures ICS 211, a second-semester programming course with a total of 86 students. As of this writing, the ICS 211 students this semester have created a total of 464 quizzes with 1410 questions, 4166

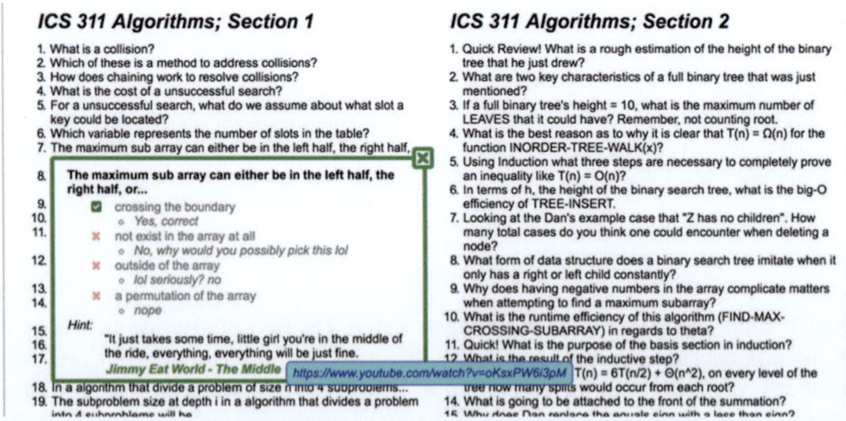

Fig. 9.14 Web page with the quizzes created in an algorithms course—top portion

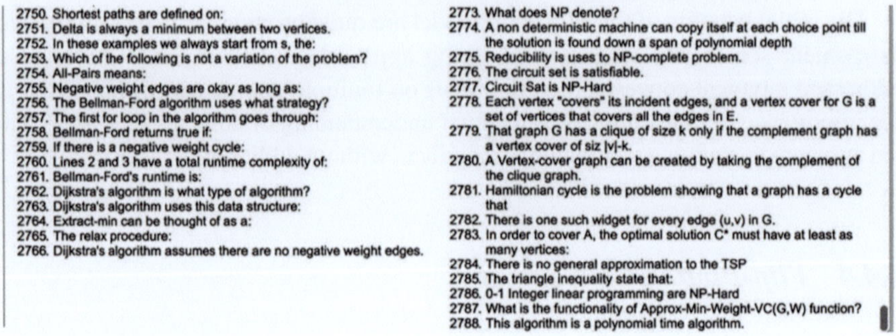

Fig. 9.15 Web page with the quizzes created in an algorithms course—bottom portion

answers, 2754 feedbacks, and 509 hints. Students were instructed to create their quizzes with a minimum of two questions with two answers each; on average each quiz had 3.04 questions and each question had 2.95 choices. Although students were provided with templates including feedbacks and hints, they did not actively use these options with 0.661 feedback items per answer and 0.361 hints per question.

Given that the ICS 211 course is a prerequisite for the ICS 311 course, one interesting option will be to reuse some of the quiz tasks created this semester for one or more of the quizzes that the ICS 311 students may take to ascertain that they have the knowledge needed to successfully continue their studies.

9.5 Conclusions and Future Work

9.5.1 Data Analysis, e.g. Can It Take Less Time?

Naturally, Flip-Flop can collect very detailed and abundant data not only while students take a quiz but also while quizzes are created. For instance, our most recent version of the framework stores the time span an author needed to come up with any of the task components: question, every answer and every feedback, every hint and hint link.

Our analysis of the collected data is still in preliminary state. However, we have developed, for instance, a visualization of the duration of the quiz tasks that allows us to compare this timing with the segmentation suggested by the template. As Fig. 9.16 shows, A. Hemmings, R. Black, and C. Carr were the only students who used exactly the same number and timing as the template proposed. (Equally wide rectangles of alternating grays.) J. Mackenzie and D. McDonald allocated twice as much time to each of the first two questions than the template suggested but while Mackenzie added more time to the last question, McDonald decided to add one more task. We can also see that K. Davies and J. Peake generated only two questions. Also, several students have already become familiar with paused type of questions that are indicated by left-pointing triangles.

While the detailed data analysis is still outstanding, we can cite several comments, critique, and improvement suggestions that students typically voice. In our experience, while the students usually see and appreciate the benefits of the Flip-Flop approach, their main objection is that they need to invest more time than in other classes. Indeed, creating a quiz is at least initially a challenging task. Since we are

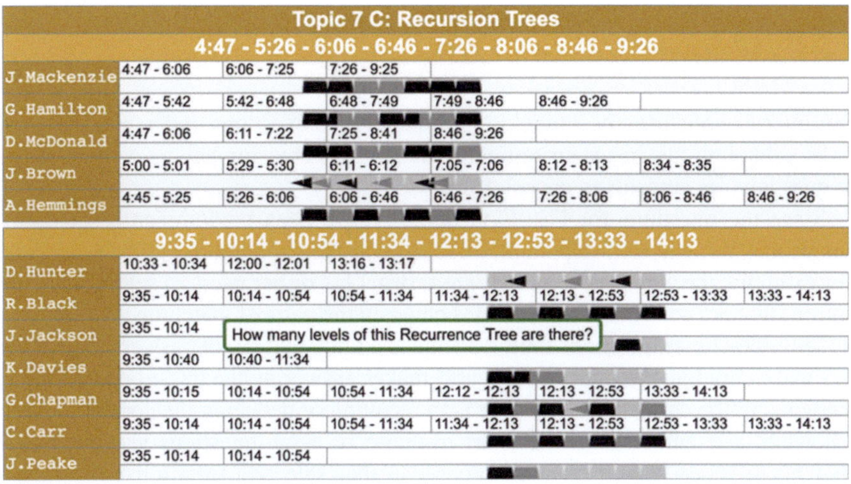

Fig. 9.16 Visualization of quiz tasks timing

now collecting data about how long it takes an author to create a quiz, we will be able to determine how much time it took at the beginning and compare it with the times at the end of the semester. (Naturally, we expect that the latter times will be shorter not only because an increased familiarity with the technology itself, but mainly because of better quiz-making skills.) If the Flip-Flop approach is applied across courses during several consecutive courses, we would also expect fewer objections and more appreciation of the acquired benefits.

Our technology, however, could help shorten the time it takes the student to take a quiz. For instance, students have raised concerns about the time spent waiting between questions on their quizzes; we could provide a button that skips the remaining portion of the screencast segment once an answer was selected and start playing the video at the beginning of the next task segment. Alternately, we could add a scale that allows the quiz taker to speed up the screencast. Another feasible approach would be to let the author who creates a quiz from a segment of one screencast to take only quizzes built from other screencasts so that he or she does not need to view any portion of a particular screencast twice. While such speedups may please the students, they may be less appreciated by the instructors—after all, viewing a lecture twice certainly reinforces the understanding of the subject. Therefore we are inclined to make them optional within the scheduling tool and let the instructor decide whether they will be available to the students in his or her course.

We expect that the integration of the *Agile Tooltip* framework discussed below in Sect. 9.5.4 will lead to a user-centered approach that gives the students ample chance to voice such concerns in and even allow them to suggest further improvements to the entire *Flip-Flop* methodology and technology. We expect that such feedback will offer valuable data that can be analyzed to ascertain the pros and cons of not just the *Flip-Flop* methodology but the concept of *Constructive Learning* as a whole.

9.5.2 Additional Question Types

Our quizzes are currently limited to multiple-choice questions, polls, and pinboard tasks. Although this has been sufficient thus far, we envision having a wider range of questions for students to choose from.

Since the questions for Flip-Flop quizzes have been predominantly multiple-choice thus far, one next step might be to support the selection of multiple answers. For example, the author of a quiz might instruct his or her peers to select all of the options that are correct or to draw lines between the pairs of matching answers.

Multiple-choice questions limit students to a finite number of answers, and while this makes grading the quiz easier it also makes answering the question a matter of recognizing the correct choice rather than recalling or deducing the correct answer. Allowing quiz authors to write short response or essay questions would compel students to generate their own answers rather than selecting from a list of options. Furthermore, the author of the quiz would have to grade the responses to these types of questions, providing the student with the perspectives of his or her peers and requiring the author to discern whether each written answer is correct or incorrect.

Many domains are more graphically oriented and an answer or feedback purely in text would take too much space on the screen. Our application currently supports images in answers, but only as a thumbnail that is displayed next to the text. Improving support for graphical answers would allow students to click on pictures of answers rather than text, increasing the versatility of the software.

On the other hand, some fields are heavily text-driven or do not have lecture videos readily available for use. Although Flip-Flop quizzes are designed for video quizzes, this system could be adapted to display a document on the left side of the window while questions and answers appear on the right as students scroll through the text. In some cases, the software might only display the questions for the quiz when the instructor does not have any material to synchronize the quiz with.

9.5.3 Improvements to Peer Improvement

Our software currently allows quiz takers to suggest modifications to the text of questions, answers, feedback, and hints. However, reviewers should also have the option to propose adding or removing quiz components as well. For example, if the author did not write feedback for an answer, the student who just took the quiz should be able to provide the author with some text that the author could eventually use when updating or revising the quiz.

Furthermore, quiz takers should be able to write comments accompanying their suggested modifications. This will allow reviewers to not just propose changes but explain why they would make those changes.

9.5.4 Agile Tooltip

We plan to integrate another novel technology into the upcoming version of Flip-Flop that we have independently developed to allow users to seek more detailed help with UI widgets as well as provide feedback such as problems encountered and suggestions for improving their user experiences. We call this technology "Agile Tooltip", as its roots are in one of the main concepts that the Agile Methodology in Software Engineering has pioneered: involving the customer in continuously defining and perfecting the software product rather than trying to make exact requirement specifications up front. The Agile Tooltip concept goes one step further in involving the end user in this process. It adds two buttons to every tooltip: A "help" button, typically represented by a "?" question mark icon, and a "feedback" button, typically depicted as a "thought bubble" icon. Both of these buttons either lead to a page or displays a dialogue where the user can find help information that is directly related to

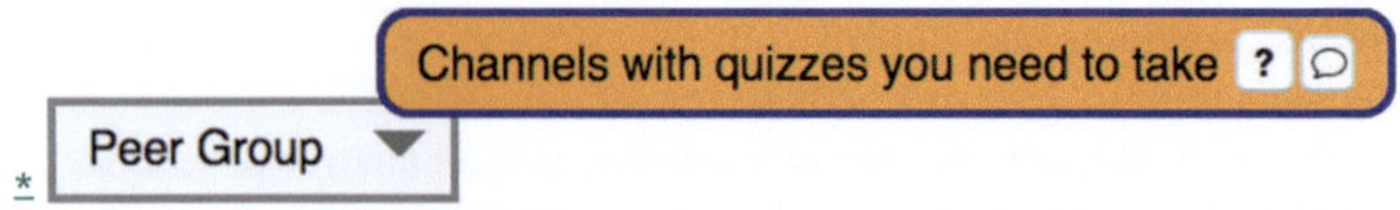

Fig. 9.17 Agile tooltip for Flip-Flop

the widget: for instance, an explanation of how this particular widget is used within a typical workflow.

In the context of Flip-Flop (see Fig. 9.17), the Agile Tooltip will assist the students while they construct and take quizzes so they can easily seek corresponding help pages as well as provide feedback about the Flip-Flop technology itself, the quizzes they take or make, and the screencasts themselves. For example, the tooltip related to the "Link" entry in the authoring system will lead to the help page that describes how the student should search for resources on the web that are related to a question, how to select and copy the web page link from the address bar of the browser, and how to paste it into the entry field. The advantage of this approach is not just that the help is targeted to the purpose of the widget, but also that the help pages can provide additional semantic information: for instance, suggesting that the linked webpage should not completely answer the question but only help with deriving the correct answer.

The "feedback" button of the Flip-Flop's tooltip will display a suggestion page or dialogue where the student will be able to choose the type of feedback he or she is providing, the entry field for the suggestion text along with a drag and drop pane where he or she can submit a screenshot, and an entry field for his or her email. We intend to support at least the following types of feedbacks:

1. Problems, errors, and suggestions how to improve the functionality and appearance of the Flip-Flop user experience,
2. Problems understanding the help pages and suggestions how to improve them,
3. Problems with the quiz the student is currently taking, and
4. Problems understanding the screencast itself and suggestions how it could be improved.

Once a student submits a feedback we will record and categorize the suggestions. The student will receive an automatic "thank you" email. Furthermore, the Agile Tooltip system will allow the instructor and/or teaching assistant to view and respond to the specific suggestion, for instance, promising to alert the student once the problem was corrected or the suggestion addressed. Such replies may be sent to all the students in the course to demonstrate that the instructors and developers do care and thus encourage them to suggest more improvements on their own.

The detailed description of the Agile Tooltip methodology, the corresponding software framework and the support app, as well as its general applications will be subject of a future research article we plan to submit to a software engineering journal.

9.5.5 *AI Support for Flip-Flop and Vice Versa*

Artificial intelligence will benefit the quiz authors as it can suggest questions based on the video content and transcript, correct answers, as well as documents to be used as hint links. An interesting aspect is that answers with a low confidence level which are normally discarded by AI frameworks can be well used in multiple-choice tasks—after all, the author must also invent the incorrect answers.

On the other hand, artificial intelligence frameworks can benefit from the experts' knowledge while they construct Flip-Flop quizzes. For instance, IBM Watson requires that a client must first 'ingest' documents and then 'train' Watson with questions and correct answers. That is exactly what the hint links and quiz tasks provide.

Moreover, an AI framework will be able to learn from both correct and incorrect answers, using feedbacks that explain why an answer is correct or not. In particular, AI will be able to learn from peer improvements—especially if the 'peer' is an expert instructor.

9.6 The Vision

The Flip-Flop quizzes have several important aspects:

- They are largely subject-independent,
- They are also grade-independent,
- They are language independent, and
- They can be easily translated into various other languages.

Most importantly, a vast number of such quizzes can be stored online, associated and linked to other online resources. If Flip-Flop and future similar technologies were widely adopted and enhanced, a vast reservoir of testing resources will become available.

In particular, an abundance of online quizzes can potentially change how we perceive testing per se.

As most educators know, when taking a test the primary motivation for students is to get the minimum sufficient number of points to achieve a desired grade. They expect that their tests will be corrected by a knowledgeable—if not infallible—instructor and that once they took the test they will not be bothered with taking another test where this knowledge will be required—except maybe on a final test that covers an entire course. So for most students, taking a test is mainly about the question "Did I get enough points?" rather than "Did I learn and understand the topic?". If students can, however, take a quiz before viewing a lesson screencast or reading a textbook chapter to ascertain that they know the prerequisites and then take a quiz after studying the topics to find out how much they learned or whether they should review the cast or reread the chapter without being stressed about how these quizzes impact their grades, their attitudes are likely change. Gradually they may perceive a test not as a threat but as a positive or even entertaining experience that helps them to learn a subject and even assess and improve their own learning progress, learning speed, and learning skills.

There are other advantages that are likely to result from the availability of online quizzes for an arbitrary subject at an arbitrary time. If there is no time limit on how long a learner can take to complete a quiz, then the lack of stress is likely to result in better scores and more satisfactory experience. On the other hand, if a learner can opt for time limitation, the increased challenge might also prove to benefit the learning effect. Moreover, online quizzes can become a competitive adventure where learners attempt to achieve better and better scores and compete. After all, the abundance of online trivia quizzes (currently 5,350,000 search results on Google) proves that testing can be very entertaining.

Furthermore, online quizzes can point the learner to resources that are appropriate for his or her current level of knowledge and learning style. For instance, if a learner performs miserably on a quiz, he or she can be guided to a learning resource that is less advanced or covers the topic in simpler terms. Moreover, quizzes may be constructed in different ways, such as using pictures rather than text. If a student performs better on the pictorial type of quizzes, he or she can be guided towards the visually rich presentations of a topic. Similarly, students who answer textual questions rapidly may learn better from a more abstract description of the subject.

In an ideal world, we are all learners who should be easily able to find out whether we understand a chapter in a book, an article in a research journal, or even a topic explained in a Wikipedia web page. Imagine that each article of an encyclopedia topic had an accompanying online quiz a reader could take before he/she starts reading it. Then the hint links could be used to point to other articles that explain the prerequisite topics that need to be covered in order to adequately digest the topic at hand. Additional quizzes interspersed within the article itself could let the readers test their grasp of each subtopics covered. Finally, at the end a quiz could not only reveal how well the entire article was understood, but even ask questions about additional related, possibly more advanced, topics with links that point to follow-up articles that can be now more easily understood. When quizzes can be taken online without any adverse consequences—such as a low score or time limit—then our attitude towards tests could be dramatically changed and we could start viewing tests positively as instruments that help us to objectively assess our knowledge and learning, and lead us through a network of knowledge while making it easy to judge whether our learning is effective, efficient and even entertaining.

Abundance of online quizzes does not benefit only the learners. Making quizzes is one of the most tedious and time consuming chores of an instructor. Coming up with a new set of quizzes with new tasks every semester is not easy. Selecting from numerous quizzes even if they are not constructed by experts but by students and possibly just improving on their wording is bound to substantially shorten the time necessary for the instructor to create quizzes. Furthermore, since such improvements are stored and classified as employed or improved by an expert, the quality of the quizzes and tasks will undoubtedly improve gradually.

Instructors and institutions may administer Flip-Flop quizzes on prerequisite content to verify that students still recall earlier concepts from other courses. The hints for these quizzes may include links to review sites so students may reacquaint themselves with the material if necessary. Much like a traditional quiz, Flip-Flop quizzes may also be used to check whether students have learned new material at the end of a module or chapter of a textbook.

Obviously the abundance of quizzes needed to achieve the aforementioned goals can only be achieved if the Flip-Flop methodologies become widely adopted. We therefore encourage the readers interested in trying Flip-Flop in their courses to get in touch with us to discuss how we could best accommodate their needs and integrate them within our technology.

Last but not least, an abundance of online quizzes might solve one of the increasingly pressing educational quandaries: how to address copying and prevent plagiarism in a time when most of the resources, exercises, problems and their solutions are accessible online. If our students were willing to take dozens of quizzes to prepare for a test, we should be confident that they have learned the subject well enough. Given this perspective, we can argue that the more quiz tasks and problem solutions are uploaded to the internet the less important it will be to penalize students for copying. Plagiarism may become a historically interesting misdemeanor rather than an educational felony.

References

Active learning. In: Wikipedia. https://en.wikipedia.org/wiki/Active_learning. Accessed 2 Mar 2018

Baggaley J (2013) MOOC rampant. Distance Education 34(3):368–378

Bishop J, Verleger MA (2013) The flipped classroom: a survey of the research. In: ASEE national conference proceedings, Atlanta

Biswas G, Segedy JR, Bunchongchit K (2015) From design to implementation to practice a learning by teaching system: Betty's Brain. Int J Artif Intell Edu 26(1):350–364

Blackboard. http://www.blackboard.com. Accessed 2 Mar 2018

Bloom's taxonomy. In: Wikipedia. https://en.wikipedia.org/wiki/Bloom%27s_taxonomy. Accessed 2 Mar 2018

D2L Brightspace. https://www.d2l.com. Accessed 2 Mar 2018

Canvas. https://www.canvaslms.com. Accessed 2 Mar 2018

Christensen G, Steinmetz A, Alcorn B, Bennett A, Woods D, Emanel EJ (2014) The MOOC phenomenon: who takes massive open online courses and why? https://dx.doi.org/10.2139/ssrn.2350964. Accessed 8 Apr 2018

Constructivism (philosophy of education). In: Wikipedia. https://en.wikipedia.org/wiki/Constructivism_(philosophy_of_education). Accessed 2 Mar 2018

Duran D (2016) Learning-by-teaching. Evidence and implications as a pedagogical mechanism. Edu Teach Int, 1–9

Flip-flop Questions. http://honza.epizy.com/slippah/questions.html. Accessed 8 Apr 2018

Flipped classroom. In: Wikipedia. https://en.wikipedia.org/wiki/Flipped_classroom. Accessed 2 Mar 2018

Goodlad S, Hirst B (1989) Peer tutoring. A guide to learning by teaching. Nichols Publishing, New York

Hanke U (2012) Learning by teaching. In: Seel NM (ed) Encyclopedia of the sciences of learning. Springer, Boston, pp 1830–1832

Hartnett K (2013) San Jose state to Michael Sandel: keep your MOOC off our campus. In: Boston Globe. http://archive.boston.com/bostonglobe/ideas/brainiac/2013/05/san_jose_state.html. Accessed 8 Apr 2018

Hill P (2017) State of higher Ed LMS market for US and Canada: fall 2017 Edition. In: e-Literate. https://mfeldstein.com/state-higher-ed-lms-market-us-canada-fall-2017-edition. Accessed 8 Apr 2018

Kahoot! https://kahoot.com. Accessed 2 Mar 2018

Learning by teaching. In: Wikipedia. https://en.wikipedia.org/wiki/Learning_by_teaching. Accessed 2 Mar 2018

Massive open online course. In: Wikipedia. https://en.wikipedia.org/wiki/Massive_open_online_course. Accessed 2 Mar 2018

Moodle. https://moodle.org. Accessed 2 Mar 2018

Ogawa MB (2018) Evaluation of flip-flop learning methodology. In: Paper presented at the HCI international conference, Las Vegas, 15–20 July 2018

Quiz It! https://devpost.com/software/quiz-it. Accessed 2 Mar 2018

Quizlet. https://quizlet.com. Accessed 2 Mar 2018

Stelovska U, Stelovsky J, Wu J (2016) Constructive learning using flip-flop methodology: learning by making quizzes synchronized with video recording of lectures. In: Zaphiris P, Ioannou A (eds) Lecture notes in computer science (Learning and collaboration technologies), vol 9753. Springer

Stelovsky J, Ogata B, Stelovska U (2018) "Flip-flop" learning by teaching methodologies: "Peer improvement", "agile tooltip", support technology, and next steps. In: Paper presented at the HCI international Conference, Las Vegas, 15–20 July 2018

Vardi MY (2012) Will MOOCs destroy academia? Commun ACM 55(11): 5

Vygotskii LS (1978) Mind in society: the development of higher psychological processes. Harvard University Press, Cambridge

Chapter 10
Using Animation to Enrich Learning Experience in Sketch-Based Physics Tutoring Systems

Salman Cheema and Joseph J. LaViola Jr.

Abstract This work describes the design of a prototype sketch-based physics tutoring system that provides animation support for a range of kinematics problems including spring systems, pulley systems, motion in 1-dimension, free-fall motion, projectile motion, kinetic and potential energy problems, and limited cases of equilibrium problems. Our key idea is to construct animations using a student's written answer to a physics problem, providing visual feedback in the given context, thus enriching the learning experience for the user. The recognition of written physics solutions and constructing animations from them are challenging research problems. We discuss design goals for providing animation support, based on analysis of 50 kinematics problems chosen from a physics textbook. We describe the high-level design of our system and discuss how animations can be generated for several classes of kinematics problems. We present the results of an informal usability test with five expert users and conclude with a discussion of the limitations and capabilities of our system.

10.1 Introduction

A well designed learning experience is an important aspect of intelligent tutoring systems. Sketch-based interaction provides the ability to manipulate a computer system with a stylus. This enables natural interaction and makes sketch-based user interfaces strong candidates for intelligent tutoring systems. In recent years, several researchers

S. Cheema (✉)
Arizona State University, Tempe, AZ, USA
e-mail: salman.cheema@asu.edu

J. J. LaViola Jr.
University of Central Florida, Orlando, FL, USA
e-mail: jjl@eecs.ucf.edu

E. Kapros and M. Koutsombogera (eds.), *Designing for the User Experience in Learning Systems*, Human–Computer Interaction Series,
https://doi.org/10.1007/978-3-319-94794-5_10

have attempted to use sketch-based user interfaces for education in domains such as Circuit Analysis (Gennari et al. 2005; de Silva 2007; Zamora and Eyjólfsdóttir 2009), Chemistry (Ouyang and Davis 2011; Tenneson and Becker 2005), Mechanical Design (Alvarado 2000; Kara et al. 2008; Oltmans and Davis 2001), Mathematics (Anthony et al. 2012; Bott and LaViola 2010; Cossairt and LaViola 2012; Jiang et al. 2010; LaViola and Zeleznik 2004), Computer Science (Buchanan and Laviola 2014; Kang et al. 2012), and Introductory Physics (Atilola et al. 2014; Cheema and LaViola 2012; Lee et al. 2012, 2007; Scott and Davis 2013).

Two important aspects of problem solving are writing and drawing.[1] Drawing (or sketching) has important benefits in science education (Ainsworth et al. 2011; Larkin and Simon 1987; Wai et al. 2009). Larkin and Simon (1987) examine the importance of visualization and drawing, concluding:

> ...Diagrams can group together all information that is used together, thus avoiding large amounts of search for the elements needed to make a problem solving inference...

Diagramming has important advantages for student learning. Diagrams represent information spatially rather than sequentially (e.g. text), enabling better spatial inferences (Larkin and Simon 1987). Spatial skills have been found to correlate strongly with improved performance in STEM[2] disciplines (Wai et al. 2009). Sketching and diagramming also tend to increase engagement and improves learning (Ainsworth et al. 2011).

Sketch-based user interfaces are excellent for providing writing and drawing support in learning environments because they closely mimic pen and paper for taking notes and communicating ideas. Sketch-based interfaces are natural and transparent (Abowd 1999), allow users to write mathematics quickly compared to typing (Anthony et al. 2005, 2007) and may help reduce cognitive load on students compared to menu-based systems (Sweller 1988, 1994). Anthony et al. (2012) and Hammond et al. (Atilola et al. 2014) present a good discussion of the advantages of sketch-based interfaces in the education domain.

Our main research goal is to investigate methods for constructing sketch-based physics tutoring systems. In order to do so, it is important to understand students' work flow in scientific problem solving. Alvarado and Lazzareschi (2007) have done preliminary work in this area for drawing logic diagrams. Figure 10.1 shows the statement of a kinematics problem that can be solved by applying $f = ma$. Figure 10.2 shows a solution acquired from a student for this problem, containing both writing and drawing. The diagram has been annotated with arrows, distance measurements and an equation for force. Both parts of the solution are clearly labeled. In part (a), the equation of motion ($x = x_0 + v_0 t + \frac{1}{2}at^2$) is used to get the answer. In part (b), the student first uses the principle of work done to compute velocity which is used to reach the required answer. It is also possible to solve part (b) with the equations of motion (Use $v_1^2 - v_0^2 = 2aS$ to derive velocity).

[1] Examples of 'drawing or sketching' include diagrams and free form art whereas 'writing' is exemplified by handwritten text and mathematics.

[2] Science, Technology, Engineering and Mathematics.

4.10 •• A dockworker applies a constant horizontal force of 80.0 N to a block of ice on a smooth horizontal floor. The frictional force is negligible. The block starts from rest and moves 11.0 m in 5.00 s. (a) What is the mass of the block of ice? (b) If the worker stops pushing at the end of 5.00 s, how far does the block move in the next 5.00 s?

Fig. 10.1 Friction problem statement taken from University Physics 13 Ed (Young et al. 2011, p. 129)

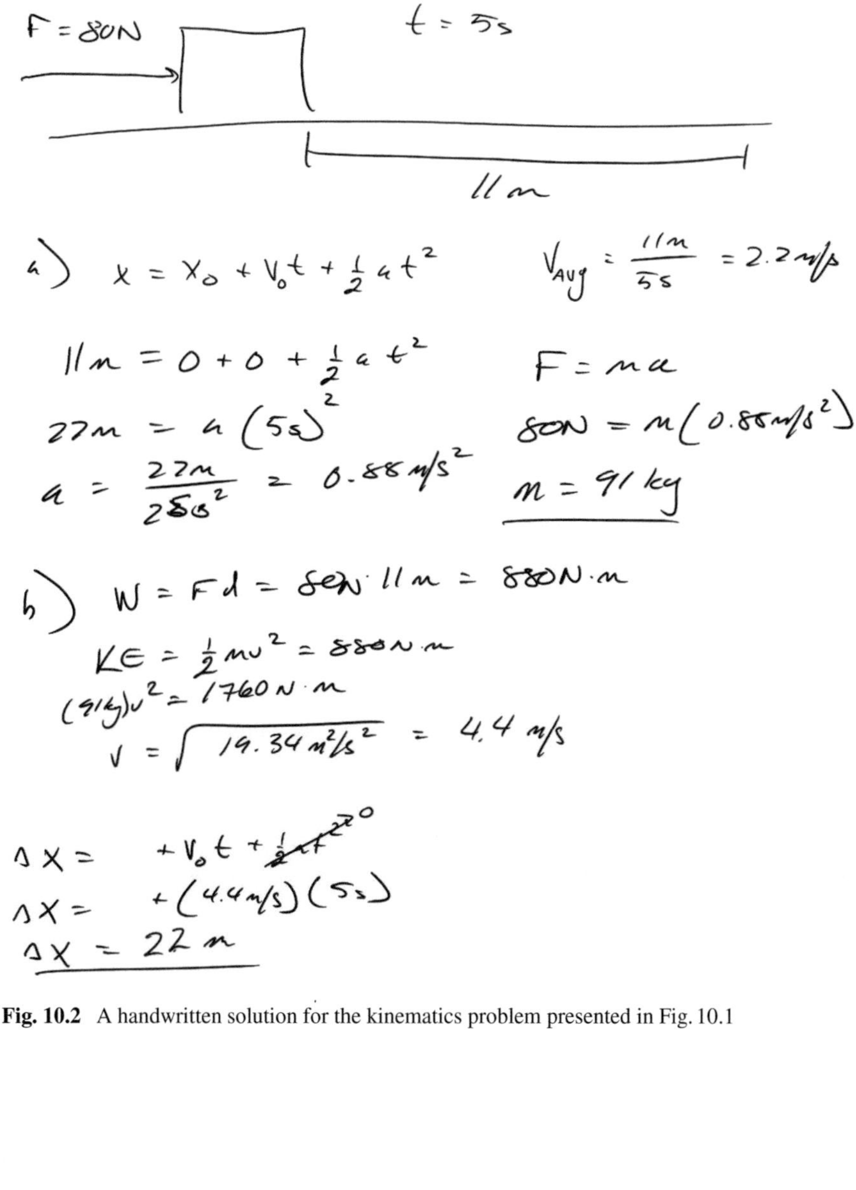

Fig. 10.2 A handwritten solution for the kinematics problem presented in Fig. 10.1

The diagram in Fig. 10.2 depicts the scenario of the assigned problem in a visual way and was annotated with the information provided in the statement. The student used physics and mathematics principles to write a series of equations which were used to compute an answer which was a numeric quantity in both parts. Generally, physics problems require student to either compute a numeric value, derive a function, make a decision or verify an equivalence. Solved on paper, a student solution is static, providing little insight into how the answer affects the given scenario. Research indicates that when solving mechanical problems, many people report consciously simulating what would happen (Clement 1994; Johnson-Laird 1998; Shepard 1978a, b). This indicates a possibility to provide deeper insight into students' solutions by constructing animations out of their solutions, thus enriching the learning experience. We can further improve the learning experience by providing rich feedback mechanisms such as the ability to construct graphs or to view the size and/or directions of scalar/vector quantities associated with motion.

This work describes a prototype tutoring system that makes significant contributions toward our research goal. Students can use a sketch-based user interface to write down solutions containing diagrams and mathematics. Our system can recognize different elements of physics solutions in several categories of kinematics problems. It can then generate parametrized animations from the recognition results. Users can specify animation parameters in a flexible manner. Our system can also infer reasonable initial values for unspecified parameters based on the appearances of simulation objects.

We first address design considerations for pen-based tutoring systems with animation support, followed by a review of existing work. We then discuss the interaction design and provide high level details of system components. We highlight the types of solutions that can be animated using our system and describe how our approach can be extended to other domains of physics solutions.

10.2 Design Considerations

Our goal of constructing sketch-based tutoring systems with animation support can be broken down into the following subproblems:

1. Recognizing the contents of written physics solutions.
2. Constructing animations from recognized solutions.
3. Control and feedback mechanisms to support experimentation and learning.

10.2.1 Recognizing Physics Solutions

A sketch-based tutoring system needs to recognize written physics solutions, parsing them into mathematical expressions, diagram elements, and annotations for diagram elements. Each solution is set of digital ink strokes representing either text (words, phrases, sentences), mathematics (numbers and equations), or diagrams. There is considerable variation in writing styles and notation between different domains and among individual users (Mahoney and Fromherz 2002). Symbols can be written in different sizes, positions, and orientations. Extracting high-level information from a sketch is yet harder. Domain knowledge is necessary to correctly recognize a given solution. It is useful to split recognition into two steps: low-level and high-level. Low-level recognition may recognize domain agnostic symbols such as text, equations, shapes, arrows, etc. High-level recognition must infer appropriate meaning from low-level recognition results. For example, high-level recognition would associate the variables in recognized mathematical equations with physics quantities and try to form links between them and recognized diagram elements.

10.2.2 Constructing Animations

Simulating physically accurate behavior in video games (Baraff 1997a, b; Eberly 2003; Millington 2007; Witkin 1997) is a well-studied problem. In such settings, approximating correct physical behavior is sufficient, rather than supporting high precision reserved for scientific modeling. Rigid body motion is a very popular method for modeling Newtonian dynamics. Popular physics engines such as PhysX (2018), Havok (2018), Open dynamics engine (2018), Newton game dynamics (2018), Cryphysics (2018) and Bullet physics (2018) all support rigid body dynamics. Rigid body motion relies on using the second law of motion ($f = ma$) in an incremental way. In each timestep, the net force on each simulation object is computed, followed by the use of numerical integration to compute changes in velocity and position, which are used to update the position of the object. Enforcing constraints such as non-penetration and friction forces during sliding contact can be challenging with rigid bodies. Alternative methods such as Lagrangian dynamics,[3] deformable bodies and penalty-based methods help alleviate some of these concerns but involve complicated software engineering.

Rigid body motion is simple to engineer and provides good approximations for several Newtonian physics phenomena such as linear motion, projectile motion, rotational and angular motion, torque, friction and sliding contact, atmospheric drag, gravitational effects, kinetic and gravitational potential energy, and momentum transfer via collision detection and resolution. These qualities make rigid body dynamics a good candidate for covering the animation requirements of physics solutions. We have explored the use of a customized physics engine to support animation of physics diagrams in (Cheema and LaViola 2010a, b, 2012). This approach yielded some promising results but indicated that a single physics engine is difficult to extend to new domains of physics problems. In this work, we outline a hybrid approach that uses a system of domain-specific simulation engines to tackle simulation.

[3] A framework for deriving the specific equations of motion in the presence of particular constraints. A good introduction is provided in (Eberly 2003).

10.2.3 Control and Feedback Mechanisms

Physics problems usually require students to either compute a numeric value, derive a function, make a decision or verify an equivalence. Students are required to reason about interesting events along the trajectory of objects or are required to predict behavior in specific scenarios. Providing animation support for these situations can be tricky, as the entire initial state may not be known. As an illustrative example, consider a problem where the student is asked to predict the range (R) of a projectile given an initial velocity (v_0) and a launch angle (θ). The equation $R = \frac{v_0^2 sin2\theta}{g}$ will yield an answer. However, more information is needed to simulate this scenario using rigid body dynamics. To compute net force, we need to know the mass of the projectile, as well as the magnitude and direction of gravity, both of which are not specified in either the problem statement or the solution. In this case, if the answer is correct, the projectile should cover the appropriate horizontal distance. However, the animation system may have a different notion of distance units from the user (pixels vs. meters).

This example highlights the importance of control mechanisms for specifying new information and/or altering properties of a generated simulation in order to verify a solution visually. In video games or traditional simulations, this information can be hand-coded or procedurally generated, but a tutoring system needs to provide intuitive and effective methods for quickly specifying this information to allow users to customize their learning experience. The user must be able to specify vector and scalar physical properties of each simulation element (e.g., mass, velocity, etc), as well as any global constraints (e.g., gravity, drag coefficient, coefficient of kinetic or static friction). Additionally, the user must also specify the spatial and temporal bounds of the simulation. We initially examined 50 kinematics problems[4] (Cheema 2014) and came up with three general categories of animation behavior that needs to be supported for sketch-based tutoring (Cheema 2014). Upon further investigation, we have chosen to extend these animation categories in the following manner:

Continuous Animation The interesting event is a continuous phenomenon such as undamped spring oscillation or simple harmonic motion. The animation runs forever.

Limited Animation The time or position of the interesting event(s) is known before the simulation starts.

Temporal Events One or more interesting event(s) occur either at specific times after the simulation starts. For each event, the student may either do a computation or reason about physical aspect(s) of the specified scenario. If only one event (at $t = t_1$) is of interest, then the simulation runs from $t = 0 \rightarrow t_1$. This category can be generalized as a series of piecemeal simulations ($t = t_0 \rightarrow t_1 \rightarrow t_2 \ldots \rightarrow t_n$, where t_i denotes a time index).

[4]The chosen physics problems can be viewed at http://www.public.asu.edu/~scheema3/dataset-description.html.

Spatial Events One or more points in the trajectory of a simulation object are interesting (e.g., find change in gravitational potential energy when a marble falls to the ground from a table). This category can be generalized in a similar manner as Temporal events, using a series of piecemeal simulations ($x = x_0 \rightarrow x_1 \rightarrow x_2 \ldots x_n$, where x_i is the position function for a simulation element).

Unknown Events One or more discrete events are interesting during the course of the simulation (e.g., momentum transfer via elastic collision). Students must make a decision or do a computation at each discrete event. This event may involve interaction of a simulation object with the environment or with other simulation objects. Usually, the nature of the event(s) is described in the problem statement, but its time or location is not, making it difficult to model.

It is important to note that constructing simulations is a well studied problem and the existing body of work provides a rich set of methods for modeling a large number of scenarios (Eberly 2003; Millington 2007). However, the process of specifying a large number of simulation parameters is time consuming, requiring users to explicitly list parameters via a customized interface or via configuration files. Techniques such as Motion Sketching (Popović et al. 2003, 2000) and Animation Sketching (Moscovich and Hughes 2001) enable interactive manipulation of simulations in select cases, allowing animators to quickly construct animations. However, these methods are not particularly suited to simulations constructed from physics solutions, because they allow users to sketch motion paths and constraints, using these to infer suitable initial parameters. In the case of handwritten physics solutions, the primary concern is using the student's solution to drive the animation, rather than inferring it. In this work, we describe methods that can (1) automatically infer some required parameters from a given physics solution and (2) allow the user to specify the remaining variables using two simple gestures (Lasso + Tap).

Feedback is an umbrella term for providing useful information to the end user. Many approaches are possible here, ranging from generating real time graphs to using visual cues to highlight errors or emphasizing important physics concepts in action. In our prototype, we provide support for viewing the interplay of physical properties of simulation elements while the animation is occurring. Our prototype can also plot physics quantities such as energy and velocity as a time series and uses visual cues such as arrows to denote direction and magnitude of forces. Finally, the animation itself can serve as a means of feedback, as a correct solution will generally lead to an intuitively correct animation.

10.3 Related Work

10.3.1 Sketch-Based Animation Systems

Motion sketching and direct manipulation are popular interaction metaphors to enable easy animation authoring in the research community (Davis et al. 2008; Igarashi et al. 2005; Santosa et al. 2013; Thorne et al. 2007). Systems like K-Sketch

(Davis et al. 2008) allow users to select an object and directly sketch its path, inserting alterations at one or more points in its trajectory. Some systems (Moscovich and Hughes 2001; Popović et al. 2003, 2000) can infer appropriate initial conditions from the user's manipulations. Special purpose applications of motion sketching have also been developed, e.g., Motion Doodles (Thorne et al. 2007) for sketching character movements in a 3D scene, and DirectPaint (Santosa et al. 2013) for free-hand painting and video annotation. These works provide useful insight into how sketch-based interfaces can be used to author animations, enabling a wide range of animations from different domains. However, they are not suitable for our research goal for the following reasons:

1. Methods that require direct manipulation to infer initial conditions are not useful for us as initial conditions must necessarily come from a student's solution.
2. Methods enabling manipulation of elements during a simulation to modify subsequent behavior are partially useful because they enable users to test physical behavior given different parameters. However, for the most part, a physics solution should drive the simulation behavior.
3. None of the existing methods in this domain use the mathematics in a physics solution to guide animation behavior.

10.3.2 Sketch-Based Animation in Education

Alvarado (2000), Oltmans and Davis (2001) and Kara et al. (2008) have constructed systems for sketch understanding in computer aided design, mechanical design and vibratory systems. These tools can recognize and animate relevant diagrams but do not allow users to write down mathematics that can influence animation. Scott and Davis (2013) have constructed PhysInk that allows users to quickly creating animations via direct manipulation and demonstration of desired behavior. PhysInk also does not allow users to write down mathematics to guide animation. While the techniques used in PhysInk have several practical applications, they are not very relevant to our research goal of understanding diagrams and context from a handwritten solution.

The MathPad^2 (LaViola and Zeleznik 2004) system is interesting because (1) it is domain independent (2) allows for unconstrained sketch input and (3) allows users to explicitly associate equations with diagrams to guide animation behavior. However, MathPad^2 is difficult to use because it includes no domain knowledge and thus cannot infer context or missing information. Additionally, users must specify all aspects of animation through hand-written mathematics. CogSketch (Forbus et al. 2011) is another sketch-based system that emphasizes conceptual labeling of sketches by its users. While CogSketch permits unconstrained sketch input and aims to aid development of sketch-based educational software, its focus is very broad, ranging from investigating cognitive aspects to running simulations. This makes it unsuitable for our goals, as it lacks the focus on understanding student solutions automatically and providing visual feedback.

Newton's Pen (Lee et al. 2007), Newton's Pen II (Lee et al. 2012), and Mechanix (Atilola et al. 2014) are important sketch-based systems targeted at the domain of Statics. Newton's Pen (Lee et al. 2007) and Newton's Pen II (Lee et al. 2012) focus on drawing free body diagrams and writing equilibrium equations. Both do not use animation or allow unconstrained sketch input. Instead, users must adhere to a particular work flow while sketching diagrams. Additionally, diagrams and equations must be drawn/written in separate pre-defined areas. Newton's Pen II (Lee et al. 2012) also describes an interesting method based on Hidden Markov Models (HMM) to correct errors in recognized equations. Mechanix (Atilola et al. 2014) is a tutoring system for statics that allows students to sketch truss and free-body diagrams. Mechanix is a deployed system and has been thoroughly user-tested, with encouraging results. It allows instructors to easily author and assign new problems to students via a web-based interface. Students solve assigned problems via a sketch-based interface. If a diagram is incorrect, the student can make corrections until it matches the instructor's correct solution (Field et al. 2011). While Mechanix allows students to sketch drawings in an unconstrained manner, it is focused on a very narrow domain, and does not support handwriting recognition. Students must enter the values for different labeled forces via a text box. While Mechanix provides useful feedback and hints, it does not provide any animation of sketched diagrams.

We have explored the use of 2D rigid body simulations for physics tutoring, constructing a prototype system called PhysicsBook (Cheema and LaViola 2012), which extended earlier work (Cheema and LaViola 2010a, b). The first prototype (Cheema and LaViola 2010b) was a simple proof-of-concept system, capable of recognizing simple physics solutions and used a customized 2D rigid body physics engine to animate diagrams. Users could associate mathematics with components of a diagram to guide animation behavior. This was extended by incorporating sketch beautification methods and additional animation capabilities in (Cheema and LaViola 2010a). In these two systems, animation parameters were limited to physics quantities directly related to motion such as position, velocity, acceleration and force, defined as functions of time (Cheema and LaViola 2010a). PhysicsBook (Cheema and LaViola 2012) extended this approach by providing recognition support for diagram annotations such as arrows and dotted lines and by using real time data transformations to enable a richer set of animations for select cases of pulley systems, work done, kinetic and gravitational potential energy. PhysicsBook's contributions overlap with our research goals, but have drawbacks. First, adding animation support for new types of diagrams was complex due to high coupling within the physics engine. Second, PhysicsBook focused exclusively on the answer step in the solution, not using any of the information provided in the problem statement or the rest of the solution.

In this work, we improve upon our earlier methods (Cheema and LaViola 2012, 2010a, b) in the following ways:

1. Use of an animation framework with multiple simulation engines instead of a monolithic physics engine.
2. Using the problem statement to identify the appropriate simulation engine(s).

3. Construction of a flexible, 2-stage sketch recognition pipeline that parses a solution into diagram, annotations and mathematics and uses these to construct a simulation.

10.4 System Overview

Our prototype tutoring system is able to provide animation support for a range of problems in kinematics, including spring problems, motion in 1-dimension, free-fall, projectile motion, kinetic and potential energy problems, and limited cases of equilibrium problems. Figure 10.3 shows the user interface for our sketch-based tutoring system, which presents a large writing area to the user. Students can solve problems on the writing area using a stylus. The system tool bar (above the writing area) provides buttons to trigger recognition and animation. A separate tab in the tool bar can be used to view graphs of interesting physical quantities. The 'Scribble' gesture can be used to erase parts of the solution. Users can scroll down for more writing space as needed. The system menu above the tool bar can be used to save and load solutions (along with problem statements) from disk. Figure 10.4 shows an animation generated from the solution depicted in Fig. 10.3, along with a graph showing vertical displacement over time.

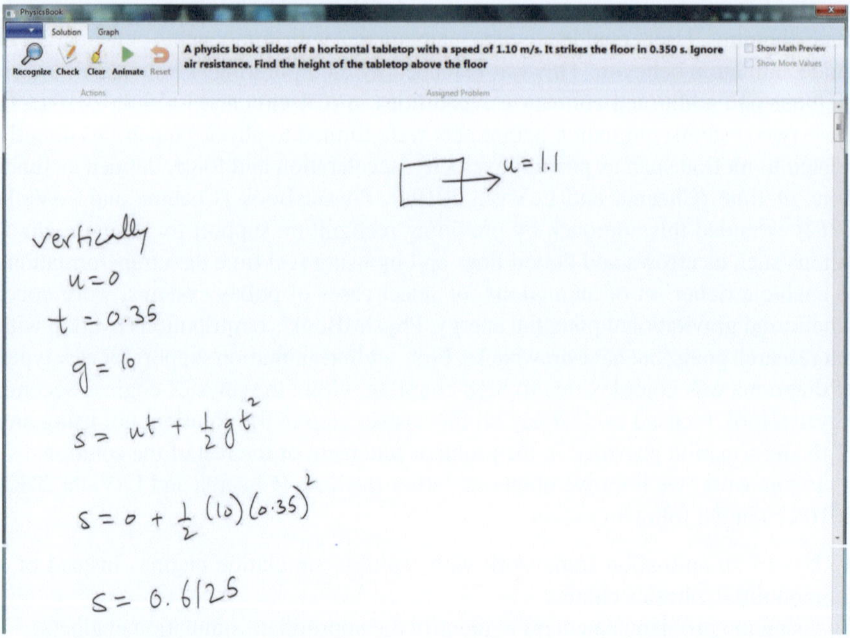

Fig. 10.3 A screenshot showing a physics solution written out using our prototype system

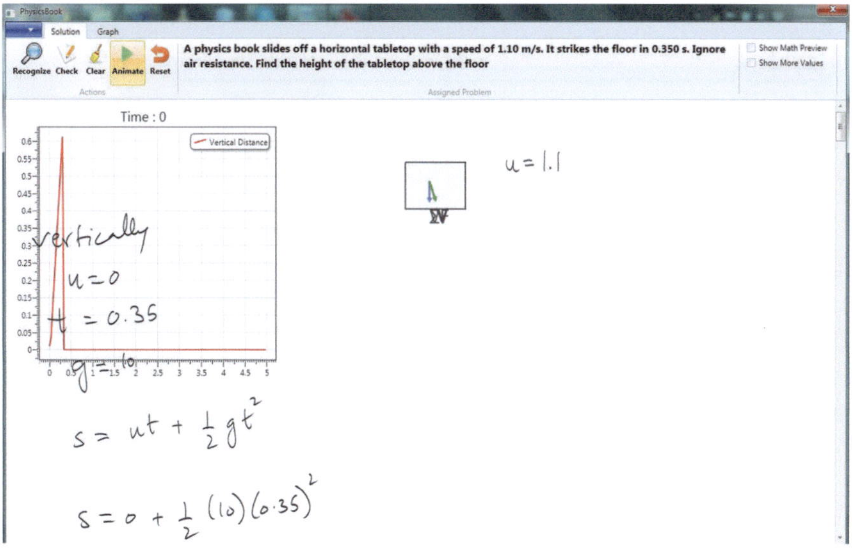

Fig. 10.4 Screenshot showing the result of recognition and animation for the solution shown in Fig. 10.3. The included graph shows vertical distance traveled by the box over time. The user can easily see that the box travels a distance of approximately 0.6 m over 0.35 s, thus verifying the solution

Our system provides support for animating sketched diagrams containing circles and convex polygons. These shapes represent diagram elements that may be attached to pulleys, wires or springs. Shapes can be floating or constrained to move along a surface (represented by a line segment or a polyline). Initial conditions can be specified by writing mathematical expressions and sketching annotations such as arrows and dotted lines. Dotted lines and intervals (parallel dotted lines) also enable students to indicate a particular event in the simulation or to define a displacement range.

The 'Recognize' button triggers recognition of the solution on the writing area and constructs an animation which can be run by using the 'Animate' button. We chose this interaction method because studies by Wais et al. (2007) suggested that users prefer to trigger sketch recognition after finishing their solution. However, experiments by Bott et al. (2011) have found that users prefer realtime recognition feedback for mathematics when they are expected to write more than one expression. We have balanced these competing concerns by running the math recognition engine (based on (Zeleznik et al. 2008)) in our prototype continuously, providing real time feedback as the user is writing. If needed, this behavior can be disabled via a check box on the tool bar.

Figure 10.5 shows the different steps in our recognition system. Complete implementation details of our recognition system can be found in (Cheema 2014). During recognition, we use the text of the given problem to identify the problem domain and select one or more relevant simulation engines for animation. The written solution

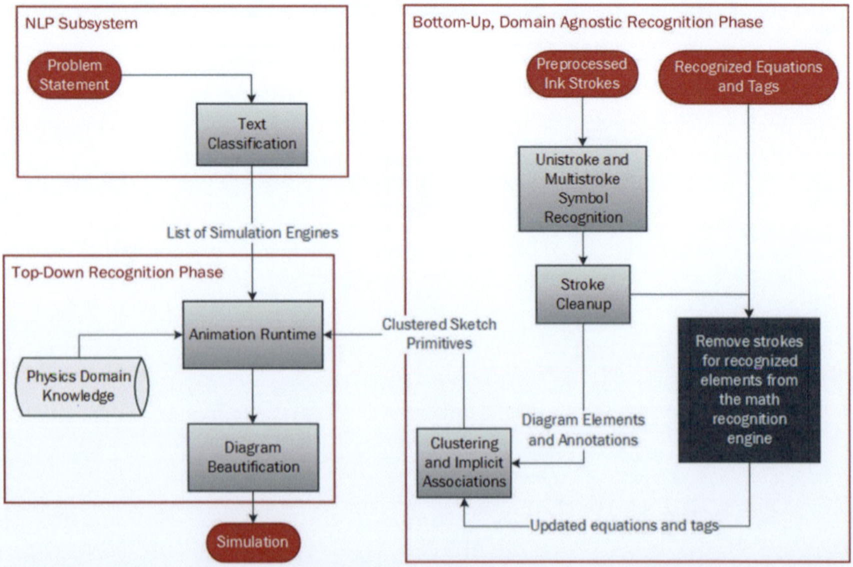

Fig. 10.5 Different stages of our recognition system. The inputs are preprocessed ink strokes (representing the entire solution), recognition results from the continuously active mathematics recognizer, and the text of the problem

is parsed in two stages. The first, bottom up recognition stage recognizes shapes, labels and annotations, which are then implicitly linked with each other using spatial proximity. Recognized mathematics is implicitly linked with shapes and annotations using both spatial proximity and label matching. The second, top-down recognition stage uses the inferred domain of the problem to assign meaning to each recognized diagram element, which are then assigned to the selected simulation engines. This approach allows our system to infer initial conditions for simulation elements directly from the handwritten solution. Any physics properties not inferred by implicit linking are filled in by the simulation engines themselves, based on the spatial characteristics of each diagram element. We do a beautification step at the end of the top-down recognition stage that resolves approximate drawings into precisely aligned simulations by (1) ensuring proper contact constraints, (2) clipping connectors (wires, pulleys, springs) against shape boundaries, (3) beautifying shapes (e.g., axis alignment), and (4) modifying physical appearance based on implicitly/explicitly linked mathematics (An example is shown in Sect. 10.5.4). Our beautification techniques are based on (Cheema et al. 2012; Cheema and LaViola 2010a).

Implicitly associated equations can be viewed by hovering the stylus over recognized diagram elements. Any associations missed during recognition can be explicitly indicated by the user. To make an explicit association, users select mathematical expression(s) with the 'Lasso' gesture and use the 'Tap' gesture to link them with a diagram element. Global variables an be specified by lassoing an expression and tapping the background canvas instead of a diagram element.

10.5 Results: Animations of Physics Problems

This section describes how animations and feedback could be generated with our system for a selected set of physics problems. It is important to note that our system is not robust enough for a full-fledged user evaluation. The examples in this section are intended to demonstrate the range of physics problems that our system can recognize and animate.

10.5.1 Example I: 3-Spring System

Figure 10.6 shows a box connected to 3 springs of different stiffness. Deriving a closed-form solution for the box's motion is non-trivial. It is far easier to sketch the spring system and view its behavior in real time. The three springs are labeled 'a', 'b', and 'c' by the user, while the box is labeled 'd'. Upon recognition, the labels are associated implicitly with each diagram element based on proximity checking. Similarly, the equations for stiffness and mass are also associated implicitly using label-matching. The graph in Fig. 10.6 shows the interplay between the kinetic and potential energy of the box once the system is released from rest. This example highlights the use of graphing as an important feedback method.

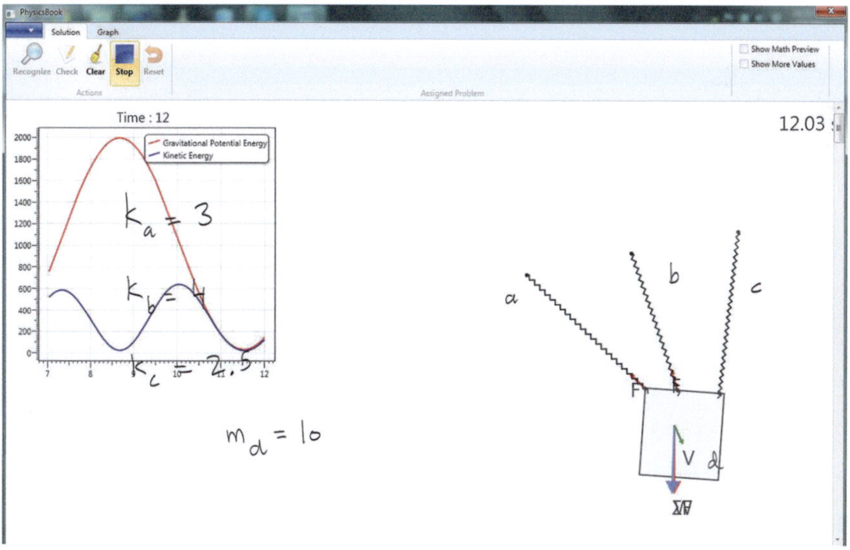

Fig. 10.6 A box suspended using three springs. Deriving a closed-form solution for the behavior of this system can be difficult whereas generating a simulation is very easy using our prototype system

10.5.2 Example II: Change in Gravitational Potential Energy

Figure 10.7 shows a free fall problem. A ball of mass $m = 10\,\text{kg}$ is dropped from a known height. The student is asked to compute the change in gravitational potential energy after the ball falls 50 m. The student sketches a circle to represent the ball, and annotates the diagram with an interval (two parallel, horizontal dotted lines) to indicate limits of displacement. From the given information, the change in potential energy of the ball is determined to be $P_e = 5000\,\text{J}$. Upon recognition, the ball is replaced by a circle. The dotted lines are interpreted as an interval. The circle is labeled 'a', and the equation indicating mass ($m_a = 10$) is associated implicitly. The student first selects the expression $dx = 50$ and associates it with the interval to indicate the displacement limit. The student then selects the answer, $P_e = 5000$ with the 'Lasso' gesture, associates it by tapping the circle, and triggers the animation. The system uses the association $P_e = 5000$ to derive the magnitude of required displacement. The simulation stops when the required displacement has been covered. If the computed change in potential energy is correct, the ball will move exactly 50 m. If it is incorrect, then the ball will come to rest either before or after reaching the end level. This example highlights the usefulness of being able to denote the starting and ending points of motion by using dotted lines.

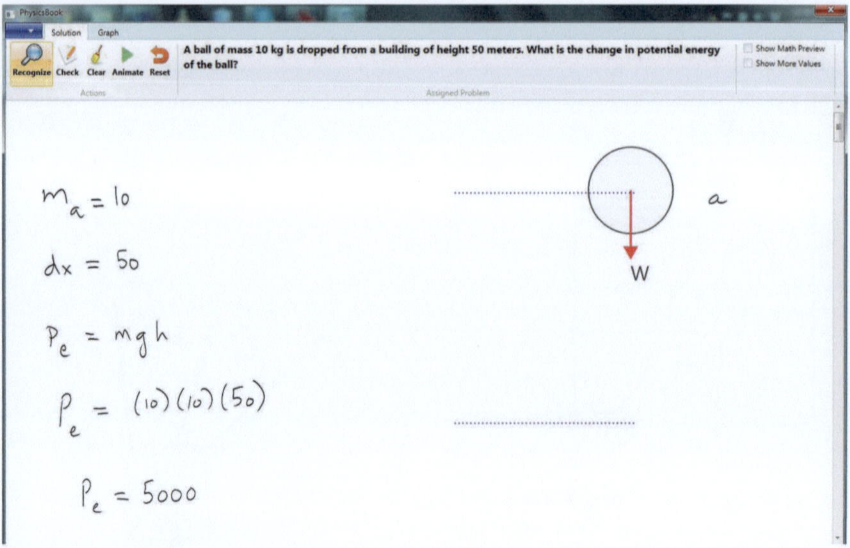

Fig. 10.7 A ball of mass 10 kg is dropped from a the roof of a building of height 50 m. The student is asked to work out the change in gravitational potential energy of the ball

10.5.3 Example III: Force and Acceleration

The simple scenario in Fig. 10.8 can be solved with the direct application of $f = ma$. A force and acceleration are provided, and the mass must be computed. However, in this instance, the answer cannot be visually verified in a simple way. If the box moves with a constant but wrong acceleration, a user may not be able to tell the difference. However, the graphing functionality in our prototype (Shown in Fig. 10.9) can be used to confirm that the acceleration precisely matches the predicted value.

This scenario is similar to the springs example in Sect. 10.5.1, from an animation point of view. A set of initial conditions are provided that yield a continuous animation (no time or distance constraints) and the result can be visually or graphically verified.

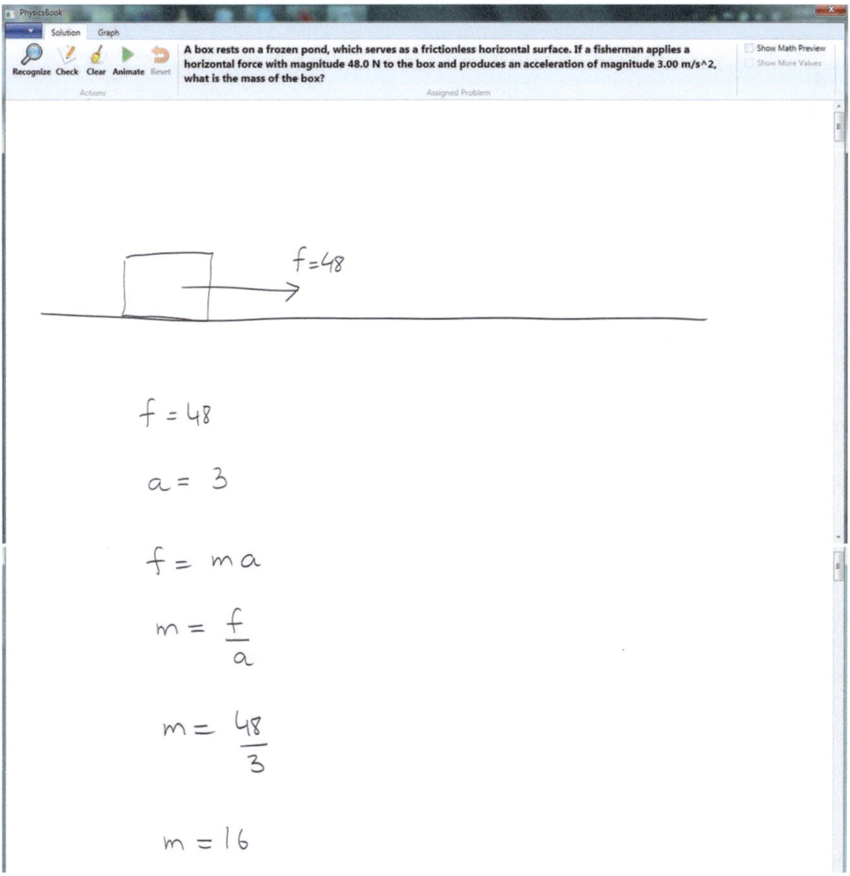

Fig. 10.8 Simple problem that requires the use of $f = ma$

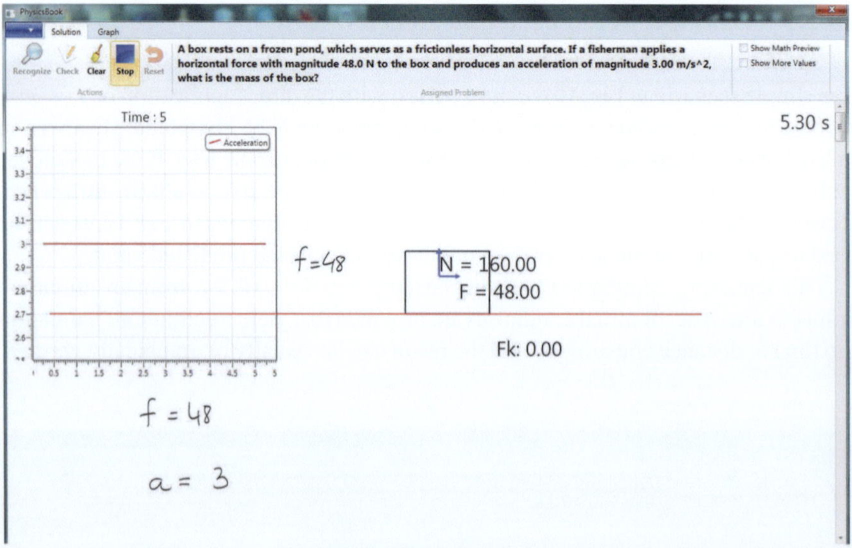

Fig. 10.9 Animation for the scenario in Fig. 10.8

10.5.4 Example IV: Box in Equilibrium

The solution in Fig. 10.10 depicts a box suspended using two wires, at angles of 60° and 40° with the horizontal. The student is asked to work out the tension in each wire such that the box is held in equilibrium. The student derives values of $0.77862w_c$ and $0.507713w_c$ for the tension in the two wires. After associating the tension with each wire, the student can hit 'Animate'. As the tension in each wire is correct, the box is held in equilibrium. If an incorrect answer for the tension had been derived, the box would move in the direction of the net force. This would cause one or both wires to stretch (depending on the direction and magnitude of the net force). If any wire is stretched beyond 20% of its initial length, it is broken, causing the box to fall freely.

This scenario illustrates several important issues. First, the answer is given in symbolic variables rather than in a numeric form. The simulation engine must be able to find and extract the value of w_c at runtime for it to work correctly. Generally, given a variable and its subscript, the simulation engine must infer the following pieces of information:

1. The physical quantity represented by the variable.
2. The simulation element to which this physical quantity belongs.
3. The value of said physical quantity at this instant in time.

Second, sketched wires may not touch the box at its exact corners and may also not make angles of 60° and 40° with the horizontal. Precise beautification after recognition and explicit association is required to mitigate these problems. Third,

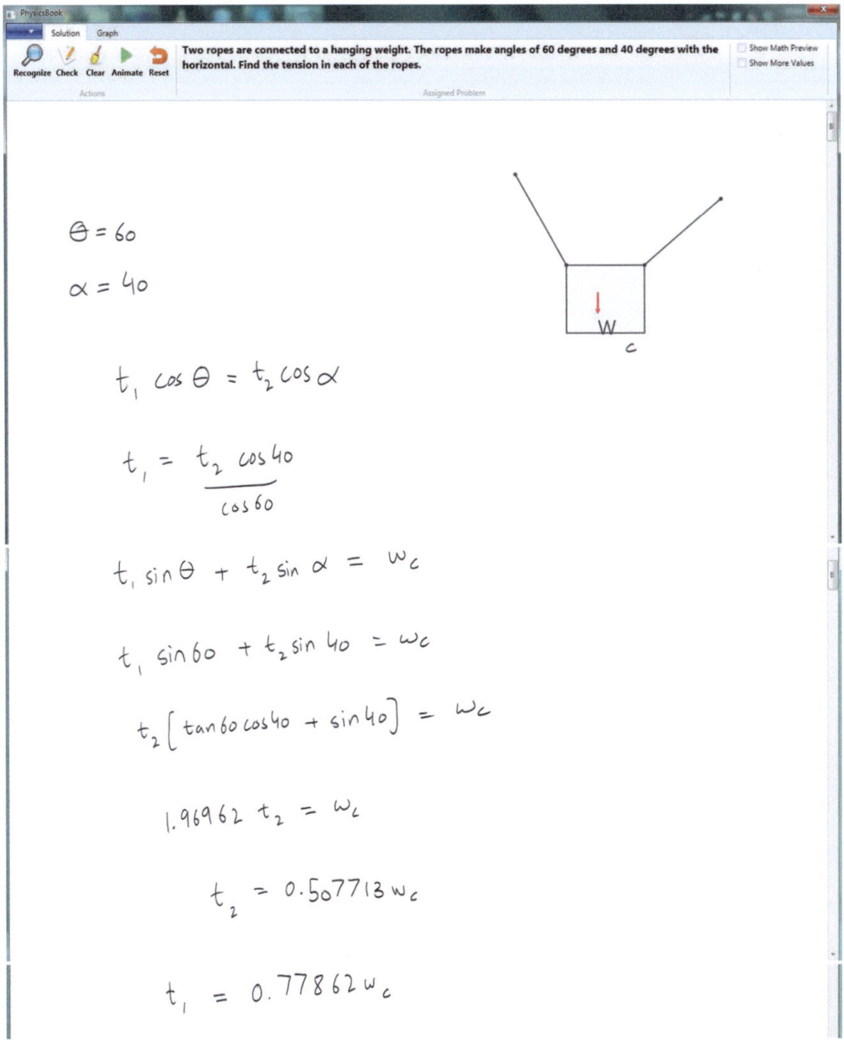

Fig. 10.10 Equilibrium problem taken from Young's University Physics (Young et al. 2011) and modeled using our system

this problem highlights an important feedback mechanism: "*the presence of motion where there should be none*".

10.5.5 Example V: Coefficient of Kinetic Friction

For Fig. 10.11, the student must work out the correct coefficient of kinetic friction that will cause a moving ball to stop in a given distance. Several factors affect the recognition and beautification of this scenario. The line denoting the surface is

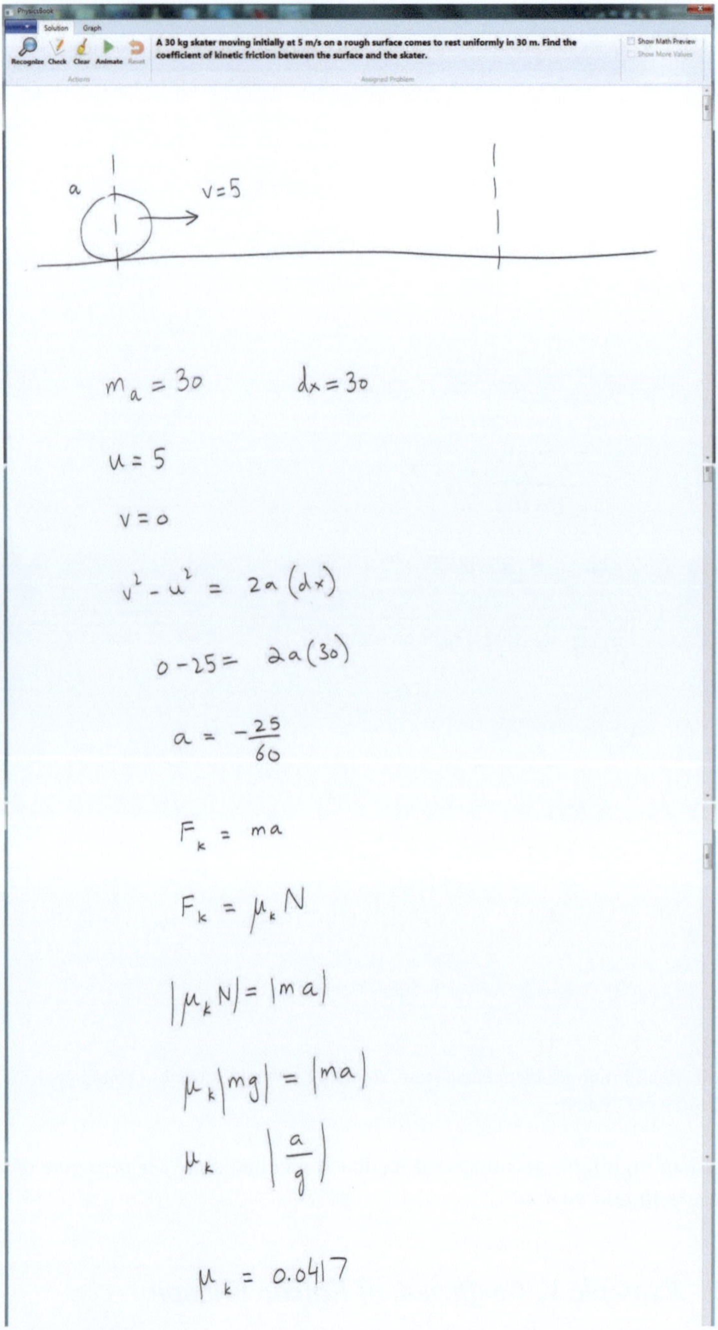

Fig. 10.11 A student is asked to work out the coefficient of kinetic friction μ_k such that a moving ball comes to rest after traveling a given distance

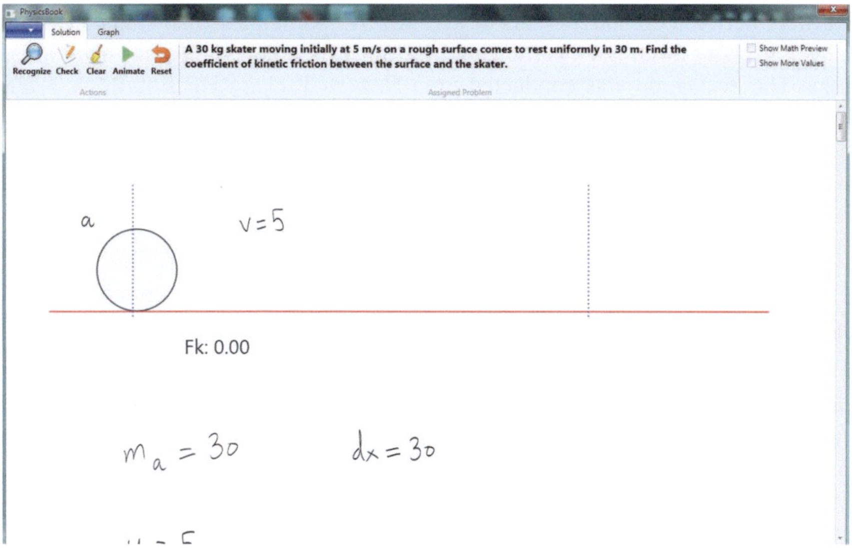

Fig. 10.12 An animation of the friction problem in Fig. 10.11

beautified so that it is perfectly horizontal. The circle is moved so that it is tangent to the line (to satisfy the touch constraint). The recognized diagram is depicted in Fig. 10.12. In this scenario, the initial velocity and mass are associated implicitly while the student must associate the distance and the coefficient of kinetic friction manually. To do this, they can 'Lasso' the $dx = 30$ and 'Tap' one of the dotted lines. Similarly, selecting $\mu_k = 0.0417$ and tapping the ball associates the coefficient of kinetic friction. When the animation is run, the ball comes to rest in the correct distance. A different value for μ_k would cause the ball to either stop before the appropriate distance or to overshoot the distance limit.

10.6 Usability Evaluation

We conducted an informal usability evaluation with five expert users[5] to get preliminary feedback about the learning experience provided by our system.

10.6.1 Subjects and Apparatus

We recruited five participants (2 female and 3 male) from Arizona State University for our informal evaluation. The participants were chosen using convenience sampling

[5]These users all had prior experience with constructing sketch-based systems, and some had hands-on experience using industry standard mathematics recognition software packages such as MyScript (2018).

and were between 26 and 28 years of age. All five participants had studied physics at the university level. Each participant took 30–45 min to complete the experiment tasks. The evaluation was conducted on a Hewlett Packard HP EliteBook 2760p Tablet PC with an Intel Core i5-2410M CPU (2.3 GHz) having four gigabytes of memory, running Microsoft Windows 7 Professional. The screen resolution was set to 1280 × 800 pixels. We disabled multi-touch capability on the tablet PC for the evaluation.

10.6.2 Experiment Procedure

Participants were first given an overview of the system's capabilities. We demonstrated the problems in Sects. 10.5.1, 10.5.2, 10.5.5. These examples indicate how to draw shapes and surfaces, as well as the use of supported annotations (arrows, dotted lines and intervals). We showed users how to associate mathematical expressions with recognized elements in a diagram. Participants were shown how to delete and redraw elements of their solution by using the Scribble-Erase gesture. Lastly, they were given an overview of the graphing functionality built into our system. Before the main experiment, participants were asked to provide five examples of each supported diagram element. We used these examples to test the accuracy of our recognition system. The main experiment consisted of two tasks. Participants first familiarized themselves with the system by drawing a shape connected to a spring and viewing a graph of a physical quantity of interest. The second task required participants to copy given solutions to two solutions to two separate physics problems. The problems chosen are shown in Sects. 10.5.3 and 10.5.4. Participants were asked to fill out a user experience questionnaire at the end of the experiment.

10.6.3 Experiment Results

Figure 10.13 shows mean likert scale values denoting participants reactions to various interface elements of our prototype system. Overall, participants were able to draw line segments and shapes (circles and polygons) fairly easily. The mean responses in Fig. 10.13 also indicate that it was easy to associate mathematics with drawing elements, to construct animations and to view graphs. However, participants were not very satisfied with the recognition performance of our system for helixes, arrows and dotted lines (also used to draw intervals). No problems involving pulleys were used in the user study, therefore they were not included in the questionnaire.

For 3 participants, the system frequently misunderstood their ink strokes for helixes as 'Scribble-Erase'. Similarly, users sometimes drew arrows with a single stroke[6] and sometimes drew the arrow head far from the shaft such that it did not

[6]This occurred even though participants were instructed to draw arrows with two separate strokes.

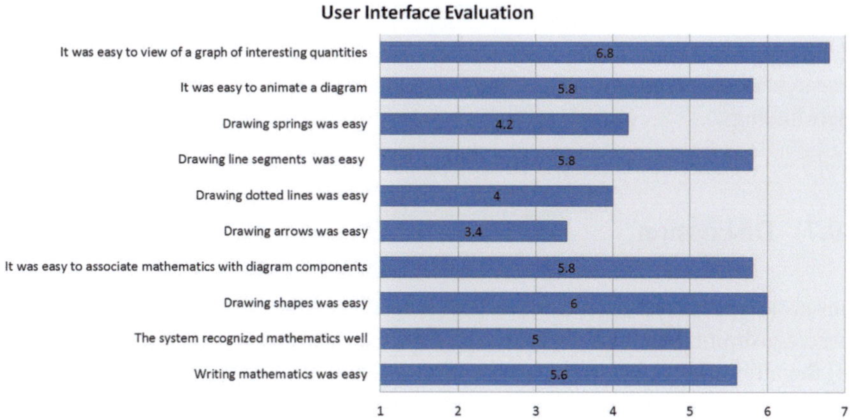

Fig. 10.13 Mean rankings assigned by participants to different aspects of our prototypes user interface. Each of these questions used a 7-point Likert scale, where 1 was the most negative answer and 7 was the most positive answer

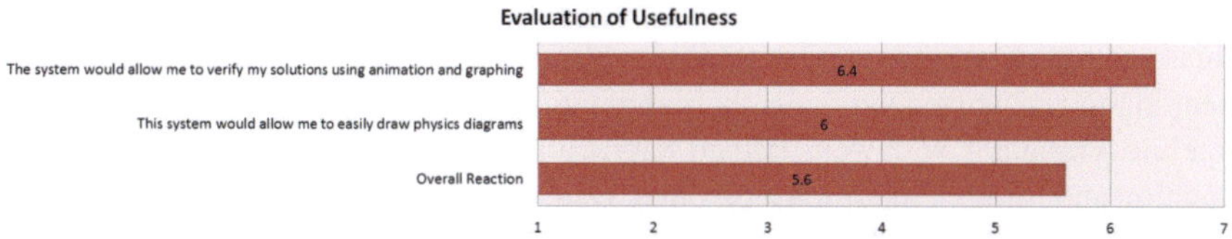

Fig. 10.14 Participants overall response to the perceived usefulness and utility of our prototype system

pass our proximity test. Such occurrences led to poor performance and frustration among participants while recognizing diagrams. Two participants reported that it was illuminating to see the interplay between gravitational potential energy and the box's displacement in the spring problem (Sect. 10.5.1). One participant reported that for the problem with the box (Sect. 10.5.3), she could not figure out how the animation showed if her answer was correct. Participants' overall responses (Shown in Fig. 10.14) indicates that despite gaps in recognition performance, participants felt positively about their experience and felt they would be able to use our prototype to verify their solutions.

We use two basic shapes (circles and convex polygons) to represent diagram elements, two different types of surfaces (polylines and line segments) to model sliding motion, 3 different types of connectors to link shapes (wires, pulleys, and springs), and four different kinds of annotations (dotted lines, arrows, intervals, and mathematical expressions) to construct simulations from diagram elements. Our recognition system achieved a mean accuracy of 85.778% across the data collected from participants. The performance of unistroke heuristics was very good (mean accuracy of 93.6%). The multistroke heuristics did not perform so well (mean accuracy of 76%), indicating a clear area of future work. We plan to investigate better clustering methods based on machine learning to improve recognition performance on diagram elements consisting of multiple ink strokes. This avenue has been explored by several researchers (Peterson et al. 2010; Stahovich et al. 2014) and we may be able to adapt their findings.

10.7 Discussion

Our prototype lets students work on physics problems in a natural manner. We place three constraints on student input (a) Only one diagram is permitted per solution (b) the allowed diagram elements are circles and convex polygons and (c) chained mathematical steps (e.g., $x_1 = y_1 = 0$) are not permitted.[7] These are soft limits which can be relaxed at a later time.

One key contribution of our work is the recognition pipeline itself. Our pipeline uses the text of the problem to infer its domain. A bottom-up recognition step identifies domain-agnostic unistroke and multistroke symbols and performs implicit linking between symbols, mathematics and annotations using proximity-based heuristics. Finally, a top-down recognition step uses physics knowledge to assign context and meaning to recognized symbols, their annotations and associated mathematics. The pipeline is modular, with well-defined stages, allowing improvements to each stage in isolation and minimizing impact on other system components. Our prototype brings together methods from sketch analysis, natural language processing and rigid-body dynamics to enable new types of animations.

Animation of sketched diagrams is our most important research goal. Earlier methods in this domain such as MathPad^2 (LaViola and Zeleznik 2004) required full specification of animation behavior. Our earlier prototype PhysicsBook (Cheema and LaViola 2012) alleviated this burden by incorporating a customized physics engine. This freed the user from having to provide a full mathematical description for animation. However, a monolithic physics engine proved difficult to extend to new problem domains. Our approach in this work goes beyond existing research by using multiple simulation engines, tailored to particular domains of physics problems. This method is more modular and extensible than our previous attempts (Cheema and LaViola 2012, 2010a, b), but poses additional challenges in terms of identifying problem domains. Specifically, our prototype provides support for the animation behaviors outlined in Sect. 10.2.3 in the following manner:

Continuous Animation Users define initial parameters by lassoing mathematical equations and associating them with recognized diagram elements before animation. The animation runs until it is explicitly stopped by the user.

[7] Our recognition mechanism only deduces links between equations and recognized diagram elements if the equations are not chained expressions.

Limited Animation

Temporal Events Users indicate a time limit by lassoing an equation for time (e.g. $t = t_1$) and associating it with the canvas. The animation runs from $t = 0$ to $t = t_1$ and stops.

Spatial Events Users indicate a limit to the motion of an object by using dotted lines to denote starting and ending points of motion. The animation runs until the moving object hits the indicated dotted line.

Unknown Events This category is currently unsupported in our prototype.

There is considerable research (See Sect. 10.1) to support the hypothesis that animation of handwritten diagrams can be useful in student learning. In support of this hypothesis, we have identified the design requirements for sketch-based intelligent tutoring systems with animation support in Sect. 10.2. Our prototype system is still under development. Although our prototype makes significant strides toward the required functionality, it is not ready for a full fledged classroom trial with pre- and post-tests for measuring the impact on student learning. Thus far, we have focused on expanding the range of animation capabilities to include several domains of physics problems and have built appropriate feedback and control mechanisms in line with specified goals in Sect. 10.2.3, which in turn were based on our exploratory analysis of student problem solving in (Cheema 2014). Section 10.5 discusses selected physics solutions to highlight the range and types of animations possible with our prototype system.

In the absence of a full fledged usability test, we have conducted an informal evaluation with five expert users to get qualitative feedback on the current learning experience offered by our prototype, and to solicit suggestions for improvements. Our informal evaluation clearly indicates the strong potential of animation and graphing to augment the learning experience in intelligent tutoring systems. Participants in our usability evaluation responded positively to the sketch-based interaction metaphor and found graphing and animation to be useful. This finding, while preliminary, allows us to optimistically conclude that providing animation support within a sketch-based intelligent tutoring system can have a potentially positive impact on student learning.

10.8 Future Work

We foresee several avenues of future work. First and foremost, we intend to improve our prototype's stability, in order to get it ready for a formal user evaluation, and thus measure its impact on students' learning experiences. Second, we want to increase the number of supported shapes and annotations for representing diagram elements. This should enrich the learning experience by letting students draw more natural shapes than circles and polygons for representing objects in physics problems. We also want to investigate more sophisticated segmentation and recognition methods for diagrams, mathematics and text. Our shape and mathematics recognizers are currently heuristic-based, and may yield better performance with machine learning-based approaches.

We want to improve the control and feedback mechanisms for sketch-based tutoring systems with animation support. One of the challenges, as outlined in Sect. 10.2.3 is having to specify a large number of animation parameters efficiently without impacting the learning experience. Our goal is for students to focus on physics rather than spending their time worrying about animation parameters. Traditional methods for specifying parameters via configuration files or manual specification are inadequate in our research domain. Our current strategy is to infer implicit relationships between diagram elements and mathematics in the solution, and use these inferences to extract a large part of the simulation parameters. Lastly, we want to support new domains of physics problems in our prototype system. This will require us to write domain-specific simulation engines to provide animation support. Supporting domain-specific mathematical notations may also require writing new recognizers for the low- and high-level recognition steps.

10.9 Conclusion

We have presented a prototype sketch-based tutoring system that uses the text of a given physics problem and a student's solution to construct an animation where a large number of parameters are automatically inferred from the solution. We believe this improves the learning experience by enabling students to focus on their solution and seeing how their answers lead to physically correct animation behavior. A range of domain-specific simulation engines are used to construct animations from recognized diagram elements. Our system provides support for three different types of animation behaviors, as well as real time graphing that can be used for visual feedback.

Acknowledgements This work is supported in part by NSF CAREER award IIS-0845921 and NSF awards IIS-0856045 and CCF-1012056.

References

Abowd GD (1999) Software engineering issues for ubiquitous computing. In: Proceedings of the 21st international conference on software engineering, ICSE '99. ACM, New York, NY, USA, pp 75–84

Ainsworth S, Prain V, Tytler R (2011) Drawing to learn in science. Science 333(6046):1096–1097

Alvarado C (2000) A natural sketching environmant: bringing the computer into early stages of mechanical design. Master's thesis, MIT

Alvarado C, Lazzareschi M (2007) Properties of real-world digital logic diagrams. In: First international workshop on pen-based learning technologies, 2007. PLT 2007. IEEE, pp 1–6

Anthony L, Yang J, Koedinger KR (2005) Evaluation of multimodal input for entering mathematical equations on the computer. In: CHI '05 extended abstracts on human factors in computing systems. CHI EA '05. ACM, New York, NY, USA, pp 1184–1187

Anthony L, Yang J, Koedinger KR (2007) Benefits of handwritten input for students learning algebra equation solving. In: Proceedings of the 2007 conference on artificial intelligence in education: building technology rich learning contexts that work. IOS Press, Amsterdam, The Netherlands, The Netherlands, pp 521–523

Anthony L, Yang J, Koedinger KR (2012) A paradigm for handwriting-based intelligent tutors. Int J Hum Comput Stud 70(11):866–887

Atilola O, Valentine S, Kim HH, Turner D, McTigue E, Hammond T, Linsey J (2014) Mechanix: a natural sketch interface tool for teaching truss analysis and free-body diagrams. Artif Intell Eng Des Anal Manuf 28:169–192

Baraff D (1997a) An introduction to physically based modeling: rigid body simulation iinonpenetration constraints. SIGGRAPH course notes, pp D31–D68

Baraff D (1997b) An introduction to physically based modeling: rigid body simulation iunconstrained rigid body dynamics. SIGGRAPH course notes

Bott JN, LaViola JJ Jr (2010) A pen-based tool for visualizing vector mathematics. In: Proceedings of the seventh sketch-based interfaces and modeling symposium, SBIM '10. Eurographics Association, Aire-la-Ville, Switzerland, Switzerland, pp 103–110

Bott JN, Gabriele D, LaViola JJ Jr (2011) Now or later: an initial exploration into user perception of mathematical expression recognition feedback. In: Proceedings of the eighth eurographics symposium on sketch-based interfaces and modeling, SBIM '11. ACM, New York, NY, USA, pp 125–132

Buchanan S, Laviola JJ Jr (2014) Cstutor: a sketch-based tool for visualizing data structures. Trans Comput Educ 14(1):3:1–3:28

Bullet physics (2018) http://bulletphysics.org/wordpress/

Cheema S (2014) Pen-based methods for recognition and animation of handwritten physics solutions. Ph.D. thesis, University of Central Florida, Orlando, FL, USA

Cheema S, LaViola JJ Jr (2010a) Applying mathematical sketching to sketch-based physics tutoring software. In: Proceedings of the 10th international conference on smart graphics, SG '10. Springer, Berlin, Heidelberg, pp 13–24

Cheema S, LaViola JJ Jr (2010b) Towards intelligent motion inferencing in mathematical sketching. In: Proceedings of the 15th international conference on intelligent user interfaces, IUI '10. ACM, New York, NY, USA, pp 289–292

Cheema S, LaViola J (2012) Physicsbook: a sketch-based interface for animating physics diagrams. In: Proceedings of the 2012 ACM international conference on intelligent user interfaces, IUI '12. ACM, New York, NY, USA, pp 51–60

Cheema S, Gulwani S, LaViola J (2012) Quickdraw: improving drawing experience for geometric diagrams. In: Proceedings of the SIGCHI conference on human factors in computing systems, CHI '12. ACM, New York, NY, USA, pp 1037–1046

Clement J (1994) Imagistic simulation and physical intuition in expert problem solving. In: Proceedings of the 16th annual conference of the cognitive science society, pp 201–206

Cossairt TJ, LaViola JJ Jr (2012) Setpad: a sketch-based tool for exploring discrete math set problems. In: Proceedings of the international symposium on sketch-based interfaces and modeling, SBIM '12. Eurographics Association, Aire-la-Ville, Switzerland, Switzerland, pp 47–56

Cryphysics (2018) http://docs.cryengine.com/display/CEPROG/CryPhysics

Davis RC, Colwell B, Landay JA (2008) K-sketch: a 'kinetic' sketch pad for novice animators. In: CHI '08, pp 413–422

Eberly DH (2003) Game physics. Elsevier

Field M, Valentine S, Linsey J, Hammond T (2011) Sketch recognition algorithms for comparing complex and unpredictable shapes. In: Proceedings of the twenty-second international joint conference on artificial intelligence-volume, vol 3. AAAI Press, pp 2436–2441

Forbus K, Usher J, Lovett A, Lockwood K, Wetzel J (2011) Cogsketch: sketch understanding for cognitive science research and for education. In: Topics in cognitive science
Gennari L, Kara LB, Stahovich TF, Shimada K (2005) Combining geometry and domain knowledge to interpret hand-drawn diagrams. Comput Graph 29(4):547–562
Havok (2018) http://www.havok.com/physics/
Igarashi T, Moscovich T, Hughes JF (2005) As-rigid-as-possible shape manipulation. ACM Trans Graph 24(3):1134–1141
Jiang Y, Tian F, Wang H, Zhang X, Wang X, Dai G (2010) Intelligent understanding of handwritten geometry theorem proving. In: Proceedings of the 15th international conference on Intelligent user interfaces, IUI '10. ACM, New York, NY, USA, pp 119–128
Johnson-Laird P (1998) Imagery, visualization, and thinking. Percep Cognit Centurys End, 441–467
Kang B, LaViola J (2012) Logicpad: a pen-based application for visualization and verification of boolean algebra. In: Proceedings of the 2012 ACM international conference on intelligent user interfaces, IUI '12. ACM, New York, NY, USA, pp 265–268
Kara LB, Gennari L, Stahovich TF (2008) A sketch-based tool for analyzing vibratory mechanical systems. J Mech Des 130(10):101101
Larkin JH, Simon HA (1987) Why a diagram is (sometimes) worth ten thousand words. Cognit Sci 11(1):65–100
LaViola JJ Jr, Zeleznik RC (2004) Mathpad2: a system for the creation and exploration of mathematical sketches. ACM Trans Graph 23:432–440
Lee C, Jordan J, Stahovich TF, Herold J (2012) Newtons pen ii: an intelligent, sketch-based tutoring system and its sketch processing techniques. In: Proceedings of the international symposium on sketch-based interfaces and modeling, SBIM '12. Eurographics Association, Aire-la-Ville, Switzerland, Switzerland, pp 57–65
Lee W, de Silva R, Peterson EJ, Calfee RC, Stahovich TF (2007) Newton's pen: a pen-based tutoring system for statics. In: Proceedings of the 4th Eurographics workshop on sketch-based interfaces and modeling, SBIM '07. ACM, New York, NY, USA, pp 59–66
Mahoney JV, Fromherz MP (2002) Three main concerns in sketch recognition and an approach to addressing them. In: AAAI spring symposium on sketch understanding, pp 105–112
Millington I (2007) Game physics engine development (The Morgan Kaufmann Series in Interactive 3D Technology). Morgan Kaufmann Publishers Inc., San Francisco, CA, USA
Moscovich T, Hughes JF (2001) Animation sketching: an approach to accessible animation. Unpublished master's thesis, CS Department, Brown University
MyScript (2018) https://www.myscript.com/
Newton game dynamics (2018) http://newtondynamics.com/forum/newton.php
Oltmans M, Davis R (2001) Naturally conveyed explanations of device behavior. In: Proceedings of the 2001 workshop on perceptive user interfaces, PUI '01. ACM, New York, NY, USA, pp 1–8
Open dynamics engine (2018) http://www.ode.org/
Ouyang TY, Davis R (2011) Chemink: a natural real-time recognition system for chemical drawings. In: Proceedings of the 16th international conference on intelligent user interfaces, IUI '11. ACM, New York, NY, USA, pp 267–276
Peterson EJ, Stahovich TF, Doi E, Alvarado C (2010) Grouping strokes into shapes in hand-drawn diagrams. In: AAAI, vol 10, p 14
PhysX (2018) https://developer.nvidia.com/physx-sdk
Popović J, Seitz SM, Erdmann M (2003) Motion sketching for control of rigid-body simulations. ACM Trans Graph (TOG) 22(4):1034–1054
Popović J, Seitz SM, Erdmann M, Popović Z, Witkin A (2000) Interactive manipulation of rigid body simulations. In: Proceedings of the 27th annual conference on computer graphics and interactive techniques. ACM Press/Addison-Wesley Publishing Co., pp 209–217
Santosa S, Chevalier F, Balakrishnan R, Singh K (2013) Direct space-time trajectory control for visual media editing. In: Proceedings of the SIGCHI conference on human factors in computing systems. ACM, pp 1149–1158

Scott J, Davis R (2013) Physink: sketching physical behavior. In: Proceedings of the adjunct publication of the 26th annual ACM symposium on user interface software and technology, UIST '13 Adjunct. ACM, New York, NY, USA, pp 9–10

Shepard RN (1978a) Externalization of mental images and the act of creation. In: Visual learning, thinking, and communication, pp 133–189

Shepard RN (1978b) The mental image. Am Psychol 33(2):125–137

de Silva R, Bischel DT, Lee W, Peterson EJ, Calfee RC, Stahovich TF (2007) Kirchhoff's pen: a pen-based circuit analysis tutor. In: Proceedings of the 4th eurographics workshop on sketch-based interfaces and modeling, SBIM '07. ACM, New York, NY, USA, pp 75–82

Stahovich TF, Peterson EJ, Lin H (2014) An efficient, classification-based approach for grouping pen strokes into objects. Comput Graph 42:14–30

Sweller J (1988) Cognitive load during problem solving: effects on learning. Cognit Sci 12(2):257–285

Sweller J (1994) Cognitive load theory, learning difficulty, and instructional design. Learn Instr 4(4):295–312

Tenneson D, Becker S (2005) Chempad: generating 3d molecules from 2d sketches. In: ACM SIGGRAPH 2005 Posters, SIGGRAPH '05. ACM, New York, NY, USA

Thorne M, Burke D, van de Panne M (2007) Motion doodles: an interface for sketching character motion. In: ACM SIGGRAPH 2007 Courses, SIGGRAPH '07. ACM, New York, NY, USA

Wai J, Lubinski D, Benbow CP (2009) Spatial ability for stem domains: aligning over 50 years of cumulative psychological knowledge solidifies its importance. J Educ Psychol 101(4):817

Wais P, Wolin A, Alvarado C (2007) Designing a sketch recognition front-end: user perception of interface elements. In: Proceedings of the 4th eurographics workshop on sketch-based interfaces and modeling, SBIM '07. ACM, New York, NY, USA, pp 99–106

Witkin A (1997) An introduction to physically based modeling: constrained dynamics. Robotics Institute

Young HD, Freedman RA, Ford A, Sears F, Zemansky M (2011) University Physics with Modern Physics. Pearson Education, Limited

Zamora SW, Eyjólfsdóttir EA (2009) Circuitboard: sketch-based circuit design and analysis. In: Proceedings of the international conference on intelligent user interfaces (IUI) workshop on sketch recognition

Zeleznik R, Miller T, Li C, Laviola JJ Jr (2008) Mathpaper: mathematical sketching with fluid support for interactive computation. In: Proceedings of the 9th international symposium on smart graphics, SG '08. Springer, Berlin, Heidelberg, pp 20–32

Appendix A
SkillTrack! Trial Details and Evaluation

This appendix details the process of the SkillTrack! trial. The focus of Chap. 4 is to explain the framework and design for the self-assessment of 21st century skills, while the purpose of this appendix is to show the experimental design, usage statistics, interview transcript quotes and their evaluation. Apart from the evaluation of specific aspects here, an overall evaluation is offered at Chap. 4.

A.1 Methodology

In regards to evaluating SkillTrack! and the SkillTrack! Teacher Dashboard, the main goal was to be able to test the application in a way that would provide insight in to the research objectives, resulting pedagogical recommendations, and technical supports (usability and data analytics). With these as the requirements, a trial structure was selected for evaluating the design in use with questionnaires, teacher and students interviews, providing end-of-use evaluation and overall triangulation.

A.2 Trial

A.2.1 Trial Overview

Prior to trialling, the following were identified as the *ideal* trial targets:

- School Profile: To be used in secondary schools with 1:1 devices and an interest in promoting 21st century skills as well as an understanding of what it means to contribute to research.
- Participants: To be trialled by multiple teacher (different subject areas) and student (different year/grade level) participants.
- Use: To be used across the full range of subject areas.

E. Kapros and M. Koutsombogera (eds.), *Designing for the User Experience in Learning Systems*, Human–Computer Interaction Series,
https://doi.org/10.1007/978-3-319-94794-5

- Time: To be used for an entire term or academic year so as to fully integrate as part of regular classroom practice and procedure.

SkillTrack! was trialled in two parts. The first trial was done with three schools of varying demographics over a short period of time. The second trial was conducted after recognising the certain challenges within the first trial may have limited the finding and was conducted in one school for an extended time period (see Trial Context for specific demographic details).

A.2.2 *Trial Limitations*

Due to the nature of the trialling environment—a school—there were certain limitations that arose and should be noted inclusive to both Trial 1 and Trial 2.

Firstly, when considering the ideal trial target around school profile (to be used in secondary schools with 1:1 devices an in interest in promoting 21st century skills as well as an understanding of what it means to contribute to research) there were innate limitations in regards to the number of schools in Ireland able to meet this criteria. This means the pool of possible trial schools was limited from the onset and that the articulation of this target may have varied across schools.

In regards to the next two ideal trial targets around participants and use, limitations also arose. Due to varying degrees of technology integration into the actual classroom as well as factors beyond our control, while an individual teacher may have been willing to participate in the trial, recruiting multiple teachers with the same level of investment, interest and skill was challenging. This in turn influenced the number of student participants: student numbers, as well as the year/grade level of the student, were influenced by the participating teachers. Additionally, this limited the use of SkillTrack! across subject areas as—while students would have the ability to use the app across subjects and classes without teacher's participating in the trial—teacher support and permission to use the app was important in supporting trial participants.

The most significant limitation in the trial is around the last ideal trial target, time (to be used for an entire term or academic year so as to fully integrate as a part of regular classroom practice and procedure). The basic premise behind successfully integrating SkillTrack! into an authentic classroom dynamic was that it is meant to be student-led and unobtrusive to the regular classroom proceedings. To do this, it must be something that is integrated into a student's classroom habits (so that it becomes just another classroom task such as taking notes) and occur over a long period of time so that the use of it does not overtake classroom instruction. To this point, SkillTrack! was designed to be trialled at the start of the term. However, due to factors outside our control in the first trial, trialling with schools was not an option until the end of March, which only allowed for 2 months of trialling. This prompted the running of the second trial the following academic year; the second trial offered the opportunity for a more robust evaluation from the beginning of October until March.

A.2.3 Trial Context

With the consideration of the above mentioned trial limitations, the first SkillTrack! trial took place within three secondary schools in Ireland and the U.S.A. starting in April 2015. Each school dictated the trial parameters (teacher participants, subject use, etc.) which led to varying demographics, varying incorporation of the trial targets and varying overall usage of the demonstrator. The second trial took place in a single secondary school (one of those that participated in the first trial) and ran from October 2015 until March 2016.

The first trial school was a fee paying, all girls school in Dublin, Ireland. While during initial talks the school was committed to the entire 2nd year class (students and teachers) using the app, due to conditions that were outside our control the trial was reduced down to one teacher. 48 1st and 2nd year Junior Cycle students (ages 12–13) began the trial—with only 22 1st years actively participating—and one classroom teacher participated in the trial from the 4th of April until the 22nd May 2015 for 4 weeks of use (with a week break for mock exams). Student use was limited to their e-learning course which met once a week. Students were onboarded by the classroom teacher and then app usage was integrated into regular classroom studies. Students accessed SkillTrack! through iOS devices.

The second trial school is a non-fee-paying coeducational secondary school in County Galway, Ireland. 96 1st year Junior Cycle students (ages 12–13) and three classroom teachers (though only one followed through) participated in the trial from the 17th April until the 22nd May 2015 for 3 weeks of use (there was a week break for mock exams). Student use was to be across all subjects with specific guidance in the two subjects (Science and Mathematics) taught by the three participating classroom teachers. Students were onboarded by the classroom teacher (with the researcher present) and then app usage was integrated into regular classroom studies. Students accessed SkillTrack! through Microsoft Surface devices. This school was the sole trial school in the second trial. The second trial ran from October 2015 until mid-March 2016 (6 months) and had one teacher participant and 67 student participants from both 1st and 2nd year (ages 12–15). Student use was to be across all subjects with the single teacher being the touch point.

The third trial school, is a fee-paying secondary school for dyslexic students located in the Eastern United States of America. This school was brought in to the trial in the hope that the systemic differences between the U.S. school system and the Irish system would allow for certain trial parameters (e.g., varying grade levels/subject, no culture against assessment, and inclusive design/universal access) to be met. Additionally, the thought was that an international trial would provide greater weight to the data collected. 26 students from grades 6th–10th (ages 11–16) and 12 classroom teachers participated in the trial from the 11th May–5th June for 4 weeks of use. Student use was across six classes a day (Science, Mathematics, Art/Design, Spanish, History, Literature). Students were onboarded by classroom teachers and then app usage was integrated into regular classroom studies. Students accessed SkillTrack! through iOS devices.

A.2.4 Trial Methodology

Prior to Trialling:

Firstly, in preparing to go to trial with SkillTrack! both times, ethical approval was sought from the University; given the age group in question, this step was especially important. From this, to trial SkillTrack!, as stated above, it was first necessary to look for schools fitting the desirable trial profile who would be willing to take on the process of the trial.

In pitching the trial to schools, one-to-one meetings were arranged with school principals and a discussion around the research model for trialling, research ethics, SkillTrack! as a trial application and the trial process were discussed. Principals were also shown what was at the time the current version of the application and given a higher level briefing document for a point of reference.

Once schools agreed to be a part of the trial, principals handed over to a teacher point of contact and all trial preparation went through that teacher.

Trial:

Students activated their app and teachers onboarded the students. Students began using the app in class for the designated time frame.

Support was offered to schools, teachers and students as glitches arose. Students were encouraged to send screenshots of glitches to the research team and contact was made with the teachers at minimum on a weekly basis (though at the start of the trial it was on daily basis).

As the trial progressed and the data was monitored by the team, additional help and feedback was given to the schools with an in-class observation of use scheduled.

Post Trial:

At the close of the trial, group interviews were conducted with participating teachers and students at the only school able to accommodate this request. Additionally, questionnaires were given to both the students and the teachers to fill out, with the students already being preloaded into the app (though these were returned with little success).

A.3 SkillTrack! User Trail Quantitative Results

A.3.1 First Trial

As described previously, the first user trialling of the Skilltrack! app was carried out across three schools with a total of 144 students using the app over a period from mid-April to the end of May 2015. Within that time the different schools used the app

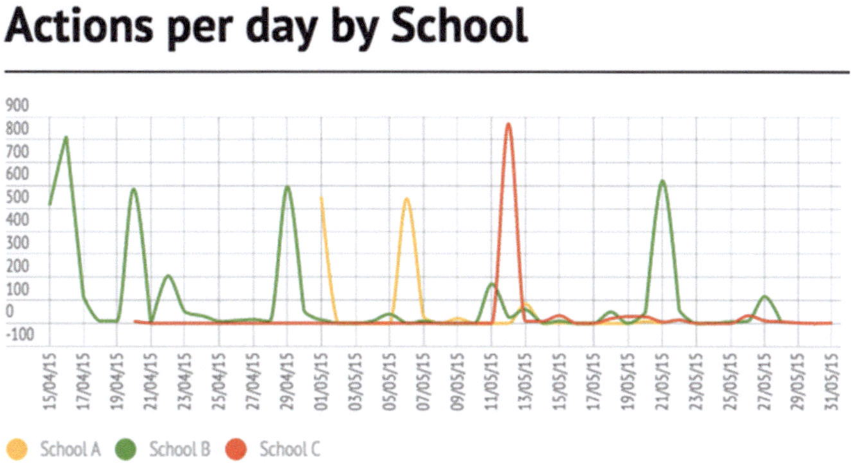

Fig. A.1 Number of interactions by students with the SkillTrack! app per day that were observed, per school

for different lengths of time. Figure A.1 provides a plot of the number of interactions by students with the SkillTrack! app per day that were observed. As shown there was a significant level of usage, which can be seen to have been generally initiated by teachers as shown by the large spikes in usage. However it is also interesting to note that there were also lower levels of usage between these spikes indicating that students were returning to the app throughout the trial period.

As mentioned previously, this trial was quite constrained due to the time of year that we were able to get the app into the classroom. As a result the students did not have enough time to progress far enough into the SkillTrack! experience for it to being to provide real benefits to them and for significant insights to be obtained from the evaluation. This was one of the motivating factors in carrying out a second trial that would benefit from being initiated much earlier in the school year and running for a longer duration that would provide a more authentic context for the evaluation. As such, the first trial effectively became a beta test for the app allowing us to refine some aspects of the experience to better meet the needs of the target user group.

A.3.2 Second Trial

Usage Data:

As described previously, the second SkillTrack! user evaluation took place over a 6-month period between October and mid-March 2015. In total 67 students used the SkillTrack! app over that period across three different classes (two first year classes and one second year class). However, it was only possible to obtain consent from

Table A.1 Number of students, total interactions for all students, and average interactions per student for each class of the trial

Class	# Students	Total	Avg./Student
One	19	2406	127
Two	17	1514	89
Three	14	2589	185
Total	50	6509	130

an appropriate legal guardian for 50 of those students. It is the data from these 50 students that will be presented in this paper. Over the entire evaluation period, 6509 unique interactions by students with the SkillTrack! app were recorded. However, there was some differences in the levels of usage of the app across the three different classes. For instance, the 2nd year class was only responsible for 23% of the total interactions despite making up 34% of the total trial participants. On average, students interacted with the SkillTrack! app 130 times each over the trial period but this does not give a clear view of the differences in usage across the three separate classes, which, when broken down by class, had averages of 127, 89, and 185 interactions per student (Table A.1).

Usage of the SkillTrack! app over the trial period is illustrated in Fig. A.2 top. As shown, there were significant spikes in usage at the beginning of the trial when the teacher was guiding the students through the onboarding phase of the SkillTrack! app. Additionally, there were spikes in usage at the beginning of the new calendar year when the students returned to classes after the holiday period. However, there was a relatively sustained level of usage of the app between the initial onboarding stage in October when the app was first introduced into the student's classroom activities and the end of the calendar year. The cyclical pattern of usage in this period is due to weekends where the students did not use the app. This period of usage is shown in greater detail in Fig. A.2 bottom. As shown the daily usage in this period does drop but can be considered consistent with expected usage for the 50 students that participated. As Skilltrack! is intended to be used intermittently over a sustained period of time rather than in intense short bursts especially high levels of usage, as seen in the onboarding stage could be taken as an indication that the students are being guided in their use of the app by their teacher while the observed usage patterns are more indicative of self-directed use. Usage of SkillTrack! had almost completely stopped by mid-March with less than 100 interactions outside of the trial period. By this stage the trial had technically ended and the teacher was no longer encouraging students to use the app. Despite the lack of any extrinsic motivation, it is encouraging to see that some students continued to use the Skill track! app.

As with any group of users the degree to which different students made use of the SkillTrack! App differed greatly. A significant proportion of the interactions with the app were carried out by a relatively small group of highly engaged and self motivated students. Table A.2 provides a grouping of students usage into 4 categories of varying

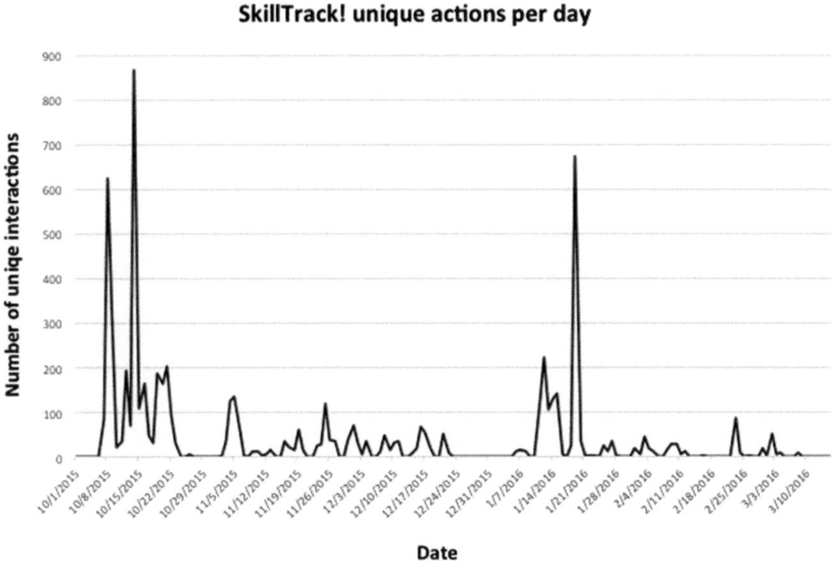

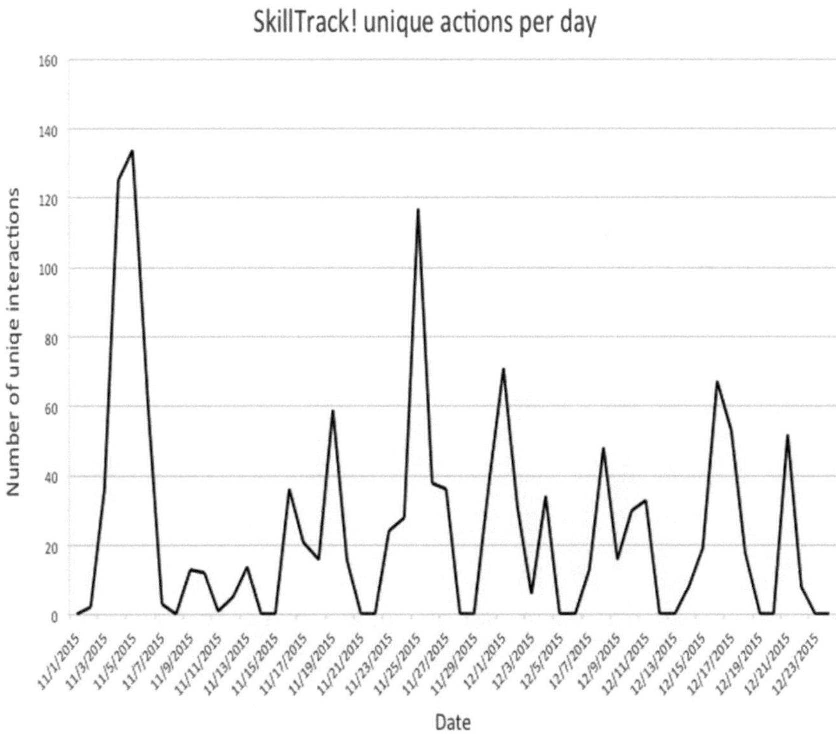

Fig. A.2 *Top* usage of the SkillTrack! app over the trial period. *Bottom* level of usage of the app between the initial onboarding stage in October when the app was first introduced into the students classroom activities and the end of the calendar year. The cyclical pattern of usage in this period is due to weekends where the students did not use the app

Table A.2 Breakdown of the usage activity by the quantity of students with such activity

Number of interactions	Number of students
0–49	4
50–99	22
100–199	16
200–600	8

size. This provides a good illustration of how the students that participated in the trial tended to fall into distinct categories depending on their usage.

An interesting observation that was made about the usage of the SkillTrack! app by students was the time of day at which it was used. As might be expected, the majority of the usage of the SkillTrack! app was during the school day between 9 a.m. and 4 p.m. However, a significant proportion of the observed interactions (22% or 1436 interactions) were outside of this time period. This can be seen as indicative of the students being motivated to engage with the SkillTrack! app (Fig. A.3).

Self-Ratings:

One of the most significant features of the SkillTrack! app is the ability for students to rate their own abilities in each of the five skills over time as they progress through

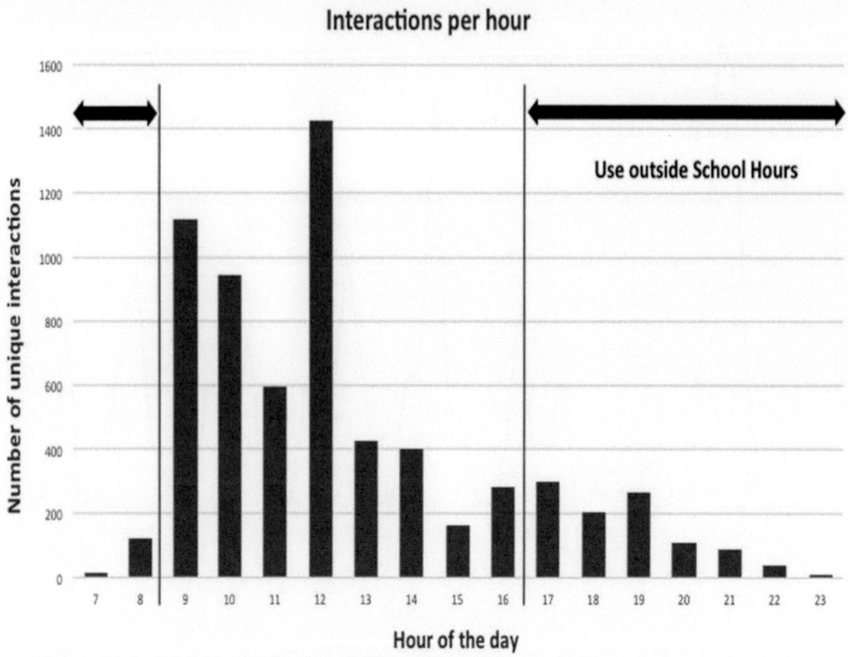

Fig. A.3 Usage per hour. A significant proportion of the observed interactions (22% or 1436 interactions) were outside of the school day, between 9 a.m. and 4 p.m., period

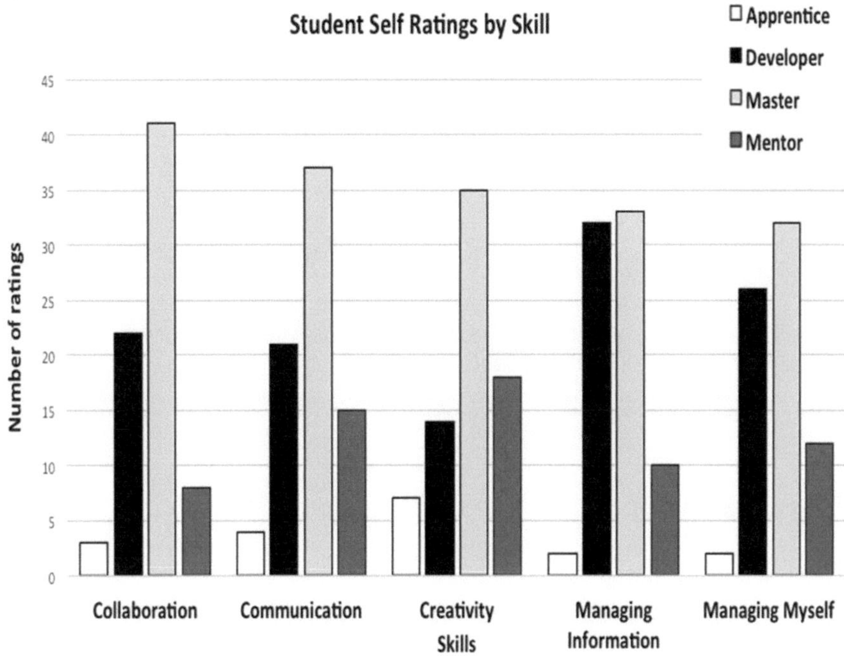

Fig. A.4 Student self ratings by skill

the different phases of the experience. Figure A.4 (data from Table A.2) provides a bar chart plotting students self-ratings, on a 4 point scale from Apprentice to Mentor, across the 5 skills tracked by the app. It might be expected that students at this age might not have the metacognitive skills to fully benefit from such an experience and that they would tend to rate themselves highly at everything. However, as the bar chart shows, students tended to rate themselves using the Developer and Master rating options rather than going to the extremes.

One of the expected outcomes of the continuous self rating as part of the Skill-Track! App is that students might initially rate themselves high and for this rating to dip as students became more aware of the skills and their use of them and finally for the students ratings to increase again as the students further developed their skills. The students' self-ratings by phase, aggregating the ratings for the five skills are provided in Table A.4 with the percentage of the total number of self-ratings generated for that phase shown in brackets. The first observation that can be made is that the number of students that progress through each of the phases diminishes over time with almost 80% of all ratings in the onboarding phase being completed to only 56% in phase 1 and so on (50 students by 5 skills means that there would be 250 ratings per phase if all students completed the phase). Despite this, it can be seen from the chart that there is a trend towards higher self-ratings as the students progress through the phases (Table A.3).

Table A.3 Breakdown of the usage activity by the quantity of students with such activity

	Apprentice	Developer	Master	Mentor	Totals
Collaboration	3	22	41	8	74
Communication	4	21	37	15	77
Creativity	7	14	35	18	74
Managing information	2	32	33	10	77
Managing myself	2	26	32	12	72
Totals	18	115	178	63	374

Table A.4 Students self-ratings by phase, aggregating the ratings for the five skills. The percentage of the total number of self-ratings generated for that phase is shown in brackets

	Apprentice	Developer	Master	Mentor	Totals
On-boarding	13 (6.5%)	77 (38.5%)	80 (40%)	30 (15%)	200
Phase 1	4 (2.9%)	34 (24.3%)	72 (51.4%)	30 (21.4%)	140
Phase 2	1 (3.5%)	4 (13.8%)	21 (72.4%)	3 (10.3%)	29
Phase 3	0	0	5 (100%)	0	5
Phase 4	0	0	0	0	0
Totals	18	115	178	63	374

Qualitative Survey:

Following their use of the SkillTrack! app as part of their day to day classroom activities, the students were given an online survey to complete. This consisted of 25 questions that were answered using a 5 point Likert scale ranging from Strongly Agree to Strongly Disagree. The aim of this survey was to gain insight into the general usability of the SkillTrack! App as well as the student's perception on how well SkillTrack! helped them in developing their 21st Century Skills. In total 27 students, whose legal guardian had provided consent, completed the online survey. The first part of the survey focused on the students experience in using the SkillTrack! app and how they perceived its effectiveness in terms of promoting skills literacy, recognition and practice. The bar chart shown in Fig. A.5 provides a summary of the results from the four questions that make up this first part of the survey. To simplify their presentation, the students responses have been converted from the 5 point scale used in the survey to a 3 point scale depending on whether the students responded positively (Strongly Agree or Agree), neutrally or negatively (Disagree or Strongly Disagree). 66% of students responded positively when asked if they felt that SkillTrack! Helped them in understanding what the '21st Skills' were with only 15% responding negatively. This is a good indication that, at least from the perspective of the students, SkillTrack! did promote skills literacy. The students were then asked if SkillTrack! Helped them to practice the Key Skills in class. Here 52% of students responded positively with 26% responding negatively. Given the young age of the students and the fact that SkillTrack! was being introduced is part of a single subject and not across all of the students subjects this is still a very positive result. Similar responses were seen when the students were asked if they felt that SkillTrack! helped

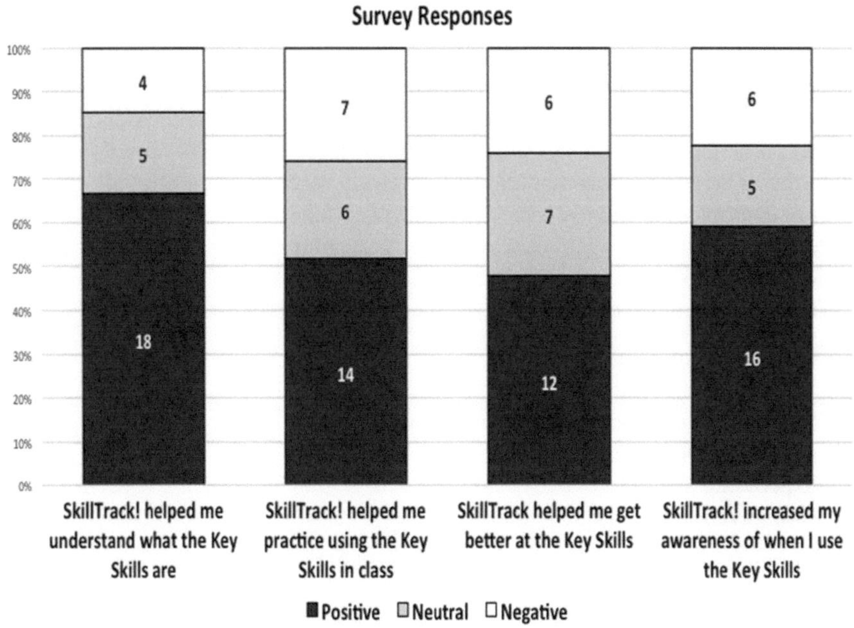

Fig. A.5 Survey responses

them to get better at the Key Skills and if it helped them to increase their awareness with only 24% and 22% responding negatively to those questions respectively (the positive responses were 48% and 59% respectively).

Apart from these SkillTrack!-specific questions, part of the survey was a System Usability Scale questionnaire, with simplified language to match the age group. The average SUS score was 61.7, and individual scores varied from 42.5 to 82.5. School average scores were 60.7 and 62.7. As this application was built as a proof-of-concept demonstrator, this score is satisfactory, as it is in the acceptable range for commercial applications.

The following section expands further on the effectiveness of SkillTrack! from a pedagogical perspective through the use of a series of group interviews with the students who participated in the SkillTrack! evaluation.

A.4 Pedagogical Evaluation

This section of the report evaluates the pedagogical frame used to create SkillTrack! in regards to the design elementals as well as the overall activity structure of the application experience. The evaluation is framed based on the two demographics of trial participants, the students and the teacher.

This pedagogical evaluation relies on the qualitative data collected from the group interviews. Individual interviews were done with 21 student participants and one teacher participant (from Trial 1 and 2 inclusive); group interviews were done at the trial schools with a random sampling of volunteer students from both a high- and low-use demographic and a teacher was present at all times.

Specifically, the following lenses, which were laid out in the pedagogical design section, will be used to view this data:

The pedagogical design elements (premise) of SkillTrack!

1. Vertical and horizontal mobility
2. Not activity specific
3. Integrates into authentic classroom dynamic
4. Activate student literacy
5. Experiential learning
6. Formative assessment.

The four main pedagogical activities within SkillTrack!

1. Onboarding,
2. Skill tagging,
3. Benchmarking tasks,
4. Exemplar stage (exemplar + self-assessment).

Due to the nature of qualitative data, participant responses were categorised under multiple headings when relevant; please note that anything in italics is a direct quote. As stated in the previous sections of this paper, two trials were conducted and the conclusions and findings should be considered inclusive.

A.4.1 Student Interviews

All student participants were volunteers and were interviewed in a focus group setting with three/four of their peers. Based on the age group being interviewed (12–15 years of age), three general questions were selected to form the base of the interview (What did you like about SkillTrack!? What did you find challenging/difficult/or did not like about SkillTrack!? How would you improve it?). Clarifying questions were asked around these questions as well as follow-up questions to any point students brought up independently. These same questions were asked at the conclusion of both trials.

As students were not specifically asked to respond to the below categories of interest, their responses occurred authentically and can be used to view their experienced strengths and weaknesses of the design.

Pedagogical Design Elements

Vertical and horizontal mobility:

Concerning vertical and horizontal mobility, the pedagogical design of SkillTrack! was interested in creating an experience that would be able to be used across year/grade level and content/subject areas.

While no student responses specifically addressed this element, some general comments can be used to provide insight into this element of design. Specifically, students spoke on teacher's support of app usage, and the overall language used in the app prohibiting their overall use of the app.

Specifically, students spoke on the difficulty of using the app in classes where teachers were not a part of the trial, stating that it wasn't easy to use as "teachers think you're like doing something you shouldn't be doing on your netbook". Additionally, it was stated that when using the app in these classes where teachers were not a part of the trial "[teachers] kind of get mad because you can't be doing something on your netbook while they're trying to teach".

While these comments do not specifically address SkillTrack!'s ability to be used across subject in regards to the content and experience of the app, it does provide insight into how the app needs to have teacher support to be successful. This is an expected finding.

Additionally, students in all focus groups mentioned that the language used in the app was challenging, difficult and, at times, confusing. Specifically, they stated that "the phrasing of the words kind of sometimes was a bit confusing" and that "the wording of the questions was hard". One student also talked about having the questions "easier worded for our age I suppose".

While these comments do not specifically address SkillTrack!'s ability to be used across year/grade level in regards to concept design, it does speak to the need of the language used within the app to be tailored to the specific age/year/grade/ability level. As the app was originally written to be used at Senior Cycle level and was instead trialled within the Junior Cycle, this is an expected finding.

A preliminary conclusion/finding for this element then is around the need for teacher support of the app in regards to horizontal mobility as well as the need for age appropriate language in regards to vertical mobility. As both of these are features are modifiable, this leads to a tentative finding that supports this design element.

Not activity specific:

In regards to being not activity specific, the pedagogical design of SkillTrack! was interested in designing an experience that would be able to be used with any classroom activity.

As no student responses addressed this feature specifically nor in the abstract possible conclusions can be made around their understanding of its holistic design; students did not need to be directed through a specific activity to identify skill usage nor do they associate skill usage with specific activities. This is an inference based on the lack of data and beyond this observation, there is not sufficient data to reach a preliminary finding on this design element.

Integrates into authentic classroom dynamic:

With regard to integrating into the authentic classroom dynamic, this pedagogical design element of SkillTrack! was interested in creating an app experience that did not interfere or prohibit regular classroom instruction but instead extended it into the space of Key Skill usage.

Within this element, while student response did not specifically address the integration of the app into the classroom, student responses spoke towards their lack of experience with self-directing their own learning. As in the comments used under the horizontal mobility element, here student responses focused on needing assistance in remembering to use the app.

Specifically, students mentioned liking doing something on their own in class about class without help from the teacher but that it was hard to remember to use: "I just think that um, some students just forgot to do it sometimes so maybe if like they had some type of notification or something to make like to remember to use it or something".

With no negative comments about the app integrating into the authentic classroom experience (students did not have a hard time figuring out how to tag activities, when to tag activities, how the app related to classroom activities, etc.) and comments really only highlighting the app moving away from the traditional classroom teacher dynamic, a tentative conclusion can be made that SkillTrack!, as is, generally fits within the authentic classroom dynamic and with the addition of reminders (and teacher support) could be integrated without issue.

Activate student literacy:

One of the underpinning pedagogical premises of SkillTrack! was in creating an app experience that addressed student understanding, experience, practice and development, or overall literacy, of the 21st century/Key skills.

Every focus group specifically—and favourably—addressed this element within their interviews in response to the question 'what did you like about SkillTrack!':

- "Um, I liked SkillTrack! um because it made me understand like to remember to use collaboration and to, to know how to use self-management and like to be able to do the Key Skills."
- "I liked the way it made you figure out what you were using, what Key skills you were using."
- "Well usually I'm kind of nervous talking but I found that kinda helped me kind of get over it like … communication."
- "Um, I liked the way that, em, you were able to think about what skills you were using in class."
- "You have to use your mind…like you use more of them skills."
- "Made you realize what you were using–you aren't really thinking until you go in to SkillTrack! and you realized 'oh, I was using creativity or collaboration…"
- "It made you aware about what the different…like self-management…what it means…"

- “Made you think of when you are doing a presentation like are you using creativity or collaboration.”

Students did mention that “just think[ing] about what you were going to put in–.which one you were going to pick [was challenging]”, a comment which could be viewed negatively but is an expected response within this user group considering the metacognitive premise behind the pedagogical design.

With students commenting specifically on this pedagogical design element, and in a unprompted and generally positive strain, a preliminary finding can be made around the app successfully activating student literacy and creating informal learning opportunities around the skills.

Experiential learning:

In regards to designing an app that would be based in experiential learning, the pedagogical design of SkillTrack! was interested in students utilising their own naturally occurring learning experiences to anchor the app experience and bring about the explicit recognition of the implicit.

Student responses in support of this pedagogical design element overlap with those regarding student literacy and centre around “like[ing] the way it made you figure out what you were using, what Key skills you were using and think[ing] about what skills you were using in class”.

These comments, while referring to the metacognitive experience of linking the skills to personal experience, offer no conclusive finding on this design element.

Formative assessment:

A key premise within the design of the SkillTrack! app is that it would offer a formative assessment experience (as opposed to a summative assessment experience) that would provide feedback, motivation and a sense of progression to the student users.

While the original conceptual premise for this formative aspect was not incorporated into the final design, the use of phases and badges at the end points of these phases was incorporated into the design as a means of providing intermediate feedback. Student response to the badges was favourable with many students stating that they “liked getting the badges and [were] proud when I got past the different levels”.

Students also like the progression feedback that home page relayed commenting that “I liked how it showed ya like when you were almost there it had like…yeah the piechart where it said like you’ve only one to go”. There was also much enthusiasm around how to develop this portion of the app by expanding it to using badges more frequent like [having] smaller ones or incorporating stars or coins or points to motivate students.

A preliminary conclusion/finding for this element then is that badging feature was considered to be a strong feedback mechanism to the students and that it could be expanded; additionally, with greater development the badges could have greater worth in providing feedback on practice and development.

Pedagogical Activities

Onboarding:

The onboarding pedagogical activity was meant to orient the student users to the app, the skills in general and the type of thinking needed to use the app with the teacher's assistance; it was an opportunity to activate prior knowledge and for teacher's to both directly instruct around the skills and model thinking and behaviour.

No student responses referred to the onboarding (beyond those about technical glitches) or could be umbrella-ed under this heading. This may mean that it was truly seen as an onboarding experience or that there was nothing within that struck the users as either positive or negative.

Beyond this observation, there is not sufficient data to reach even a preliminary finding on this activity.

Skill Tagging:

The foundational pedagogical activity, and design feature, of SkillTrack! is the student tagging of skills. This activity supports the majority of design elements and provides an anchor for the two other app activities. For those comments on the tagging feature, it was the metacognitive portion of the tagging that drew attention as they "liked the way it made you figure out what you were using, what Key skills you were using". Additionally, one student linked tagging to achievement in regards to liking to "tag and stuff that you done or like achieved that day".

As this was the main activity student participants engaged with, it seems significant to note that it was not explicitly stated as problematic or too difficult (in the cognitive sense) and was even identified as "not being repetitive". Any negative student responses around this activity was more on teacher behaviour—"it is not easy to do cuz teachers think you're like doing something you shouldn't be doing on your netbook"—than the feature itself.

Based on these responses, a preliminary finding can be made that tagging feature was simple enough for students to understand as well as to activate their metacognition around the skills. Additionally, as there were no negative comments around the act of tagging (beyond the teacher allowance of it) it may also be tentatively suggested that it was an executable and unobjectionable activity.

Benchmarking Tasks:

The secondary activity within SkillTrack! is holistically termed the benchmarking tasks; this is where students are, after tagging, occasionally given a pedagogically scaffolded question or task based on their tagging action.

Student responses around these tasks themselves were positive, though, as noted earlier, there was the feeling that the language used within them was at times too difficult. Specifically, it was mentioned that they liked "the different questions and stuff like that…you know you are not just tagging for no reason and that [the questions] made you think". Additionally, it was felt that the questions helped students to know that the app was working and that you were progressing.

In regards to the types of benchmarking tasks, students showed a preference to those that did not require free text entry as they felt that those questions were harder (required them to think more).

Based on this, a preliminary finding can be made that students appreciated the benchmarking tasks but felt that they were at times too difficult (either from the language used or the type of task free text they were asked to do).

Exemplar Stage (exemplar + self-assessment):

The final activity in the build of the application, the exemplar stage that required an uploaded picture as exemplar evidence and a self-assessment of the skill, is the last activity required in each phase.

Primarily, students liked the concept of uploading a picture stating that "I liked how when we got to the exemplar stage we'd have to upload a picture of the work we did in class so I think that was very helpful and it makes you feel like you have a sense of achievement and done".

However, they did find it just took a while to get to the exemplar stage and that it was hard to get a photo as "we don't bring our [devices] everywhere". There was also interest in "see[ing] other pictures that people put up".

Not one student interviewed commented on the self-assessment portion of the app, even when prompted. This can generally be seen to mean that the students had no feelings, positive or negative, about this as a task, and accepted it as a part of the overall experience.

Generally then, based on these responses, a preliminary finding around this pedagogical activity is that this activity was both enjoyable enough, and easily accomplished.

Conclusion (Students):

In summary, generally in regards to the pedagogical portion of the app, from the student users point of view, the pedagogical design and activities accomplished what they intended to (with certain noted reservations).

In all of the evaluated areas, the strongest feedback given was in support of use of the app activating student literacy of the skills. The strongest drawbacks within the app design were around the language and the difficulty in using the app without teacher support.

A.4.2 Teacher Interviews

The teacher in charge of both the first and second trial at the County Galway school was the sole teacher interviewed regarding the classroom use of SkillTrack! due to availability limitations. The following questions were used to generally guide the interview after both trials:

- What did you like about SkillTrack!?
- What do you think the students liked about SkillTrack!?

- What was challenging about using SkillTrack! From the teacher perspective? From the student perspective?
- Do you think that there was any change in student understanding of the Key Skills for those who were using it?
- Was SkillTrack! adaptable to various class activities?
- What would your comments be on the Teacher Dashboard?

Additionally, clarifying questions and follow-up questions were asked.

At the end of the second trial, the teacher was specifically asked to respond to the pedagogical design elements and activities. Answers from both interviews are integrated below.

Pedagogical Design Elements

Vertical and Horizontal Mobility:

With regard to vertical and horizontal mobility, the pedagogical design of SkillTrack! was interested in creating an experience that would be able to be used across year/grade level and content/subject areas. In regards to the the horizontal portion of this element, the teacher commented on it being an app that "went across subject…nothing was subject specific (math and science); nothing limited it, especially as there is the exposure to skills in multiple subjects".

When thinking about the intention of the app to be vertically mobile, the teacher did not speak against the premise but did feel, as did the students, that the language used within the app was problematic:

> So I think the language was too hard for our age group. It would have been ideal for 5th years, which is three years ahead of us. I think it is probably quite sophisticated language for our group which I didn't realise until I introduced it until I showed the app to other staff members who said 'whoa, how are they going to use that, they're first years, it's really hard, isn't it.' That was the first time I had considered that cuz I was just so like, this is exactly what we want to be talking about, stretching them, but actually our kids are too young. And I think that age group lose a lot when it's reading. And literacy. Actually, that is another thing, literacy is a big issue with first years.

Additionally, the teacher felt the design of the app could have been more tailored to the age group:

> Yeah, like even if the elements were floating bubbles around the page and they had to pop the bubbles that they thought were the right ones. That would tie them in a little bit more. Really simple things like that I think would gain that age group.

As with the student comments, while these comments do not specifically address SkillTrack!'s ability to be used across year/grade level in regards to concept design, it does speak to the need of the language used within the app to be tailored to the specific age, year, grade, or ability level as well as certain design features. As the app was originally written to be used at Senior Cycle level and was instead trialled within the Junior Cycle, this is an expected finding.

Not activity specific:

Concerning being not activity specific, the pedagogical design of SkillTrack! was interested in designing an experience that would be able to be used with any classroom activity. The teacher felt that "students can do it whenever, it's not even class specific or about the what of what they are doing…it actually doesn't even have to be academic it could be extracurricular".

This series of comments offer a strong validation of this design feature.

Integration into authentic classroom dynamic:

In regards to integrating into the authentic classroom dynamic, this pedagogical design element of SkillTrack! was interested in creating an app experience that did not interfere or prohibit regular classroom instruction but instead extended it into the space of Key Skill usage. Concerning this design element, the teacher said:

> The other really good thing about it is how minimal it is in interfering in the class work. They can either have it totally minimised…I have them pinning it to their start menu so they always see it. But they literally just have to touch it and it doesn't interrupt the lesson so I have no problem suggesting to teachers to encouraging them to use it in their lesson.

This is quite positive in support of this design element.

However, she did note that:

> Yeah and so the only other thing that came back with them and challenges is them literally forgetting or not being used to doing it…If it is not run by every teacher in every class, it doesnt work actually…if it was done the way you designed it which is over a full academic school year it would probably become more inherent…And if it was permanently there for the kids to have it. They would use it all the time. And you know if it was always visible you are going to get a much more engaging experience…

This mirrors student comments and speak towards the need for teacher engagement and investment in the use of the app as well a tweaking of the home screen design to help facilitate full engagement and integration.

A finding, then, from the teacher's experience is that SkillTrack! does integrate into the the authentic classroom dynamic; a more successful and complete integration would take full teacher buy-in and support as well as a slight design modification.

Activates student literacy:

One of the underpinning pedagogical premises of SkillTrack! was in creating an app experience that addressed student understanding, experience, practice and development, or overall literacy, of the 21st century/Key skills.

With regard to this design element, the teacher response was quite positive in praising the pedagogical content of the app promoting literacy:

> So…we have been trying to find something like SkillTrack! for the students to introduce them to the Key Skills. So the fact that the SkillTrack! app identifies the Key Skills and has a really really good onboarding introduction to the Key Skills for us fits perfectly in with what we were looking for which was how do we kind of give them an engaging way of interacting with the skills and coming up with examples themselves of where they are using the skills and then being able to identify next time in the lesson did they use that skill. This was the

> most positive outcome from it…kids who engaged were developing language around it and because of the app. The app forces the interaction with the language.

as well as the resulting metacognitive reflection and informal learning on both the student's and teacher's part:

> I also think one of the skills that seemed to be really misunderstood was creativity. And I think we did look a lot about problem-solving within creativity. And I know that at different times when I said to them, so what skill are we using here? In Maths. And one or two of them were able to kind of say, we are kind of being creative because were looking at…And that was good for me because I suppose I always think that the subjects that I teach are not creative. And I would think as well…well, when we do STEM, and projects and building stuff, it's creative, but I think definitely the students started to see problem-solving as a creative skill. Which I thought was very positive, I found that really positive even for me, cuz I would now promote it as you are being creative because you came up with a solution. Whereas…definitely before that it was like you were colourful…You did your Maths in blue and red. Which is like [terrible] creativity. So you know, I think it probably it increased my literacy on it as well, like I'm using the language a little bit more, which was my goal from the beginning. I wanted something that would make me engage with the skills with the kids. And I think this is doing that, definitely.

Additionally, the teacher speaks towards the app making the implicit explicit:

> And I think actually [the skills] has to be forced because it is not a natural thing for us to be doing, like we are even though naturally we are using the skills, we are never naturally talking about them. So we are never naturally talking about them, so I think that…you have to force it then. So I think that's really good and it has been really good that way…I think definitely there is [a change in student understanding of the Key Skills].

With the teacher commenting directly on this pedagogical design element, the metacognition it supports and the assistance it gives to supporting the practice and development of these skills in the classroom, a strong finding can be made around the app successfully activating student literacy and creating informal learning opportunities around the skills.

Experiential learning:

Concerning designing an app that would be based in experiential learning, the pedagogical design of SkillTrack! was interested in students utilising their own naturally occurring learning experiences to anchor the app experience and bring about the explicit recognition of the implicit.

In regards to this design premise, the teacher speaks on:

> Which I suppose we don't want them to be like skill hawks but we do want them like to recognise the use of the skill and to that just become…And I think if it starts in first year that will becomes that more natural for them in an interview situation to recognise the use of skills when they see them and are using them.

Additionally:

> [The students] were able to say what it looks like in practice; a lot of what we do is 'today we will be using…' But we don't usually say 'we did work together as a team, you were very creative'—we don't often reflect and validate because you are moving on to the next one—there is a bigger spiel in pre-teaching than post-teaching…the app caters for that post-teaching bit.

This comment positively highlights the experiential premise of the app as well as the extension—and value—of this premise beyond the classroom. A finding can be then that the experiential design element is executed sufficiently and a desirable premise for the classroom setting.

Formative assessment:

A key premise within the design of the SkillTrack! app is that it would offer a formative assessment experience (as opposed to a summative assessment experience) that would provide feedback, motivation and a sense of progression to the student users. Here, teacher feedback once again mirrors that of the students with the badging component being recognised as a key motivator:

> The other thing that is really motivating for them is the badges…I mean you've got competitive. Even the competitive kids who wouldn't be academically motivated are motivated by getting a badge and I think probably, that that is definitely the only buy in for kids who are not interested in the content is the badge and so you know that is something, that is what's keeping them in there…

Additionally, the design feature that shows the student how they are progressing through the phase was highlighted as a means of providing feedback and motivation:

> And I think that's (the pie pieces filling up) a motivator for them especially for the high achievers are wanting to get that all done so they are on the look out for where these skills are and the definitely diligent kids don't want to be mistagging. So they don't want to just gamify and go it…tick tick tick…they want to wait until they…and so they are on the lookout for that skill.

Furthermore, when discussing the app with other teachers not involved with trial the focus was on how the app would provide teachers a means of formatively assessing students' engagement with the Key Skills. Specifically:

> I suppose their interaction with it is that's a good way of monitoring it. And that is what they said. And that is definitely what they said 'oh yeah, that is a good way of monitoring it.

A finding for this element then is that badging feature was considered to be a strong feedback mechanism for this age group and that the app provides the needed support in this realm.

Pedagogical Activities

Onboarding:

The onboarding pedagogical activity was meant to orient the student users to the app, the skills in general and the type of thinking needed to use the app with the teacher's assistance; it was an opportunity to activate prior knowledge and for teacher's to both directly instruct around the skills and model thinking and behaviour.

In regards to the onboarding, the teacher feedback was very positive and enthusiastic as it was the first thing mentioned in response to the general question of 'what did you like about SkillTrack!':

> So I think the onboarding for me was brilliant. Was the best part of it. Because it started a discussion. My favorite part of the onboarding is here's an example of what someone thought was their best work. And then that was–there was just a really good rich discussion around that.

> I think other things that maybe, the onboarding is long — now the onboarding is my favourite part — but the onboarding…I would have liked to spend a term on the onboarding, like literally 6 weeks, where we do one skill 1 week, where we talk about it, I have it on the staff board, the skills this week. Like the onboarding in computer science is 'collaboration', can you highlight any use of it in your lessons? All the kids are looking at it, all the kids are aware of it…

These comments not only highlight the need for instruction, practice, and development of the skills (prior to assessment) of the skills, but also the natural instinct of the teacher to be a part of the delivery of the content. This then supports the design element of the onboarding as a means for teacher involvement with the app.

Skill Tagging:

The foundational pedagogical activity, and design feature, of SkillTrack! is the student tagging of skills. This activity supports the majority of design elements and provides an anchor for the two other app activities.

With regard to the tagging mechanism within SkillTrack! as a means of identifying skill usage, the teacher did not speak to this feature specifically except in regards to how minimal it is in interfering in the class work and how "[students] need to make a choice—their own choice—about what they were doing, what skill, and it's quick and then done".

Beyond this observation, there is not sufficient data to reach even a preliminary finding on this activity.

Benchmark Tasks:

The secondary activity within SkillTrack! is holistically termed the benchmarking tasks; this is where students are, after tagging, occasionally given a pedagogically scaffolded question or task based on their tagging action.

The teacher comments around the tasks focused more on the language used within the tasks than the task themselves and as shared earlier the belief was that "the language was too hard for our age group".

This response pairs with that in the first design element in regards to the app's vertical mobility and reaffirms the preliminary finding that the language used to articulate the pedagogical structure must be age appropriate.

Exemplar Stage (exemplar + self-assessment):

The final activity in the build of the application, the exemplar stage that required an uploaded picture as exemplar evidence and a self-assessment of the skill, is the last activity required in each phase.

Teacher comments focused on the exemplar portion of this stage:

> And then I love the uploading of an exemplar piece of work because I think it is really important that they make a judgement call on a piece of work surrounding that particular skill that they seemed to have followed to that level. So I really like that.

And on the self-assessment piece:

> So the self-assessment and like progression level increasing in complexity…there is an element of education in that; they are learning what they are being. This is the best tool to get them to consider their use of skills and to consider their progression with school…and that it is self-assessment, that is the best place to put it for the classroom, that is what we want.

This response allows for a strong validation of both concepts and the finding that the exemplar stage as well as the self-assessment are appropriate and are strong anchor features in the design.

Conclusion (Teacher):

In summary, the teacher's response paralleled those of the students, with the pedagogical design and activities accomplishing what they intended to.

In all of the evaluated areas, the strongest feedback given was in the design areas of integrating into the authentic classroom dynamic, activating student literacy and experiential learning. In regards to the pedagogical activities, the onboarding received strong praise as did the exemplar and self-assessment portion, validating both the choice and design of them. The strongest drawbacks within the app design were around, as in the student feedback, the use of age appropriate language as well as the ability of students to remember to use the app.

MIX
Papier aus verantwortungsvollen Quellen
Paper from responsible sources
FSC® C105338
FSC
www.fsc.org

If you have any concerns about our products,
you can contact us on
ProductSafety@springernature.com

In case Publisher is established outside the EU,
the EU authorized representative is:
Springer Nature Customer Service Center GmbH
Europaplatz 3, 69115 Heidelberg, Germany

Printed by Libri Plureos GmbH
in Hamburg, Germany